Learn SQL Server Administration in a Month of Lunches

Learn SQL Server Administration in a Month of Lunches

DON JONES

MANNING

SHELTER ISLAND

For online information and ordering of this and other Manning books, please visit
www.manning.com. The publisher offers discounts on this book when ordered in quantity.
For more information, please contact

Special Sales Department
Manning Publications Co.
20 Baldwin Road
PO Box 261
Shelter Island, NY 11964
Email: orders@manning.com

⊗ Recognizing the importance of preserving what has been written, it is Manning's policy to have
the books we publish printed on acid-free paper, and we exert our best efforts to that end.
Recognizing also our responsibility to conserve the resources of our planet, Manning books
are printed on paper that is at least 15 percent recycled and processed without the use of
elemental chlorine.

Manning Publications Co.
20 Baldwin Road
PO Box 261
Shelter Island, NY 11964

Development editor:	Suzie Pitzen
Copyeditor:	Elizabeth Martin
Proofreader:	Barbara Mirecki
Typesetter:	Dennis Dalinnik
Cover designer:	Leslie Haimes

ISBN: 9781617292132
Printed in the United States of America
2 3 4 5 6 7 8 9 10 – MAL – 19 18 17 16 15 14

To the Atlantis Team, who helped me stay on track with my writing schedule: Malcolm, Ellen, Michael, Gregory, Randy, Adam, and Momma, along with Brit Lee.

And to Christopher, for helping me stay on track every day.

brief contents

contents

ix

preface

I've been working with Microsoft SQL Server for a very long time—it was, in fact, one of the first Microsoft server products I was responsible for in a production environment. I do so much with Windows PowerShell these days that not many folks know I have a strong fondness for good ol' SQL Server.

Learn SQL Server Administration in a Month of Lunches exists in large part because I've met so many administrators who came to SQL Server the same way I did: "Hey, you know Microsoft stuff, why don't you have a look at our database server and see why it's running so slowly?" The "Reluctant DBAs," as I call us, aren't typically involved in database development. We might not have access to the code that's connecting to SQL Server; in many cases we simply need to know how to run a reliable backup, keep indexes maintained, and keep the server running as smoothly as possible. That's what this book will try to teach you.

This book won't try to make you an expert DBA, and I doubt this book will be the last one you read on SQL Server. But this book is a good *first* book to read on SQL Server: it'll help you understand the less-than-obvious things going on under the hood, and hopefully give you a solid foundation for working more effectively with SQL Server.

Good luck!

acknowledgments

Books don't write, edit, and publish themselves, although I keep looking for book elves who'll do just that! Until I find them, I'm always grateful to everyone at Manning Publications who worked so hard to make this book happen, given our rapid schedule. Thanks to Michael Stephens, development editor Suzie Pitzen, the production team of Elizabeth Martin, Barbara Mirecki, Mary Piergies, Janet Vail, and Dennis Dalinnik, and the many others who worked behind the scenes.

I'd also like to acknowledge everyone who provided feedback for this book, particularly all of the MEAP (Manning Early Access Program) readers, and the following peer reviewers who read the manuscript during its development: Adam Dutko, Carm Vecchio, Christopher Morgan, Chuck Henderson, Daniel Kreeger, George Laframboise, Ian Stirk, Maqbool Patel, Nick Selpa, Spike Xavier, and Stan Bice. Their input and insights have made this a better book.

Finally, special thanks to Richard Siddaway for his careful technical proofread of the final manuscript shortly before it went into production.

xviii

about this book

Most of what you'll need to know about this book is covered in chapter 1, but there are a few things that we should mention up front.

First, if you plan to follow along with our examples, and complete the hands-on exercises, you'll need a virtual machine or computer running Windows 7 or later. You'll need at least 2 GB of RAM, and 10 GB of free disk space. You could also use Windows 8, or Windows 8.1. Whichever you use, you'll need to be able to log on as the computer's Administrator. One more decision: do you want to go with the free SQL Server Express Edition or another edition of SQL Server. We cover that in more detail in chapter 1, and it's an important decision that will impact how you move through this book.

Second, be prepared to read this book from start to finish, covering each chapter in order. Chapters are short, meaning, as the title says, you can read a chapter on your hour lunch break. (You don't have to, but each chapter takes about 40 minutes to read and digest, giving you time to enjoy your sandwich.) The human brain can absorb only so much information at once, and by taking on SQL Server in small chunks, you'll learn faster and more thoroughly.

Don't feel the need to read ahead. A chapter a day will give you time to read and practice what each chapter shows you.

Third, this book contains short code snippets so you should be able to type them in quite easily. In fact, I recommend that you do type them, since doing so will help reinforce an essential skill: accurate typing!

That said, there are a few conventions that you should be aware of. Code will always appear in a `fixed-width font`. In a few examples, **`bold fixed-width font`** will be used to highlight the information you'll need to insert in the code. I have tried to format the code so it fits within the available page space in the book by adding line breaks. But the neat thing about SQL Server is that it isn't terribly sensitive about line breaks in code. For the most part, you can type everything exactly as shown here in the book and it'll work, or you can type it out as one long line and it'll still work. The formatting shown here in the book is mainly to keep everything fit to the page size, and to enhance readability.

Author Online

The purchase of *Learn SQL Server Administration in a Month of Lunches* includes access to a private forum run by Manning Publications where you can make comments about the book, ask technical questions, and receive help from the authors and other users. To access and subscribe to the forum, point your browser to www.manning.com/ LearnSQLServerAdministrationinaMonthofLunches or www.manning.com/jones5 and click the Author Online link. This page provides information on how to get on the forum once you are registered, what kind of help is available, and the rules of conduct in the forum.

Manning's commitment to our readers is to provide a venue where a meaningful dialogue between individual readers and between readers and the author can take place. It's not a commitment to any specific amount of participation on the part of the author, whose contribution to the book's forum remains voluntary (and unpaid). We suggest you try asking the authors challenging question, lest their interest stray!

The Author Online forum and the archives of previous discussions will be accessible from the publisher's website as long as the book is in print.

About the author

Don Jones is a multiple-year recipient of Microsoft's prestigious Most Valuable Professional (MVP) Award for his work with Windows PowerShell, but one of the first Microsoft products he ever worked with in production was SQL Server—way back in version 6.5. He's since found a sideline teaching "reluctant DBAs" how to be effective with SQL Server maintenance and administration. Visit MoreLunches.com and click this book's cover image to learn more about Don, and to find out how to contact him online.

Don is the author of a number of books published by Manning, including *Power-Shell in Depth* (a second edition is in the works); *Learn Windows PowerShell in a Month of Lunches, Second Edition*; and *Learn PowerShell Toolmaking in a Month of Lunches.*

Before you begin

SQL Server is Microsoft's relational database management system (RDBMS), and it's at the heart of many corporate applications. Its job is, quite simply, to store data. Application developers write applications that add, remove, and change data constantly. As a major platform component, SQL Server requires a bit of ongoing maintenance—and that's what this book is designed to teach.

1.1 Is this book for you?

Let's start by making sure this is the SQL Server book for you. This book doesn't set out to make you a Database Administrator (DBA), nor does it cover anything in the way of SQL Server development or programming. Instead, this book is meant as a starting point, and from here you could go on to being a DBA or developer. This book is about maintaining SQL Server, monitoring it, and doing a bit in the way of performance tuning. Mostly, this book focuses on how to spot problem situations that you might not even have permission to fix, and that you'll have to report to someone else, such as an application developer. I'll help you understand where to look, and what data to collect, so that your report can be as useful as possible to whomever you send it.

In a traditional organization, DBAs are something of a hybrid. They're familiar with the server itself, meaning they often deal with its security, backups, availability, and performance. They're also into the code, meaning they can troubleshoot SQL queries, write stored procedures, and perhaps even code a bit in C# or Visual Basic. They tend to work primarily with in-house applications, meaning they either have access to application code or work directly with someone who does.

But more and more organizations are finding themselves supporting numerous SQL Server installations for slightly different reasons. Increasingly, SQL Server is used as the back end to commercial software applications, meaning you do not have access to the application code—it's owned by a vendor. In those cases, you're a bit more limited in what you can do, since you can't actually change the code. But you still have to maintain SQL Server and keep it running. If performance does falter, you'll need to figure out why, and be able to send an intelligent, actionable report to the vendor. This book is meant for folks working in those organizations, to help them accomplish those exact tasks. I'll show you how to perform backups and restores, how to look for major performance problems, and in many cases how to collect "evidence" that you can provide to a vendor or developer to help correct problem situations. I'll share a bit about underlying design concepts, but mainly as a way of helping you understand why SQL Server works the way it does. For this book, I'm assuming you can't change database or software designs, and that you have to work with what you've been given.

I find a lot of "reluctant DBAs" out there, folks who work with Microsoft server technologies in their organization, perhaps administering Active Directory or working with file servers. The organization implements SQL Server to act as the back end for some application they've bought, and belatedly realizes that someone actually has to maintain that SQL Server installation. So one of the "Microsoft people" in the organization gets SQL Server "dumped" on them, making them a reluctant DBA. This book is really written for them.

1.2 *How to use this book*

The idea here is that you'll read one chapter each day. You don't have to read it during lunch, but each chapter should take you only about 40 minutes to read, giving you an extra 20 minutes to gobble down your sandwich and practice what the chapter showed you. You really should focus on just one chapter a day, then let your brain process that information overnight. Blasting through a third of the book in a single day won't actually let the information digest and stick the way it needs to.

THE MAIN CHAPTERS

Of the chapters in this book, chapters 2 through 23 contain the main content, giving you 22 days' worth of lunches to look forward to. This means you can expect to complete the main content of the book in about a month. Try to stick with that schedule as much as possible, and don't feel the need to read extra chapters in a given day. It's more important that you spend some time practicing what each chapter shows you, because using the product will help cement what you've learned. Not every chapter will require a full hour, so sometimes you'll be able to spend the additional time practicing (and eating lunch) before you have to get back to work.

HANDS-ON LABS

Most of the main content chapters include a short lab for you to complete. You'll be given instructions, and perhaps a hint or two, but you won't find any answers in the book. The answers are online, at MoreLunches.com, but try your best to complete each lab without looking at the online answers.

The MoreLunches.com website contains additional supplementary content, including extra chapters and companion videos.

A few chapters only skim the surface of some cool technologies, and I'll end those chapters with suggestions for how you might explore those technologies on your own. I'll point out additional resources, including free stuff that you can use to expand your skill set as the need arises.

You'll notice a few ABOVE AND BEYOND sidebars in the book. They're designed to provide additional information or insight that you don't really need, but that you might find interesting. If you're pressed for time, or just feeling "full," feel free to skip them, or to come back and read them later.

1.3   Setting up your lab environment

The best way to learn SQL Server is to use it, and that's one reason this book comes equipped with hands-on labs, as I described previously. To perform those labs, you'll need a lab to work on. The best and easiest way to set this up is to turn to the appendix of this book. More on that at the end of this section; for now, let's start with a quick overview of what you'll need.

To begin, you'll need a computer running Windows 7 or later. You'll probably need at least 2 GB of RAM, and 10 GB of free disk space. You could also choose to use Windows 8 or later, but no matter what, you'll need to be able to log on as the computer's Administrator. You'll need to decide if you want to go with the free SQL Server Express Edition, or another edition of SQL Server. The next few sections offer guidance on choosing an edition.

You'll also want a sample database to play with, so head over to http://msftdbprod-samples.codeplex.com/downloads/get/478214, where you can download the "Adventure Works for SQL Server 2012" sample database.

TIP   If you'd like help setting up SQL Server, including getting that sample database installed, turn to the appendix, a screen-by-screen walkthrough of the installation process. The screen shots make it a pretty long document, which is why the publisher and I decided to make it an appendix, rather than adding the material to this chapter. For more supplementary materials, log on to MoreLunches.com. Click on this book's cover image, and you'll have access to hands-on lab answers as well as database, SQL Server, and index inventory sheets.

1.3.1   Choosing a SQL Server edition for your lab

SQL Server's Express Edition is great for practicing, primarily because it's free. For that reason, this book's appendix will direct you to download it, and walk you through installing it. However, it isn't 100% identical to what I call the "big boy" versions of the product (Standard, Enterprise, and even Developer). Express behaves differently if you're not logged on as Administrator, or if your computer has User Account Control (UAC) enabled. Express doesn't include some of the auditing and performance tuning features that I'll cover in this book. It also lacks a few of the management tools and options I'll show you.

My goal with this book isn't to teach you how to use the Express Edition; it's to teach you how to maintain the real, production-quality editions of SQL Server that you would find in a business environment. If you decide to use Express as your "let's play with this product" software, understand that there *will* be differences, and that I'm not going to call attention to all of them, because you won't encounter those differences if you're maintaining a production SQL Server installation that's part of a business application.

If you'd prefer to work through this book's labs using a "real" edition of SQL Server, you can download and install a free 180-day trial from Microsoft. Visit www.microsoft.com/en-us/sqlserver/get-sql-server/try-it.aspx (or, if Microsoft changes the URL, go to http://microsoft.com/sqlserver and look for trial downloads). If you choose to go with the trial edition, then the setup instructions in this book's appendix should still be completely valid. That 180-day trial can either be Developer or Enterprise, depending on the version of Windows you install it on.

1.3.2 *Selecting a version of Windows for your lab*

Windows comes in two broad flavors: client and server. The client OSes are Windows 7, Windows 8, and later; the server OSes are Windows Server 2012, Windows Server 2012 R2, and so on.

SQL Server has two editions that will run on a client OS: Express and Developer. Express is the free one I mentioned earlier. Developer is a paid edition of SQL Server that's intended for software developers. Developer is a lot closer to the real, business-level editions of SQL Server than Express. If you use Developer, you'll get a much closer taste of what the real SQL Server is like than if you use Express, because Developer offers basically the same feature set as the Enterprise edition of SQL Server. Developer isn't free. But, if you download the 180-day trial of SQL Server, you should be able to install it on a client version of Windows and you'll end up with Developer.

TIP   To see the differences between editions of SQL Server 2012, visit http://msdn.microsoft.com/en-us/library/cc645993(v=SQL.110).aspx.

Here's the thing: I'm assuming that you want to learn SQL Server maintenance because you want to maintain SQL Server in a business environment. Well, business environments don't use Developer or Express as the back end to production applications! So if you want to *really* practice what you'll do in the real world, you need a *server* version of Windows running the Standard or Enterprise editions of SQL Server. You can certainly get a trial of Windows Server 2012 or later, and you can get a trial of SQL Server Enterprise Edition. Those trials are good for only about 6 months, but that should be long enough for you to get through this book.

1.3.3 My recommendation for your lab environment

So while you *can* practice on a client OS using Express, I *recommend* you at least work on a client OS using the 180-day Developer trial, and I *prefer* that you work on a server OS using the 180-day Enterprise trial. I know that's a lot to set up. You may need Windows 8 or later on a computer that supports Hyper-V, so that you can install Windows Server into a virtual machine (that'll require your computer to have at least 4 GB of memory, too). SQL Server isn't something you can easily "play with" cheaply or with low-end hardware, unless you're willing to go with Express and deal with its differences. Let's summarize:

- *Good:* Windows 7 or later, 2 GB of RAM or more, 10 GB of free disk, and SQL Server Express (with Advanced Services). There will be some differences in functionality, and you won't be able to practice everything in this book. The appendix will get you through setting up SQL Server.

- *Better:* Windows 7 or later, 2 GB of RAM or more, 10 GB of free disk, and the 180-day trial of SQL Server (which will install as Developer Edition, functionally equivalent to Enterprise Edition). The appendix should still work for getting SQL Server installed.

- *Best:* Windows Server 2012 or later (180-day trial is okay), 2 GB of RAM or more, 10 GB of free disk, and the 180-day trial of SQL Server (which will install as Enterprise Edition). The appendix will get you through installing SQL Server, but you're on your own for installing the Windows Server OS.

1.3.4 A word about SQL Server versions

I wrote this book for SQL Server 2012, and everything in it should be accurate for that version. Because this book focuses on foundation-level maintenance tasks, everything here should be valid for SQL Server 2014 also.

Many organizations run multiple versions of SQL Server, usually because each version is supporting some application that's certified (by its vendor) to work with only that version. Again, because this book's tasks are foundation-level, they haven't changed much over the years. You should find that most of what I share here works with SQL Server 2005, SQL Server 2008, and SQL Server 2008R2. However, my focus is on SQL Server 2012. I won't be exhaustively pointing out version differences, because doing so becomes really complex to test and verify. Just understand that, with some older versions, things may be in different places in the tools, or certain features I discuss might not exist. That's one of the joys of working with SQL Server in a production environment!

1.4 SQL Server documentation

Throughout this book, I'll refer to SQL Server Books Online (often calling it Books Online), which is SQL Server's official documentation. I *don't* tend to send you directly to a web page for Books Online, because Microsoft periodically reorganizes its website, and my links end up being useless. Instead, I'll direct you to search terms, which you can then use to find the intended material no matter what Microsoft does to the website. Search terms are also better if you need to look up something for a previous version of SQL Server.

Books Online is capable of installing locally on your computer, meaning it copies content from the internet for offline use. That can take up a lot of space, and it's obviously possible for the download to get out of date, so many administrators rely on the web-based Books Online. That starts at http://technet.microsoft.com/en-us/library/ms130214.aspx, and you'll find an Other Versions link at the top of most pages that let you switch between the documentation for different versions. Just make sure you're reading the documentation that matches whatever version of SQL Server you're trying to use!

1.5   *Online resources*

I've mentioned the MoreLunches.com website a couple of times, and I hope you'll find time to visit. A number of supplementary resources for this book are available there:

- Example answers for each end-of-chapter lab
- Downloadable code listings (so you don't have to type them in from the book)
- Additional articles and bonus chapters
- Links to Q&A discussion forums related to SQL Server

I'm pretty passionate about helping folks understand SQL Server maintenance, although my travel schedule doesn't give me a lot of time to get online and answer questions. But you're always welcome to contact me through Twitter (@concentrateddon), and I'll do my best to either help, or get you to a forum where someone else can. I can't answer technical questions via email.

1.6   *A word on my recommendations*

Nearly every organization I work with has multiple versions of SQL Server: 2005, 2008, 2008R2, 2012, and so on. For that reason, I've tried to keep this book as version-neutral as possible. The vast majority of what you'll learn is applicable to every version, as I've already mentioned.

I also try to avoid giving too much version-specific advice. For example, Microsoft may have offered guidance for SQL Server 2005 in terms of how to configure such-and-such a setting, but it may have negated that guidance for a subsequent version. In those version-specific instances, unless there's a really strong, impactful reason to mention something, I'm going to steer clear.

Be on your guard when you start doing your own research on things like performance, and when you read someone else's advice—even mine—validate it for the specific version of SQL Server you're using, down to the edition (Enterprise, Standard, etc.). What someone wrote in his or her blog about SQL Server 2008 might not be applicable to SQL Server 2012. Sometimes, advice gets out there in the world, doesn't get attached to a specific version in people's minds, and becomes some kind of legendary cure-all for a specific problem. The problem with that is Microsoft: it's always meddling around and improving the product, which often makes older advice either unnecessary or downright wrong! Be really cautious of following advice unless you know what version it's applicable to.

1.7   *Being immediately effective with SQL Server*

Immediately effective is a phrase I've made into my primary goal for this entire book (in fact, I authored a book on how to write immediately effective books). As much as possible, I'll try to have each chapter focus on something that you could use in a real production environment, right away. Immediately. That means I'll sometimes gloss over some details in the beginning, but when necessary I'll circle back and cover them at the right time. In many cases, I had to choose between first hitting you with 20 pages of theory, or diving right in and accomplishing something without explaining all the nuances, caveats, and details. When those choices came along, I almost always chose to dive right in, with the goal of making you immediately effective. But all of those important details and nuances will still be explained at a different time in the book. And of course, I want to emphasize that this book should only be your starting point for SQL Server—there's a lot more to explore, and I'll post recommended resources on MoreLunches.com so you have some next steps available.

OK, that's enough background. It's time to start being immediately effective. Your first lunch lesson awaits.

Server assessment and configuration

2.1 Identifying instances and versions

SQL Server was one of the first products to support what we'd now probably call virtualization. In SQL Server 2000, Microsoft designed the product to support multiple *instances*. In other words, you can install multiple copies of SQL Server on a single computer, and run them at the same time. Each copy, or instance, is separated from the others. You can even run multiple versions side-by-side on the same computer!

> **NOTE** When you install SQL Server, it includes several common components, network access libraries being one of them. If you install multiple versions, these common components will always be the latest version of the product. Normally, that doesn't cause any problems, but be aware that it's happening in case something crops up.

The idea between multiple instances is similar to the idea of running multiple virtual machines on a single host. Each instance can have its own configuration, its own version, and its own security settings. Rather than having a dedicated physical computer for each installation of SQL Server, you can combine them on a single computer, saving resources. If each instance's workload is less than the total capability of the computer, then it might make sense to consolidate at least some instances. Instances also

It's important to start off on the right foot, and that includes figuring out what you're dealing with. In this chapter, I'll cover some of the basics of SQL Server architecture, and look at your existing server (or servers) to see what you've got. We'll also dive into the server-level configuration settings, and I'll explain what the most important ones mean to you.

play a role in SQL Server clustering, since instances can be logically moved from computer to computer in the event of a failure or of a maintenance need.

When a client computer connects to a computer running SQL Server, it needs to indicate which copy of SQL Server it wants to talk to. Each computer can have one *default instance*, which is the instance you connect to if you connect to just the computer itself. Any other installed copies of SQL Server need to be *named instances*, meaning that in addition to the computer name, you also have to know the name of the SQL Server instance you want. If you have a computer named SQL01, then connecting to just SQL01 will get you the default instance, if one is installed. (It's possible to have only named instances installed.) If you connect to SQL01\SQLEXPRESS, you'll connect to the named instance called SQLEXPRESS running on the computer SQL01.

NOTE SQL Server Express installs, by default, to a named instance called SQLEXPRESS. If you modified that during the installation, you'll need to know the new instance name.

There are a few ways to figure out what instances are running on a given computer. Some of them require that SQL Server's graphical management tools be installed, which might not always be the case, especially on a server computer. The easy way to check is simply looking and seeing what's running on the computer. SQL Server runs as a Windows service, so checking out the list of installed services will quickly reveal SQL Server instances and their names. I like to use Windows PowerShell for this: open a PowerShell window, as shown in figure 2.1, and run Get-Service. As you can see, I

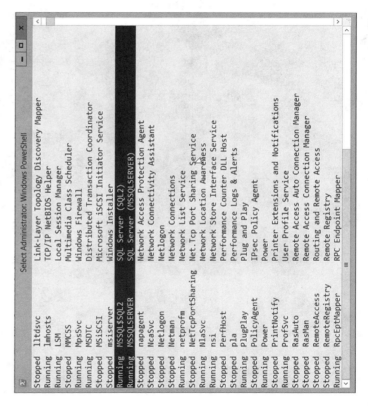

**Figure 2.1
Two instances of
SQL Server are
installed.**

have two instances installed. By the way, PowerShell is preinstalled on Windows Server 2008 and later; you can get the latest version from http://download.microsoft.com. Search for "Windows management Framework," and read the prerequisites closely to make sure the version you're grabbing can run on your server.

- The MSSQLSERVER instance is the default instance, meaning you don't specify an instance name when connecting to it.
- The MSSQL$SQL2 service is the SQL2 named instance. Every instance but the default will run under a service named MSSQL$, followed by the instance name.

This is an excellent way to quickly figure out what instances are included on the computer, so that you know what to try and connect to. Now we need to connect to those, and figure out what version they're each running.

Open SQL Server Management Studio. Prior to Windows 8, this is easy to find in the SQL Server 2012 folder on the Start menu; in Windows 8 and later, go to the Start screen and type SQL to find SQL Server Management Studio.

TIP   Once I find the SQL Server 2012 folder on a computer, I tend to pin the icon to the Task bar, so that I can get to it faster in the future.

As shown in figure 2.2, you'll be greeted by the Connect to Server window. I'll start by connecting to the local SQL2 instance, by providing the server name localhost\SQL2 and using my Windows logon for authentication. Since I'm logged on as Administrator, this should usually work. Keep in mind that if you didn't install an instance named SQL2, you shouldn't expect this to work.

The management console can connect to multiple instances at once, so I'll click Connect on the Object Explorer, and select Database Engine to connect to the default instance. This time, I'll provide localhost as the server name. As shown in the figure 2.3, I now have two instances in Object Explorer, and I can see their version numbers.

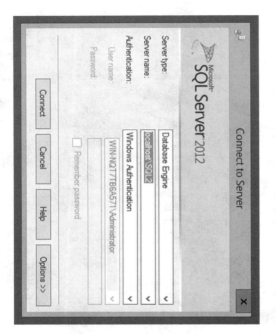

Figure 2.2   Connecting to SQL Server

Here's a rundown of the common major version numbers:

- 11: SQL Server 2012
- 10.5: SQL Server 2008R2
- 10: SQL Server 2008
- 9: SQL Server 2005
- 8: SQL Server 2000
- 7: SQL Server 7.0

You shouldn't run across anything older, although it's possible. SQL Server 6.5 and prior usually ran on Windows NT 3.51—that's going back quite a ways.

TRY IT NOW Connect to the SQL Server instance on your lab computer, and make sure you can identify the version number. If you have access to other SQL Server computers (and permission to connect to them), see if you can figure out what version they're running.

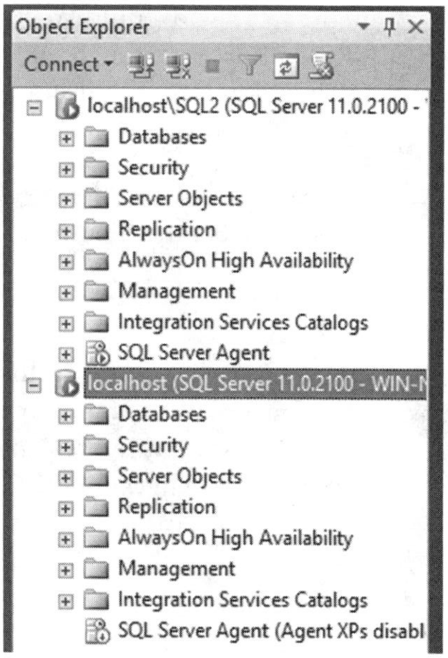

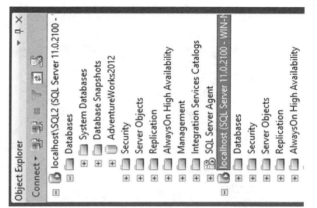

Figure 2.3 Observing SQL Server version numbers

Figure 2.4 Inventorying the databases in localhost\SQL2

2.2 Identifying databases

The basic unit of management in SQL Server is a *database*. If you've set up your lab computer, then you've already seen how a database (such as the AdventureWorks sample database) can be easily moved between computers. Databases are more or less all-inclusive, meaning they contain almost everything they need to function. It's always a good idea to know what databases are connected, or attached, to a SQL Server instance, and what each one is used for. It's also a good idea to know where the database's files physically live.

In Object Explorer, expand the Databases node to find installed databases. For now, you don't need to worry about the System databases or the database snapshots; you're just looking for any actual databases, such as Adventure-Works2012, shown in figure 2.4. If you've just installed SQL Server, you won't find any databases—but you can (and should) install

Microsoft's AdventureWorks database so that you'll have something to play with. Remember that this book's appendix discusses installing that database. That said, please don't install AdventureWorks on one of your company's production servers—keep it in your lab environment.

NOTE   If you accidentally close Object Explorer, you can get it back by selecting it from the View menu in SQL Server Management Studio. Or, press F8.

Right-click a database, select Properties, then select the Files page, as shown in figure 2.5.

Most of the settings in this Properties dialog will be covered in upcoming chapters, but for now it's useful to know the physical path of each database file, as well as their sizes. My AdventureWorks database is set to grow in 16 MB increments, with no maximum size, whenever the database gets full. Scrolling left and right in the Database files

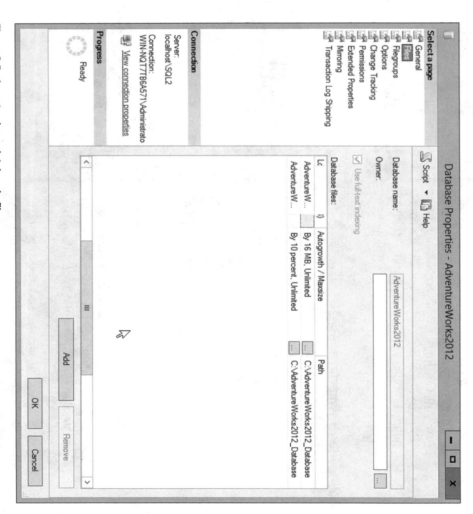

Figure 2.5   Inventorying a database's files

table lets you see additional information, such as the fact that my database is currently 189 MB in size, and its log file is just 1 MB in size.

The last piece of information you'll want to know is what each database is used for. SQL Server doesn't have that information; you'll need to ask around in your organization if you're not sure.

2.3 *Identifying other server objects*

There are a few things apart from databases that you'll want to know about. In Object Explorer, expand your instance's Security folder, then expand the Server Roles folder. Right-click sysadmin and select Properties. As shown in figure 2.6, you can now see

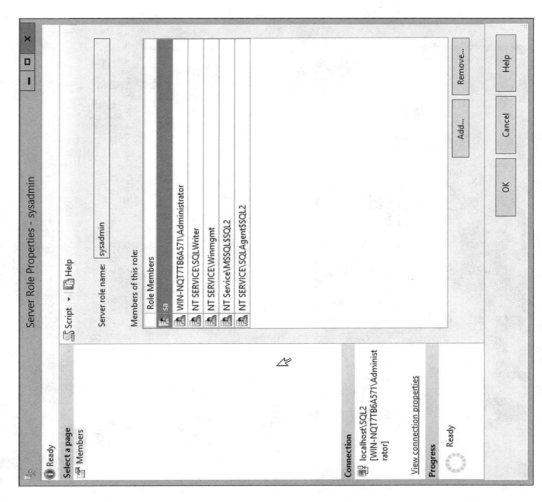

Figure 2.6   Members of the sysadmin fixed server role

who belongs to the sysadmin fixed server role. The members of this role have total control over SQL Server, so it's good to know who they are.

NOTE   On client OSes like Windows 7, you may need to double-click instead of right-click. Because absolutely no business runs SQL Server on a client OS for production purposes, I'm going to proceed with server-oriented directions. If you're using a client OS for practice, remember that you're not getting the "real" experience, and there may be operational and feature differences that I won't discuss.

Here, you can see that I have four members that are service accounts, one member that's a Windows logon (Administrator), and one member that's a SQL Server login (sa). This is a common configuration for a newly installed SQL Server instance; the sa account will be present only if the server is configured for Mixed Mode Authentication, instead of using Windows Authentication only. In a domain environment, it's also common to see the domain's Domain Admins group here.

TRY IT NOW   Take a moment to inventory the other fixed server roles. We'll cover the permissions assigned to these roles later; for now, it's enough to see who belongs to each one, so that you have an idea of who is accessing the server.

2.4   *Inventorying the server configuration*

The last thing I like to do with an unfamiliar server is inventory its configuration. The information I'm after now isn't easily accessible from within SQL Server Management Studio; instead, I'll launch SQL Server Configuration Manager. Mine is shown in figure 2.7, where I've selected the SQL Server Services node to see the services installed on my computer.

NOTE   This is another good way to see what instances are installed on the computer.

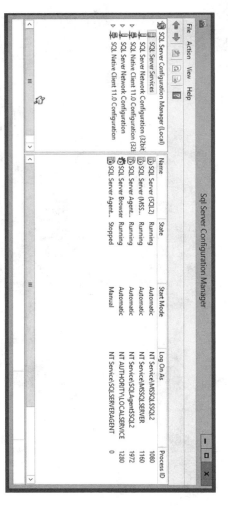

Figure 2.7   Viewing installed SQL Server services

The information I'm after here is the user accounts being used to run each service, as well as the start mode of each service. I notice that the SQL Server Agent service assigned to the default instance is set to start manually, and isn't currently running. That suggests the default instance isn't using any of the Agent features. That's good to know: if I'm working with that instance, I know that I can't rely on any of those features unless I set Agent to start automatically, and get the service running. You'll learn more about Agent in an upcoming chapter.

NOTE If you're using SQL Server Express to follow along, you may find that it lacks SQL Server Agent, or that Agent can't be started. As I've mentioned, Express isn't really the focus of this book, because in a business environment you won't find yourself maintaining Express instances.

2.5 *Hands-on lab*

For your first hands-on lab, go ahead and practice what you've learned in this chapter. Start by going to MoreLunches.com. Select this book's cover image, and look for the Inventory Worksheet download. That's a Microsoft Office Word document, and you'll use it in this lab.

If you have access to only your lab computer, complete the following inventory information for it. If you have access to (and permission to use) another SQL Server, complete an inventory sheet for it as well.

T-SQL crash course

SQL Server operates using a language called Transact-SQL (T-SQL). It's a Microsoft-specific variation of the industry-standard Structured Query Language, or SQL. T-SQL is compliant with the industry-standard SQL elements, and adds its own features for things like server management and schema definition. While much of SQL Server can be operated using the GUI, SQL Server's real power lies in T-SQL (some of the GUI runs T-SQL under the hood). In this chapter, we'll explore some of the basic data manipulation language (DML) queries in T-SQL.

It's difficult to understand a lot of how SQL Server works, and even difficult to really work with SQL Server, without knowing a little bit about T-SQL. However, I don't have a goal in this book of trying to make you a T-SQL programmer. So I'm going to go through some of the major T-SQL queries in this compact chapter. That way, you'll get the context you need for much of the rest of the book to make sense, but I won't bog you down with stuff that isn't directly related to the goal of effectively maintaining SQL Server.

3.1 SELECT queries

A SELECT query is designed to retrieve data from a database. It's the most common of the four basic DML queries (the others being DELETE, UPDATE, and INSERT), and it's one you'll use a lot as you work with SQL Server.

Start by getting SQL Server Management Studio up and running. Connect to your instance, then click the New Query button in the toolbar. A second toolbar will also open underneath the main one, and you'll need to use the drop-down box there to select your database. It will probably default to master, which is where SQL

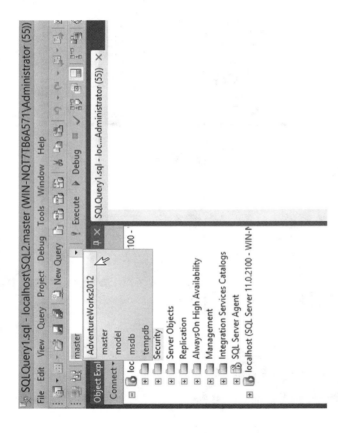

Figure 3.1   Selecting a database for the query window

Server keeps its configuration settings—we don't want to mess with that! Instead, select AdventureWorks2012, as shown in figure 3.1.

That selection tells the console that our queries will be run in that database.

3.1.1   A basic SELECT query

Let's start with a simple query. Type the following in the query window, then press Alt+X to run the query.

```
SELECT * FROM Person.Person
```

The results are shown in figure 3.2. You can also see that I've expanded the database's structure, showing a list of its tables, and near the bottom of that list is the Person.Person table. Within a database, data is actually stored in tables, which are a lot like a spreadsheet in Microsoft Office Excel. Each table consists of a predefined set of columns, and each entry in the table consists of a single row. In the query results, you'll notice that some rows contain NULL for some columns, meaning they don't define a value for that column.

NOTE   In most cases, SQL Server is not case-sensitive. Query keywords like SELECT and FROM can be typed in lowercase, but the common convention is to show them in uppercase. Object names like Person.Person are normally not case-sensitive, but it's common practice to type them as they're defined in the database itself.

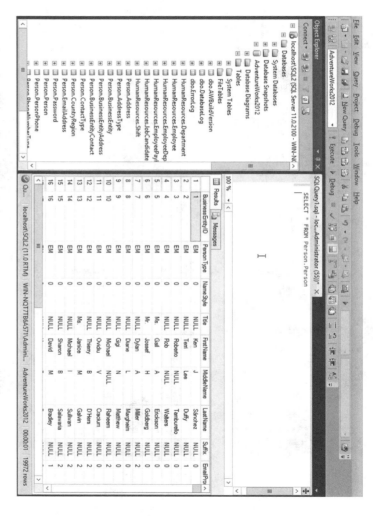

Figure 3.2   Running a sample query

Let's talk a bit more about what the SELECT query can do.

- The query starts with the keyword SELECT. That tells SQL Server we want to retrieve data.

- The * tells SQL Server to retrieve all of the columns from the table. It's a poor practice to use * in production queries, because it forces SQL Server to take the extra step of going and figuring out what all the columns are. Instead, you'd use a comma-separated list of column names, such as:

SELECT BusinessEntityID, PersonType, NameStyle FROM Person.Person

- The FROM keyword, followed by a table name, tells SQL Server which table we want to retrieve the data from.

NOTE   Throughout this chapter, I'm expecting that you will follow along, and run each of the queries I give you. If you are going to follow along, you'll need the AdventureWorks database installed. I'm assuming that you've at least read this book's appendix and installed AdventureWorks as directed.

This query retrieves all rows from the table.

3.1.2 *Returning specific rows from the table*

In production, it's more common to retrieve just a subset of the rows that meet whatever need you're trying to fulfill. To do so, you add a WHERE clause to your query. Try this query:

```
SELECT FirstName,MiddleName,LastName,Title
FROM Person.Person
WHERE Title IS NOT NULL
AND FirstName LIKE 'D%'
```

There are a few things to note about this query:

- The query still starts with the SELECT keyword.
- I used a comma-separated list of column names instead of *, but I listed the columns in a different order than they occur in the database. My results will appear in the order I listed them.
- I still used FROM to specify the table name.
- I added a WHERE clause, which in this example has two criteria. These are connected by the AND Boolean operator, meaning only those rows where both of my criteria are true will be included. The first criteria specifies that the Title column not be null, and the second specifies that the FirstName column start with the letter D.

TRY IT NOW You should definitely run this query. Much of the SELECT statement's complexity comes from the WHERE clause, so we're going to spend more time working with it.

SQL Server provides a number of operators for the WHERE clause to use. Some of the major ones are:

- = (the equal sign), which specifies that a value must be exactly the same as the one given. For example, WHERE FirstName = 'Daniel' will return only rows where the FirstName column contains "Daniel." Notice that, in T-SQL, strings like "Daniel" are delimited with single quotation marks.
- < (less than) and > (greater than), along with variations like <= (less than or equal to) and >= (greater than or equal to), which usually work with numeric and date values. For example, WHERE TotalSpent > 100.
- LIKE, which can use the wildcard % (percent sign) to perform simple pattern matches in strings. For example, WHERE LastName LIKE '%s%' will return all rows where the LastName column contains the letter "s" anywhere in the value.
- NOT, which is a Boolean operator that reverses true and false. For example, WHERE FirstName NOT LIKE 'D%', which will return all rows where the FirstName column does not start with "D." You can also use <> (not equal to), such as in WHERE FirstName <> 'Daniel'.

- IN, which specifies a set of values to match against. For example, WHERE Last-Name IN ('Banks','Bruno','Lee') will return all rows having one of those values in the LastName column.

- AND and OR, which are Boolean operators that each connect two criteria. You've seen AND at work already; using OR might look something like WHERE FirstName LIKE 'D%' OR LastName LIKE 'D%'. Notice that each side of the OR operator contains a complete criteria, in the form *column <operator> value.*

3.1.3 *Delimiting string and date values*

As already described, SQL Server expects strings to be contained within single quotation marks. But what if you have a string value that includes a single quote, such as the last name "O'Malley?" Consider this query (you don't need to run this, because it won't work):

```
SELECT * FROM Person.Person WHERE LastName = 'O'Malley'
```

SQL Server will read this as an instruction to select all rows where the LastName column contains "O," and will get upset about the "Malley'" part. One way to solve this is to double the single quotes that are a part of the string:

```
SELECT * FROM Person.Person WHERE LastName = 'O''Malley'
```

SQL Server will now properly read this as "O'Malley." Two single quotes in a row are read as a literal single quote, rather than as a string delimiter.

Date values also go in single quotes:

```
WHERE EnrollmentDate > '01-01-2013'
```

With date criteria, > (greater than) means "later in time," while < (less than) means "earlier in time." SQL Server treats dates and times a bit like numbers, so you can't use string-specific operators such as LIKE.

3.1.4 *Sorting results*

SQL Server normally returns data in whatever order it's stored in the database, which is often the most recently added data will be last on the list. You can use the ORDER BY clause to change the sort order:

```
SELECT FirstName,MiddleName,LastName,Title
FROM Person.Person
WHERE Title IS NOT NULL
AND FirstName LIKE 'D%'
ORDER BY FirstName ASC, LastName DESC
```

TRY IT NOW Please run this query so that you can see it change the order of the results.

Notice that SQL Server isn't terribly picky about formating. I was able to break this query onto multiple lines, or you could have typed it all on one, long line. I tend to start each major clause at the beginning of its line, and on a new line; additions like the logical AND I'll often put on a new line and indent a space or two. SQL Server doesn't care, but it makes it easier for me to read the query.

Here, I've asked SQL Server to sort on two columns. It will first sort the entries alphabetically by FirstName in ascending (A to Z) order. Ascending is the default; I could have left out the ASC keyword. For people with the same first name, they'll be sorted next in reverse alphabetic order (descending, or Z to A) by last name. You must specify DESC to reverse the sort order, since ascending is the default.

NOTE The WHERE and ORDER BY clauses are not connected to each other. You can use them together in the same query, or you can use just one or the other. However, when you use both of them, WHERE comes first.

Notice something interesting about the WHERE clause in that query: when you want to grab rows that have a column which is NULL or which isn't NULL, you can't use the normal comparison operators, such as the equal sign (=). In other words, you wouldn't write WHERE column = NULL or WHERE column <> NULL; you have to use IS and NOT: WHERE column IS NULL or WHERE column IS NOT NULL.

3.1.5 *Finding T-SQL documentation*

This is probably a good time to point out the SQL Server Books Online application, which contains SQL Server's documentation—including documentation on the T-SQL language. On Windows 7 and earlier, Books Online can be found (if you installed the feature) on the Start menu. On Windows 8, search the Start screen. You can also just choose View Help from the Help menu in SQL Server Management Studio, where you'll be given the option to use a locally installed Books Online, or view the help on Microsoft's website.

NOTE While local, offline help is convenient, I prefer the online, web-based help, because it gives me easier access to multiple versions of the help. Because I work with multiple versions of SQL Server, that access is pretty handy.

Figure 3.3 shows the online help. I've navigated to Database Engine, Transact-SQL Reference, Data Manipulation Language (DML), and SELECT to find the documentation for the SELECT query. Notice the Other Versions drop-down, where I can switch to the documentation for a different version of SQL Server.

You'll find all of the basic queries, and their clauses, under this DML section of the help.

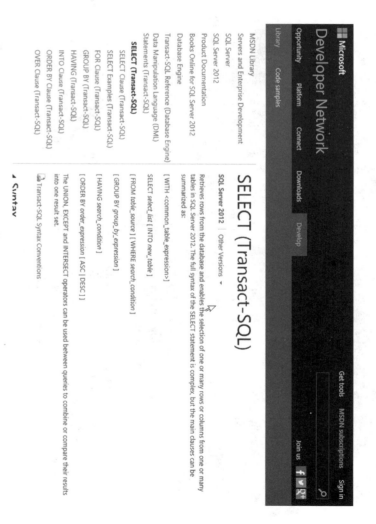

Figure 3.3   The online documentation is easy to access from anywhere.

ABOVE AND BEYOND

You don't need to remember all of the three-letter acronyms (TLAs) associated with SQL Server, but it sure helps navigate help and online examples. Some of the major ones:

- SQL—Structured Query Language
- DML—Data Manipulation Language
- DDL—Data Definition Language
- SSRS—SQL Server Reporting Services
- SSIS—SQL Server Integration Services
- SSAS—SQL Server Analysis Services
- DMO—Database Management Objects
- SMO—SQL Management Objects (superseded DMO in SQL Server 2005 and later)

You'll encounter some of these throughout this book, and I'll explain what they mean when we cover them. Expect to see coverage on SQL, DML, and DDL, in particular.

3.2 *DELETE, UPDATE, and INSERT queries*

Of the four common DML queries, only SELECT is pretty harmless, because it simply retrieves data without affecting any of it. DELETE, UPDATE, and INSERT are potentially dangerous because they change, or manipulate, data (which is where the DML acronym comes from). Fortunately, we're working on our AdventureWorks database: if you mess it up, you can always delete it (right-click it in Management Studio to find the Delete option, making sure you close any open query windows first), redownload it, and attach the downloaded files. You'll lose any work you've done, but that should be fine for your lab environment.

NOTE I want to point out that, as an administrator—especially as a beginning SQL Server admin—you might not have much opportunity to *run* these queries in production databases. But you'll *see* these queries, and I want you to recognize what they are. We'll use some of these in upcoming chapters' labs, so I can have you set up particular situations, which is why we're covering T-SQL so early in the book. But if you're thinking, "Wow, I didn't expect to get into programming by now," don't worry. This stuff isn't super-important at this stage in your SQL Server administration career.

3.2.1 *DELETE queries*

DELETE queries, as the keyword implies, remove data from a table. You'll almost always add a WHERE clause to these queries, since otherwise you'll delete everything in the specified table. Because you can't delete single columns (you have to delete entire rows), you don't specify a column list.

CAUTION There's no need to try the following query—it'll delete a number of rows from your database. Also note that, because of the way the database is constructed, this query may not complete without error. That's okay. We're not interested in its results, we're interested in the query itself.

For example:

```
DELETE FROM Person.Person
WHERE BusinessEntityID IN (
    SELECT BusinessEntityID
    FROM Person.BusinessEntity
    WHERE rowguid LIKE 'A%'
)
```

This query makes use of a *subquery*. In other words, the query inside the parentheses will execute first, just as in a mathematical expression. The result of this subquery is a list of BusinessEntityID values, because that's the column that the subquery selects. Those in turn correspond to the BusinessEntityID column in the Person.Person table, so whatever is selected by the subquery will be deleted in the Person.Person table. Subqueries like this are expensive for SQL Server to execute, especially for large tables, so they're often considered a poor practice. In this case, I wanted to make sure you knew what they looked like. A simpler DELETE query might look like this:

```
DELETE FROM Person.Person
WHERE FirstName LIKE 'D%'
```

3.2.2   UPDATE queries

UPDATE queries change existing information in the table. You'll specify the table to modify, and if you don't want to change every row you can specify a WHERE clause. Your actual changes are specified by a SET clause, which includes a comma-separated list of things to change.

For example, imagine that we had people entering both "Sr" and "Sr." for name suffixes in the Person.Person table. We could standardize those by changing the wrong ones:

```
UPDATE Person.Person
SET Suffix = 'Sr'
WHERE Suffix = 'Sr.'
```

An example of changing multiple columns at once might look like this:

```
UPDATE MyTable
SET Column = 'Value',
    OtherColumn = 'OtherValue'
WHERE This = 'That'
```

Obviously, that's just a simple example.

3.2.3   INSERT queries

An INSERT query adds new rows to the database. There's no need for a WHERE clause here, since you're not working with existing data. You usually specify a list of the columns for which you're providing values, and then a list of those values. The column and value lists must come in the same order, and must have the same number of items. You're required to include any columns for which SQL Server has not defined a default value, and where a NULL value isn't allowed. For example:

```
INSERT INTO Person.Person
(BusinessEntityID, PersonType, NameStyle, FirstName, LastName,
EmailPromotion)
VALUES (1861, 'SC', 0, 'Danica', 'Roberts', 0)
```

Some notes about that query:

- Numeric column values aren't delimited.
- Strings are delimited, as always, in single quotes.
- I omitted some columns that allow null values or that provide a default value of some kind; you'll learn how I knew that in the next section.

An INSERT query is one of the few SQL queries that affects only a single row—the one it is adding. There are other variations of INSERT, such as INSERT INTO, which can insert multiple rows. We won't cover those in this crash course chapter.

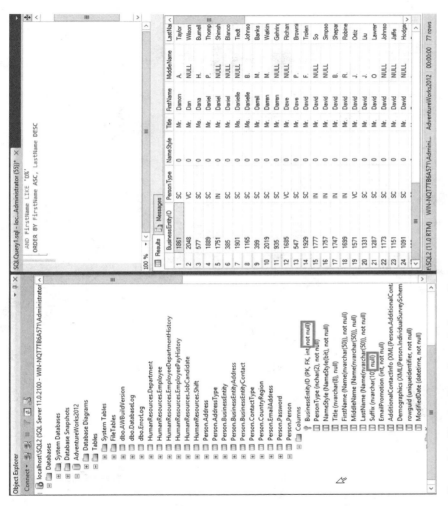

Figure 3.4 Viewing the columns in Person.Person

3.3 Assessing a database's structure

As shown in figure 3.4, Management Studio provides plenty of information about the structure of the database. I've used Object Explorer to drill down into the columns of the Person.Person table.

You can see all of the columns in the table listed, including BusinessEntityID,Person-Type,FirstName. I've marked two spots where you can see how Management Studio notes columns that may be null, and those which are not null, meaning they must contain a value. You can also see the type of data required for each column. For example, FirstName requires data of the type nvarchar(50), meaning it is a 50-character string that supports double-byte character sets (DBCS). A DBCS is used to support languages that have a large number of characters, such as most Asian languages. Some of the main data types are:

- *Bigint, Int, Smallint, and Tinyint*—Represent whole numbers of varying lengths.
- *Varchar and Nvarchar*—String fields that can hold values of varying lengths up to the maximum size specified. The "N" denotes a DBCS-compatible column.

- *Char and Nchar*—String fields that hold values of a fixed length, up to the maximum size specified. In other words, a char(10) will always contain 10 characters. If you provide a smaller value, it'll be padded with blanks to create the desired size (which wastes space). Again, "N" denotes a DBCS-compatible column.

- *Datetime, along with variations such as Datetime2, Date, and Time*—Hold date and time values.

- *Uniqueidentifier*—A globally unique identifier (GUID) that SQL Server creates for you. These are guaranteed to be unique within the table.

Some columns here are set to be not null, but I didn't provide a value for them in my INSERT query. I got away with it because the table structure defines a default value for them, which is used when I don't provide a value of my own. You can see these in Object Explorer under the Constraints column, but it won't tell you what the defaults are. Instead, right-click the table and select Design. You'll see a screen like the one in the next figure.

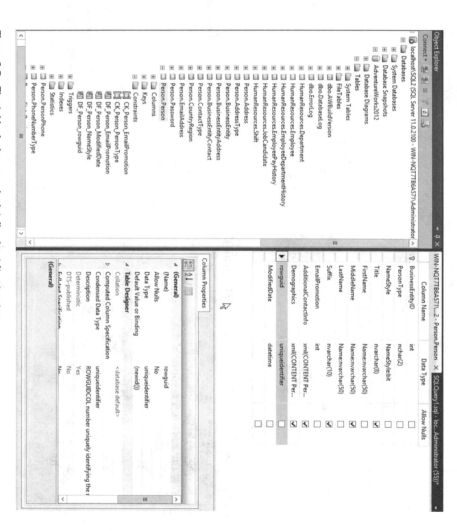

Figure 3.5   The table design reveals details about its structure.

Clicking the rowguid column in the upper pane reveals that it provides a default value, which is the output of SQL Server's built-in newid() function. That's what inserts a new unique ID into the column, so I get a new, unique ID each time I make a new row. That happens automatically thanks to the default. The ModifiedDate column uses the built-in getdate() function for its default, which returns the current date and time. The NameStyle column provides a static default value of 0, as does the EmailPromotion column.

TRY IT NOW Make sure you can spot these details in Management Studio. It's important that you know how to look up these pieces of information yourself, because it's the only place they're formally documented.

There's another important piece of structure, which I relied upon (but didn't explain) when I showed you the INSERT query. Where, exactly, did I come up with that value for BusinessEntityID? I did the same thing in the DELETE example, where I queried BusinessEntityID values. How did I know which table those came from?

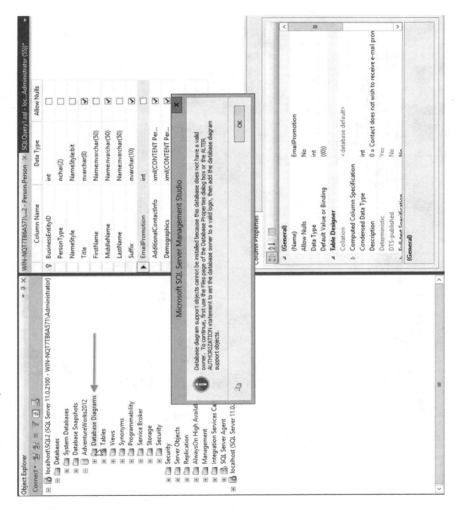

Figure 3.6   Database Diagrams folders are located in each database.

There are a few ways I could have found that out, but the easiest way—and the way that will provide the maximum number of other benefits—is to create a *database diagram*. SQL Server can generate the diagram automatically for you, and they're a visual representation of how various tables *relate* to one another. To create one, look for the Database Diagrams folder on Object Explorer. It'll usually be the first thing under the database itself, as shown in figure 3.6.

The first time you click this folder in a new database, you may see the warning message that I got in the previous figure. This is just telling you that SQL Server can't create database diagrams in this database until the database has a valid owner. Let's take care of that. I'll click OK on that message, right-click the database, and select Properties. On the Files page, in the Owner text box, I'll use the … browse button to select my Administrator account. The result is shown in figure 3.7; I'll click OK to save that information.

Now, when I click Database Diagrams, I get a different message, telling me that the database needs some support objects to make diagramming possible. Just answer Yes. Then, right-click Database Diagrams and select New Database Diagram.

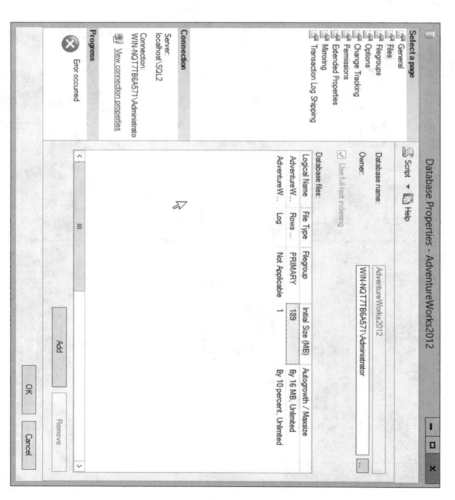

Figure 3.7   Adding an owner to the database

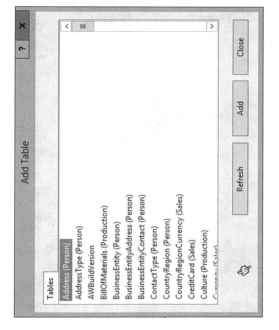

Figure 3.8   Database Diagrams start with a list of tables.

As shown in figure 3.8, you'll get a list of tables in the database. Since I want all of them in the diagram, I'll click the first table (Address), scroll to the bottom of the list, and hold the Shift key while clicking the last table (WorkOrderRouting). All of the tables should be highlighted now, so I'll click Add.

The result, figure 3.9, is an impressive, visual layout of the tables and how they relate to one another—and since this database has a lot of tables, it may take some time for your computer to complete the drawing.

TRY IT NOW   If you haven't done so already, start following along and get your basic diagram started. Be sure to include all of the tables from the Adventure-Works database.

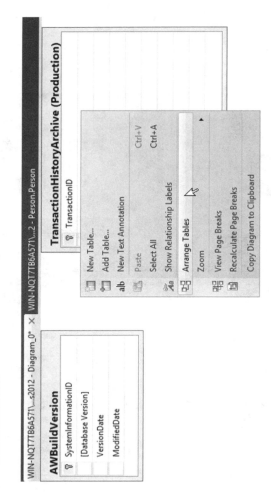

Figure 3.9   Arranging the tables creates a better layout.

When the diagram is ready, the table list will be empty (since there are no more tables to add), and you can click Close. The default layout isn't all that useful, so I'll right-click in a blank area of the diagram, as shown in the next figure, and select Arrange Tables. I'll then right-click again, in a blank area, and select Zoom, and then select To Fit. The result is a huge diagram.

You'll notice a zoom factor drop-down list in the toolbar—mine went to 10%, although yours may be different depending on your screen size. I'm going to change that to 100%, which zooms in a bit. I'll then scroll up and down, left and right until I find the Person (Person) table. For me, it's on the far left.

As shown in figure 3.10, the table has a bunch of key icons on the side, which connect to other tables. Those are the tables that have a relationship with Person.Person, meaning they share some kind of data with it. Hovering your mouse over the keys displays details about each relationship. You can click the attached line to highlight it, and then trace that to the other end.

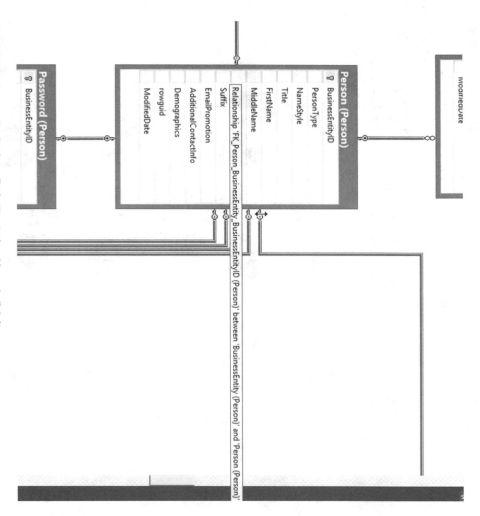

Figure 3.10   Locate the BusinessEntityID relationship and click it.

The other end of this relationship is the Person.BusinessEntity table. This is how I knew that the BusinessEntityID column in Person.Person contained values from the Person.BusinessEntity table—the two tables are connected, or *related*. Now, right-click that relationship line and select Properties. A Properties pane pops up, and the Description field says, "Foreign key constraint referencing BusinessEntity.BusinessEntityID." Here's what that means:

- *The Person.Person table's BusinessEntityID column has a foreign key constraint applied to it.* That means the field can only hold values that come from a corresponding field in another table.
- *The other table is Person.BusinessEntity, and the field is BusinessEntityID.* Person.Person's BusinessEntityID column must draw its values from Person.BusinessEntity's BusinessEntityID column.

Read that a few times, and study your diagram, until it makes sense! Then, let's put your new diagram-reading skill to use.

TRY IT NOW Take a look at the Sales.SalesOrderDetail table, and its columns. One column is named SalesOrderID, and in Management Studio you can tell that it has a foreign key constraint (in the column list, FK means foreign key).

From what other table, and what column in that table, must the SalesOrderID column of Sales.SalesOrderDetail draw its values?

Here's your answer: the SalesOrderID column of Sales.SalesOrderDetail is linked to the Sales.SalesOrderHeader table, and specifically to the SalesOrderID column of that table.

Now, why do you care?

3.4 Multitable SELECT queries

Once you know what columns link to tables, you can create multitable queries that combine, or *join*, those tables. For example, try running the following query in figure 3.11, which combines information from a sales order "header" table with a sales order "detail" table to construct a complete order:

```
SELECT sod.ProductID, sod.OrderQty,
    soh.OrderDate, soh.[Status]
FROM Sales.SalesOrderHeader AS soh
INNER JOIN Sales.SalesOrderDetail sod
    ON sod.SalesOrderID = soh.SalesOrderID
```

Let's break down that query:

- I start with the SELECT keyword.
- I've referred to four columns. Note that I've put the prefixes "soh" and "sod" in front of them. Those are called *aliases*, and they represent the SalesOrderHeader (soh) and SalesOrderDetail (sod) columns. I used those aliases because they

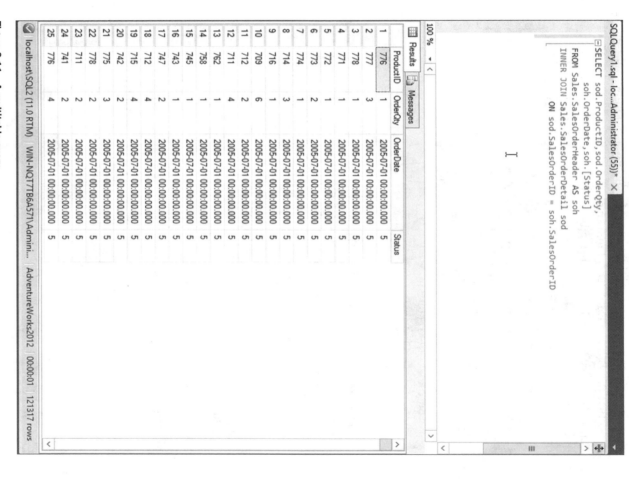

Figure 3.11 A multitable query

- remind me of the full table names, but are easier to type. I could have just used "fred" and "Wilma," but those wouldn't make as much sense to me.

- Notice that the [Status] column is contained in square brackets. That's because "status" is a special keyword in SQL Server; the square brackets tell SQL Server that I'm referring to a column name, not the keyword.

- Next I specify my first table, in the FROM clause. I used the AS keyword to assign that "soh" alias. It's a bit weird to see the alias used first, in the column list, and then actually defined later in the query, but that's how SQL works.

- The INNER JOIN keyword tells SQL Server that I'm connecting two tables, and I give it the second table name. I also define an alias, although this time I skipped the AS keyword and just gave it the alias name—that's legal.

- The ON keyword tells SQL Server *how* the two tables are joined. I specified the two columns that match them up: the SalesOrderID column from each table.

OK, I'll be honest—this is pretty advanced stuff, and if it doesn't make sense right now, that's fine. You'll see this a lot more later, and I'm quite frankly not concerned about your ability to write join queries. What's important is that you be able to recognize one when you see one, because they play a big role in performance in SQL Server.

3.5 *Hands-on lab*

Let's practice what you've just read about in this chapter. See if you can complete the following tasks:

- Write a SELECT query that will retrieve the Title, FirstName, LastName, and Suffix columns from the Person.Person table.

- Write a SELECT query that will list the FirstName and LastName from Person.Person, as well as the CustomerID from Sales.Customer, all in a single result table. Include only those customers who have a PersonID that is not null.

Remember, you can find answers at MoreLunches.com. Click this book's cover image, and look under the Downloads section for the Lab Answers.

Managing databases

Databases are the basic unit of management and work within SQL Server. A database is an almost entirely self-contained package that bundles security settings, configuration settings, your actual data, and much more. That makes databases a good place to start your education in SQL Server maintenance. Some of the things you'll look at in this chapter will need a much more complete explanation, which will come in later chapters; the goal right now is to focus on the database container itself. We'll be covering database configuration options and some basics of how to manage databases.

4.1 Configuring database options

If you don't have it open, get SQL Server Management Studio on your screen. Right-click a database, such as AdventureWorks2012, and select Properties. You should be looking at the General page of the Database Properties dialog, as shown in figure 4.1.

There's not really anything to change on this tab, but it does give you a quick glance at who owns it, when it was last backed up, and how big it is—all useful information. The next page is Files, and this is where we can start assessing database storage. You'll do that in an upcoming section of this chapter, so just remember where you saw the information. That goes for the Filegroups page as well.

The other main page we need to look at right now is the Options page. Here's what you should see:

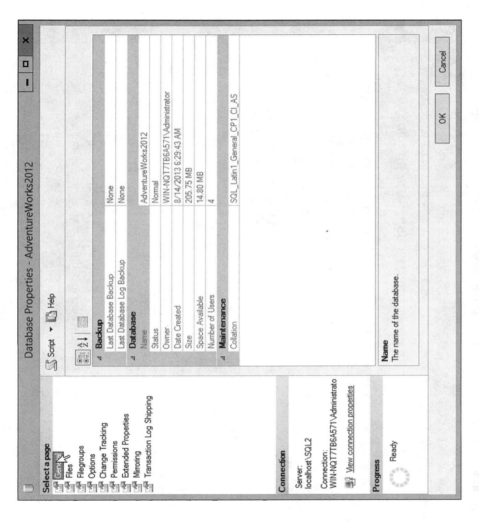

Figure 4.1   The General tab includes basic information about the database.

- *Collation* defaults to the collation setting of the SQL Server instance (and you incur a performance hit if you select a collation other than that). It refers to the way SQL Server treats data for sorting and comparing purposes. For example, in Lithuania the letter "Y" comes between "I" and "J," so SQL Server would need to know if you wanted to use those rules. The "Latin" collations work well for English and most Romance languages.

- *Recovery model* determines how the database can be recovered. Production databases should use the Full model; nonproduction databases, or databases that are primarily read-only, may use Simple. You'll learn more about these in the next chapter.

- *Compatibility level* can be used to change the behavior of the database to correspond with a previous version of SQL Server. This is mainly used when you migrate a database from an older version to a newer version.

- *Containment type* specifies exactly how standalone the database is. Normally, databases have a few dependencies on certain instance-wide objects, meaning you can't easily move *only* the database to a different instance. A contained database has fewer, or zero, dependencies, making it more standalone—but less centrally managed. Chapter 6 will go into some of these details.

- *Auto Close* should, in general, be False. This specifies that SQL Server should close the physical database files when the database isn't being used. When someone does try to use it, there will be a delay as SQL Server opens the file. For a large database, or on a busy server, that delay can be significant.

- *Auto Create Statistics* should usually be True. This tells SQL Server to automatically create certain statistical information used to optimize query performance. You'll learn a lot more about statistics in several upcoming chapters, and you'll also learn about the Auto Update Statistics and Auto Update Statistics Asynchronously options.

- *Auto Shrink* is typically set to False. Setting it to True causes SQL Server to periodically try to make the database files smaller by returning unused space to the OS. Later in this chapter, you'll learn why that's often a bad idea.

Those are the main settings that you need to focus on for now. There are some others that will come up in discussion in upcoming chapters, so just remember where you found the database properties, and how to get back to that dialog.

4.2 Detaching and attaching databases

When you need to move a database between instances, or even copy a database—perhaps to a test environment—detaching and attaching can be an easy way to do it. Detaching tells SQL Server to close the database and forget that it exists. At that point, the database is just some files on disk. You can copy them, move them, or do whatever else you want.

Attaching is the opposite—and you've already done it if you set up your lab environment, since you attached the AdventureWorks database. Attaching "connects" the database to a SQL Server instance, so that administrators and users can work with the database.

To detach a database, right-click it, select Tasks, then select Detach.... As shown in figure 4.2, you have two options.

Drop Connections, the first option, will forcibly disconnect anyone using the database. That could result in a user being upset, so you don't want to do that on a production database in the middle of the workday. Update Statistics, the second option, tells SQL Server to make one last update of the database's performance statistics before detaching. That way, when the database is attached to a new instance, it's ready to go right away—provided the new instance is the same version of SQL Server; statistics aren't compatible across versions.

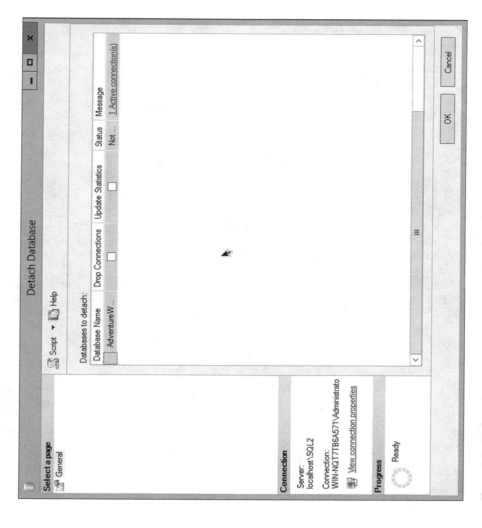

Figure 4.2   You have two options when detaching a database.

You should already have seen how to perform an attach operation; if not, turn to the appendix and follow the lab setup procedure.

ABOVE AND BEYOND

There's another way to copy a database that you should be aware of, although we're not going to use this technique in this book. It's called the Copy Database Wizard, and you start it by right-clicking the database, choosing Tasks, then selecting Copy Database....

This Wizard is capable of copying a database to a different instance, with the advantage of not taking the database offline as a Detach would do. The Wizard is also capable of copying the instance-level dependencies that a database may need to function properly.

4.3   Assessing database storage

Go back to the Files page in the database properties. Every SQL Server database has at least two, and possibly many more, files:

- Files with a .MDF filename extension are a database's primary files. This is where everything in the database is normally stored. Every database has a .MDF file. In cases where you have multiple database files (see .NDF files in the third item of this list), the .MDF file will always store the database's internal configuration information and other internal system data.

- A .LDF filename extension indicates the database's transaction log file. This file serves several important operational and recovery purposes, and you'll learn about it in the next chapter. Every database has one of these, and only one, although databases in the Simple recovery model automatically empty the log so it'll *usually* never be very large. We're going to discuss the Simple model in the next chapter, and I'll share more details about it then.

- Databases can also have zero or more .NDF, or secondary data, files. These are usually created as a tactic to improve performance or to make backing up a large database more manageable.

Start your assessment by figuring out what files you have, and where they are physically stored. If possible, work with a server administrator to understand how the server is accessing the files. For example, if .LDF files are stored on one Storage Area Network (SAN), and .MDF files are on another, try to discover if the server is accessing both SANs by means of a single network adapter, or if it's using different adapters for each. Those answers will become important in the next section.

Also try to learn more about what *type* of storage is being used. Are files being written to a single local disk? A local array, or mirror? If they're being written to a SAN, how is the SAN configured? Are there any solid-state drives (SSDs) in use? Again, these are all important answers as you try to identify any potential concerns with the storage subsystem.

4.4   Identifying potential performance concerns in storage

Storage is the absolute single biggest bottleneck for SQL Server performance. As such, one of your biggest concerns should be whether or not the storage layout is optimized for performance. Storage is also one of the biggest potential failure points, since disk drives do indeed fail every now and then. That means reliability and recoverability will be another concern. Your final concern relates to whether or not you're able to efficiently back up and restore the database, should the need for restoration arise. How your database storage is laid out can affect that significantly.

4.4.1   Problems with file layout

Let's start with a few major problem areas. You should make sure that, unless there's a good reason, none of your databases have any of the following situations:

- *Colocated log and data files.* For both performance and reliability reasons, you want your data (.MDF and .NDF) files separated from your log (.LDF) files. Separated ideally means on different physical disks.

- *Unnecessary secondary files.* If your database is split into one .MDF and one or more .NDF files, and they're all located on the same storage volume, then those secondary files may be unnecessary. On a huge database, the .NDF files may serve to break up the backup tasks into more manageable chunks; on smaller databases, there's no reason to have .NDF files if they're going to live on the same disk volume as the .MDF file.

- *Heavy disk fragmentation.* Use Windows' disk defragmentation tools to look at the level of physical disk fragmentation. Ideally, you want SQL Server's database files to come from a single contiguous block of space on whatever disk volumes they live on. Anything else slows down SQL Server. Note that you can't defragment these files without either detaching the database or shutting down the SQL Server instance.

The last thing to look at is a bit more of a judgment call, and that's how your database uses any .NDF files it may have. When you create a .NDF file, you choose which database objects are moved to that file. Similarly, when a developer creates a database object, they pick which file it lives in. Those objects can include tables, which house all of your actual data, and programming objects like views, stored procedures, and the like. If your goal is to improve performance, or to split up a large database to make backups more manageable, then you can't just move any old files into a .NDF: you have to be strategic.

Let's say your database includes two heavily used tables, A and B. There are a bunch of other tables, but those two get the majority of the traffic. Moving A and B to separate .NDFs, while leaving everything else in the main .MDF, can be a good way to improve performance *if*—and only if—the three files live on separate disk volumes, and ideally if those disk volumes are accessed by different controllers (either actual disk controller cards for local storage, or SAN adapters for SAN storage). That way, SQL Server can access each of the three without the other two getting in the way.

Imagine that you run a freight train. You have three boxcars full of merchandise that you need to get to three different destinations. One way to do so would be to tack all three boxcars behind a single engine, and run it to each of the three destinations. That'd be pretty slow, and it's what SQL Server does when all of your data is in a single .MDF file.

Another approach would be to attach each boxcar to a different engine. If they're all sharing track for a portion of the journey, you're really not getting much benefit. This is like having multiple .NDF files, but only one controller channel to the storage.

The best approach would be to have three boxcars, three engines, and three separate tracks. Everyone can go their own way, without worrying about what the others are doing. This is the same as having multiple .NDFs, with different controller channels to each storage volume.

Modern SANs can help alleviate the need to have multiple .NDFs. SANs are fast, so controller channel contention may not be a problem. SANs inherently spread your data across many different physical disks, further reducing contention and improving performance. With a fast, well-built SAN, you may not need .NDFs for performance purposes.

4.4.2 *Problems with file size*

Sizing is also something to look at. Go back to the database properties dialog's Files tab and look at the properties for each file. You'll notice that each has a current size, as well as a growth option. Most folks leave their files set to autogrow by some size or percentage. Autogrowth is a bad thing, although you may want to leave it on for specific reasons. Here's why it's bad:

- Autogrowth puts a significant burden on a server, and when it happens during production hours your users will be impacted.

- Autogrowth results in the physical fragmentation of the database files, which slows down database access. This is because disk space is requested from the OS in chunks (set by the autogrowth size you've configured), and those chunks won't be all lined up in a contiguous space.

- Autogrowth isn't managed. Either you'll allow unlimited growth, which will eventually consume available disk space, or you'll cap the growth, forcing you to deal with the capacity problem anyway.

Without autogrowth won't your database eventually fill up and stop working? No—not if you're monitoring it. *Growth* is fine. Databases grow. When a database *starts* to need more room, you should plan to manually increase its size during a scheduled maintenance window, to avoid the downsides of autogrowth. That maintenance window can involve taking the database (or the entire SQL Server instance) offline, so that Windows can defragment the physical layout of the database file. In other words, *manage* your database sizes. You can do that right from the properties dialog box. Some administrators prefer to leave autogrowth turned on as a kind of last-ditch safety net—it's a way to ensure the application doesn't stop working unexpectedly. I personally don't like to rely on that safety net, because, in my experience, autogrowth has caused me a lot of grief over the years.

Autogrowth on a log file is also bad. Typically, your log files should remain at a more or less constant size. The backup process should empty out the log, leaving it ready for new entries. Your log may need to grow if there's an increase in overall workload, meaning the log has more to keep track of between backup operations, but once it hits its new "comfort zone" size, the growth should stop. Again, that growth should, as much as possible, be managed manually.

Autogrowth is a good last-ditch emergency measure (which is why some folks leave it on), but your goal should be for it to never happen. So how can you properly size your database? You do so through monitoring. Pay attention to how much of the database file is being used, and monitor that figure. Get a feel for how much larger a database grows every day, for example, and you'll be able to predict when it will need more room. You'll also know about how much room to give it to have it last for a specified number of additional days. To perform that monitoring, you can pop into SQL Server Management Studio every few days and look at the databases' properties. You'll see the file sizes, and, if you like, you can record them in an application such as Microsoft Office Excel. That way, you can have the spreadsheet generate charts that show you database growth over time. Charts help me visualize when the database size is going to become too large for the disk it's on, for example.

4.4.3 Filegroups

We haven't yet discussed *filegroups*. If your database consists of a single .MDF file (and a .LDF file), you won't use filegroups. Filegroups come into play when you have one or more .NDF files. In that scenario, filegroups act purely as a convenience. They let you target specific operations—primarily backups and restores—to a single filegroup, thereby affecting a bunch of files.

Let's say that, for performance reasons, you've split your database across three .NDF files in addition to the main .MDF file. Each of those four files is located on a separate disk volume, and each volume is accessed by a different disk controller. That's great for parallel operations, and it should help performance in the system. But now you have to back up and recover four files, making a lot more work for yourself. Instead, you can group those into a single filegroup, and then run backups against that filegroup, grabbing all four files at once.

On a huge database, you might have many different .NDF files to spread out the data. If, taken altogether, they're too large to back up in a single maintenance window, you might group them into different filegroups. That way, you can back them up separately. Of course, recovering becomes a lot more complicated, since you won't have a single point-in-time backup that includes everything. You'll dive more into this topic in the next chapter.

4.5 System databases

We should spend a few minutes discussing the four system databases in SQL Server.

- *Master* is where SQL Server stores its own configuration information. This database doesn't change often—mainly when you add or remove a database, or make a server-wide configuration change—but you should back it up regularly. There are special procedures for restoring this database, and for moving it to a different location. Consult SQL Server's documentation for instructions.

- *Model* is a template from which all new databases are created. Unless you've made changes to it (which is rare), there's no real need to back it up or move it.

- *TempDb* is a temporary database. This should be located on a fast storage volume, ideally separate from the volumes used by your databases. It doesn't need to be backed up (SQL Server makes a new one each time it starts, anyway), and its disk volume doesn't need to be redundant (meaning it doesn't necessarily need to be on a disk array). Many organizations install a local SSD (often chosen because they're fast) and put TempDB on it.

■ *MSDB* is technically a system database, but it's really used just like any of your databases. SQL Server Agent uses it for all of its tasks, which you'll learn about in several upcoming chapters. MSDB should be backed up, and treated more or less like any of your own databases.

TempDB is worth discussing a bit more. There are a number of different query operations that might need to use some space in TempDB, and there are certain administrative options that use it as well. Developers can explicitly put things into TempDB as part of their code. It's used for *lots* of things. In terms of properly maintaining SQL Server, you don't need to worry so much about what it's used for as you do about how to position it properly for maximum performance. That's something we'll touch on in several upcoming chapters.

4.6 *An overview of storage hardware*

It's almost impossible to talk about SQL Server performance without talking about disk storage, because the disk system contributes most of SQL Server's performance overhead. Since I brought up the topic of arrays and SSDs, I will quickly review some of those options for folks that might not be familiar with them.

A disk is a basic unit of storage hardware. SQL Server is completely capable of running itself from a single disk, provided it's big enough to store the data you'll be keeping. But a single disk can only do so much in a given period of time, and it can quickly become a performance bottleneck. Imagine asking someone to read the contents of this book aloud: their mouth is a single output channel, and it's going to take some time for them to stream all of those words out into the air.

An *array* is a group of disks that work together. There are many different types of arrays. A *mirror*, for example, is one or more disks that retain an exact copy of another set of disks. Mirrors provide *redundancy*, meaning if the first group of disks dies, you've got a live backup ready to go. *Stripe arrays* take data and spread it across multiple disks, reducing the bottleneck that a single disk would create. So instead of having one disk reading and writing your data, you've got several disks working together to do so. Some of those arrays can include *parity* information, which helps provide redundancy for the data on the array. With parity, you could have one or more disks (depending on how the array is set up) fail, and not lose any data.

An SSD is a solid-state disk, which stores data in microchips rather than on magnetic platters. They're generally much faster than disks, because they don't have mechanical bits that have to spin and move.

A SAN is a big box full of disk arrays that sits on the network. Servers are assigned pieces of the SAN's total storage, and they use their pieces just like they'd use a locally attached set of disks. SANs are a way of centralizing disks for management purposes. SANs are nearly always configured as large arrays, providing resilience against the failure of individual disks inside the SAN. Rather than plugging in disks using a copper cable, you connect a server to the SAN over a network of some kind. Most SQL Server instances keep their data on a SAN, because the SAN itself can provide a high level of both performance and reliability. SANs are commonly managed by specialized administrators, so as a SQL Server administrator you might have to work with them to understand how your servers' data is being physically stored.

4.7 *Hands-on lab*

Let's practice what you've just read about in this chapter. Go to MoreLunches.com, click this book's cover image, and find the Database Inventory Sheet download. Complete one sheet for each database on one of your SQL Server instances. If you don't have a production environment to inventory, complete the worksheet for your AdventureWorks database instead.

Backup and recovery

5.1

The transaction log

Before we can talk about backups, we have to talk about how SQL Server works, internally, and about its transaction log. This process is crucial to how backups work, along with a dozen other maintenance and performance-related tasks.

SQL Server stores all data in 8 KB chunks called *pages*. A page typically contains all of the data for a single row in a single table, and it can contain multiple rows, if they're small. There are some exceptions: SQL Server supports certain data types that can span several pages, but for right now think of each 8 KB page as being the basic unit of management.

When you issue a query that makes a change—that is, an UPDATE, INSERT, or DELETE query—SQL Server starts by finding the page that contains the affected data (or in the case of an INSERT, the page that *will* contain the new data), and loading it into an area of memory called the *buffer pool*. Figure 5.1 illustrates that action.

Backups are perhaps the most common task people think of when you say "server maintenance." Without a doubt, they're important. I have to be honest: many organizations don't use SQL Server's native backup facilities. Instead, they rely on other backup software, like Backup Exec, BrightStor, or even Microsoft System Center Data Protection Manager. Those solutions let a company manage all of its backups—including SQL Server—in a single place, whereas SQL Server's native backup abilities only apply to SQL Server. This chapter won't cover those other solutions. What it will cover is what's built into SQL Server—and plenty of organizations do use that, even if they only use SQL Server to create a backup file that is subsequently picked up by another backup solution.

INSERT INTO Table (ColA,ColB) VALUES('ValA','ValB')

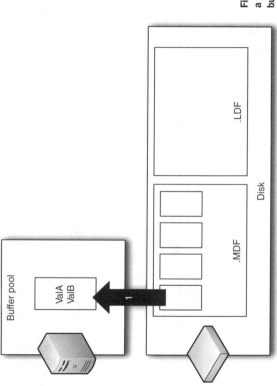

Figure 5.1 Loading a page into the buffer pool

At almost the same time, SQL Server makes a copy of the actual query in its transaction log, as shown in figure 5.2. The log isn't a database file. Think of it as a big list of all the queries that SQL Server has been asked to run.

INSERT INTO Table (ColA,ColB) VALUES('ValA','ValB')

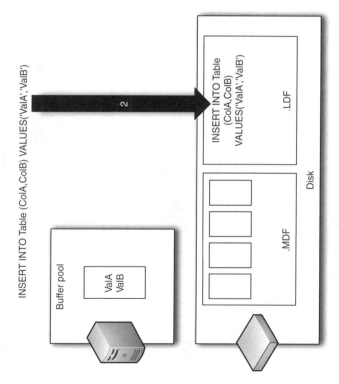

Figure 5.2 SQL Server copies all queries into the transaction log.

At this point, the changes SQL Server has made only exist in memory, although the query itself is on disk. If SQL Server were to crash, when you restarted it the server would go into *recovery mode*. It would read all of the queries sitting in that log, and reexecute them to reproduce those same changes. This is how SQL Server protects against data loss. You can see why it's important that the log file be on a different disk than the database file! If you lose one, you've still got the other as a backup.

Eventually (usually just milliseconds, but that's forever to a computer) SQL Server will save the changed, or *dirty*, page back to disk, as shown in figure 5.3. At the same time, it marks, or *checkpoints*, the log file to show that the query was successfully committed to disk. Now, if the server goes into recovery mode, it knows not to worry about this query, because it's already been made and saved.

Every query executes like this when a database is in the Full recovery model. The committed query is still in the log, but it's specifically marked as having been committed. It's also timestamped, so that SQL Server knows when the query took place. If SQL Server ever ends up in recovery mode, it replays queries in the same order they originally took place, and the timestamp helps ensure that.

In the Simple recovery model, checkpointed log entries are deleted. That means you can never again reexecute them, but it means you never have to worry about the log file getting full. Well, *mostly* not worry. A very large transaction can certainly fill the log, since the entire transaction has to fit in the log until the transaction completes. Certain maintenance tasks like rebuilding indexes are very large transactions, so in some cases you may need to worry about the log size. But the idea behind the Simple model is that completed transactions are removed automatically from the log.

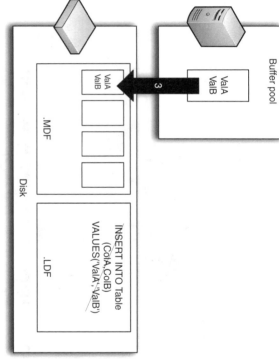

INSERT INTO Table (ColA,ColB) VALUES('ValA','ValB')

Buffer pool

ValA
ValB

3

ValA
ValB

.MDF

.LDF

INSERT INTO Table
(ColA,ColB)
VALUES('ValA','ValB')

Disk

Figure 5.3 SQL Server commits the page and checkpoints the log.

When a database uses the Bulk-Logged recovery model, most regular queries are logged just as they are in the Full model. However, certain bulk operations are logged as a single entry, which means SQL Server can't reexecute them. Typically, if you need to bulk-load or bulk-change data, you switch to the Bulk-Logged recovery model, do your work, switch back to Full, then immediately back up the database to capture those bulk changes.

5.2 How backups work

SQL Server supports four kinds of backup:

- *Full*—Backs up the entire database either to a locally attached tape drive, or to a file on disk.
- *Differential*—Grabs all of the data that has changed since the last full backup. You run these when your database is too big to do a regular full backup. Each differential you do will be larger than the last, since it contains the changes since the last full backup.
- *Copy*—Grabs all of the data, the same as a full backup, but doesn't reset the differential marker. Any differentials taken after a copy will still refer back to the most recent full backup, not to the copy.
- *Transaction log*—Works only on the database's transaction log. By making this kind of backup, you also gain the ability to clear the log, making room for more transactions. I'll discuss this in just a bit.

Backups are physically saved to a *media set*, which can contain multiple backups. Backups can be given an expiration date, too, to help ensure that nobody accidentally uses them when they're too old to be accurate.

None of these backups automatically empties, or *truncates* the log. That's a separate and important step. Truncating means you permanently delete all of the checkpointed queries from the log, freeing space in the log for new queries. This is how you keep the log from eventually filling the entire disk. But you can't truncate the log without backing it up (at least, not in newer versions of SQL Server; it used to be possible).

The *transaction log* backup, as the name implies, backs up only the transaction log, doing nothing else to it. As part of backing up the log, you can also opt to truncate it, which empties out all the checkpointed transactions and frees space in the log file. Transaction log backups can be very quick, since most transaction logs aren't that big. You'll want to be sure to back up to a different disk than either the database or the log file is on, so that if you lose a disk you don't lose your data *and* your backups!

We'll discuss how you decide how often you'll do each of these kinds of backup later in the chapter. But for now, let's walk through how to do each one first.

TRY IT NOW In the next three sections I'm going to walk you through a complete backup process. Then, I'll explain how to restore data and walk you through that process. I suggest you follow along with the steps I'm taking, since they're your hands-on lab for this chapter.

5.2.1   *Making a full database backup*

Start by right-clicking the AdventureWorks2012 database and choosing Properties. On the Options tab, change the Recovery model to Full, then click OK. SQL Server will need a few seconds to complete that change.

Now make the backup.

1   Right-click the AdventureWorks2012 database, choosing Tasks, then Back Up…. By default, you'll be set to make a full backup of the database, which will not expire. SQL Server will make a new backup set, which is designed to contain one or more backups. It will also default to creating a new media set on disk.

2   On the Options page, we'll back up to the existing media set, but since this is a new full backup, select the option to Overwrite all existing backup sets.

3   Click OK to start the backup.

4   Click OK on the success dialog.

That's it! AdventureWorks is a small database, so this should only take a few seconds to complete.

5.2.2   *Making a differential database backup*

With AdventureWorks2012 selected in the Object Explorer of SQL Server Management Studio, click New Query. In the query window, type the following, and press Alt+X to run it:

```
UPDATE Person.Person
SET MiddleName = 'G'
WHERE BusinessEntityID = 3
GO
```

This will give us a change in the database, so that there will be something for the backup to capture. Now let's make a differential backup:

1   Right-click the AdventureWorks2012 database, choosing Tasks, then Back Up….

2   For Backup type, select Differential. Notice that SQL Server creates a new default backup set name, but we're still saving the backup to the same media set.

3   On the Options page, verify that we're set to Append to the existing backup set.

4   Click OK to run the backup.

5   Click OK on the success dialog.

You're done!

5.2.3   *Making a transaction log backup*

For this last step, you're going to run the following query. It should already be in your query window; change the "G" to an "X". Just before you press Alt+X to run the query, make a note of the exact time on your computer, in seconds. Here's the query:

```
SELECT * FROM Person.Person
```

```
UPDATE Person.Person
SET MiddleName = 'X'
WHERE BusinessEntityID = 3
GO

SELECT * FROM Person.Person
```

You're going to change the "X" to a "B" now, and run the query again. Make a note of the exact time, in seconds, just before you press Alt+X to run this:

```
UPDATE Person.Person
SET MiddleName = 'B'
WHERE BusinessEntityID = 3
GO

SELECT * FROM Person.Person
```

Now let's make a t-log backup:

1 Right-click the AdventureWorks2012 database, choosing Tasks, then Back Up....

2 Change the Backup type to Transaction Log. Again, you'll get a new backup set, but the same disk media set.

3 On the Options page, select the option to Truncate the transaction log. It should be selected by default, just as it was in the previous two backup operations.

4 Click OK to run the backup.

5 Click OK on the success dialog.

At this point you should have three backups: full, differential, and t-log. Your database has gone from its original value for that guy's middle initial, through three different variations. This will give us something fun to work with in the next section.

You'll notice that we didn't take the database offline to perform these tasks. That's right, backups can happen while the database is online and in use! Transaction log backups don't present a problem when you do that, but full and differential databases might. SQL Server takes a pretty big performance hit when you run a backup while the database is under heavy use, which is why most organizations schedule it for a maintenance window during off-hours.

5.3 *How restoration works*

When you restore, you typically start by making a *tail-end* t-log backup. You should have seen that option when you made the t-log backup in the previous section. That grabs the *active*, or uncheckpointed, queries in the transaction log. That's different than a normal t-log backup, which grabs the checkpointed transactions. When you make that tail-end backup, the database will go into a *restoring state*, which allows you to restore backups, but prevents normal use of the database.

You then restore your full backup, and tell SQL Server that you're not done. Then you restore your differential, and again tell the server there's more coming. You then restore all of your transaction log backups, including the tail-end backup, which goes last. All the while, you keep telling SQL Server, "Wait! There's more!"

When you restore your *last* backup file, you tell SQL Server that you're done, and it'll go into recovery mode.

Recovery mode reexecutes all of the queries in your restored t-logs, bringing the database up-to-date. The database goes online after the recovery mode is complete, and should be ready to use.

One neat variation on this is to do a point-in-time recovery, which lets you restore all of your transaction logs, but tell recovery mode to stop reexecuting queries once it reaches a certain point. Remember how I had you make a note of the exact time when you ran those queries in the previous section?

5.3.1   *Preparing for recovery*

Let's run through a recovery. I'll start by making a tail-end backup:

1   Close all open windows within SQL Server Management Studio, leaving only the Object Explorer open.

2   Right-click the AdventureWorks2012 database, choosing Tasks, then Back Up....

3   For the Backup type, select Transaction Log.

4   On the Options page, select Back up the tail of the log, and leave the database in the restoring state.

5   Click OK to start.

6   Click OK on the success dialog. Notice that the icon on the database now indicates it's in restore mode.

NOTE   If you get an error that the backup couldn't complete because the database is in use, make sure you've closed any other windows. Wait a few minutes, and try again.

5.3.2   *Starting the recovery*

Let's get the recovery under way.

1   Right-click the AdventureWorks2012 database, choose Tasks, then Restore, then Database....

2   You should see a dialog something like the one in figure 5.4. Your full backup, differential backup, and t-log backups should all be present. Remember those two times you noted when making the transaction log backups in the previous section? Change the Restore to time to be somewhere in between the two times you noted.

3   Click OK to start. We'll review the other pages and options in this dialog in a moment.

4   You should get a success dialog; click OK.

5   With AdventureWorks2012 selected in the Object Explorer, click New Query in the toolbar.

6   Run the following query:

```
SELECT * FROM Person.Person
```

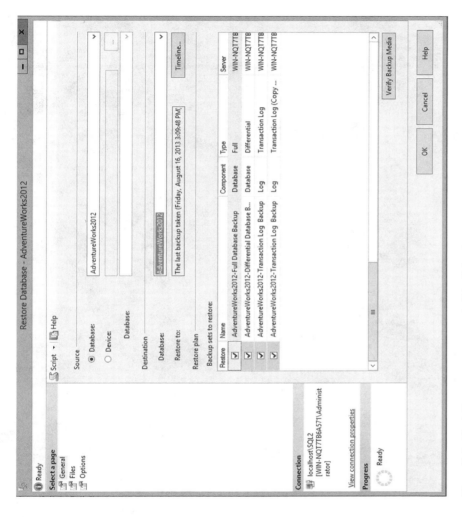

Figure 5.4   Start the recovery process in this dialog.

If you were careful with your time notations, the middle initial will be "X". That means you restored one of the three queries you ran, but not the last one, which should have happened after the time you specified in the restore dialog. Neat, right?

Now, back to the Restore dialog and its Files page, shown in figure 5.5. This lets you decide where the database's physical files will be restored. The default is to restore them to their original location, but if you're trying to restore the database to a lab, or to keep the current database available, you can choose a different location.

The Options page, in figure 5.6, provides a built-in option to take a tail-end t-log backup (which the UI calls a *tail-log backup*). This is selected by default if you try to perform a restore and haven't already done a t-log backup (the UI is trying to watch out for you and make sure you don't lose any data). There's also an option to close existing connections, if the database isn't already in the restoring state. Another option is to overwrite the existing database that you're restoring to.

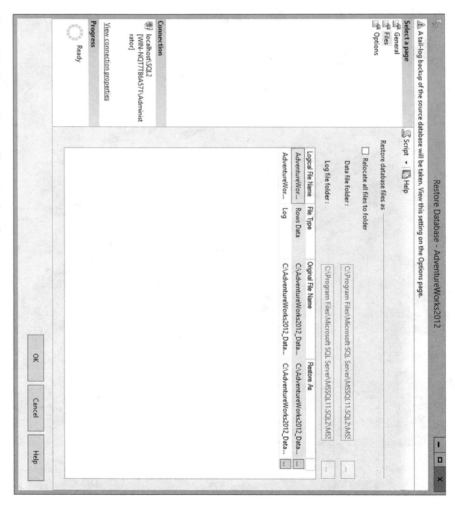

Figure 5.5   Choose alternate file restore locations.

5.4   *Model backup and recovery scenarios*

So now that you know which buttons to push, when do you push them?

As you'll find with many things in SQL Server, the answer is, it depends. However, there are certainly some guidelines. Start by taking a full backup as often as you can. If that can be once a day—perfect! You won't need to deal with differentials. If not, then try to grab a full backup weekly, and a differential nightly. Then, throughout the day, grab a t-log backup, making sure you get that backup onto separate storage from the actual t-log file.

How often do you run a t-log backup? Every 15 minutes, if you can. Every 10. Every 5. It depends on your *recovery point objective*, or RPO, which is the amount of data you can stand to lose. Although a t-log backup every 5 minutes might be a bit much, I know folks who do that. They have a super busy database, so it's a convenient way to get a backup and to clear out the log for further use. When the time comes to recovery,

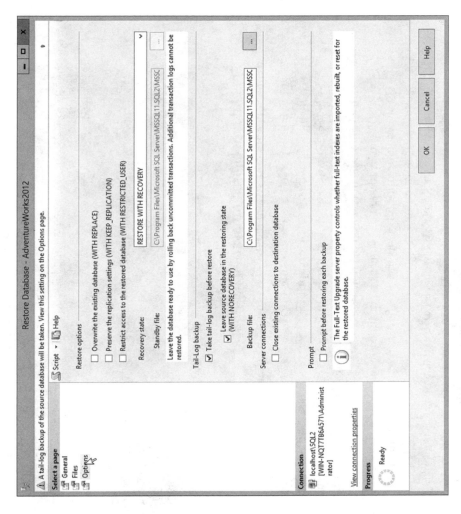

Figure 5.6 Selecting database recovery options

they have to accept a somewhat long *recovery time objective*, or RTO, meaning the actual recovery can take a while since they have so many files to restore.

Many, many, many organizations use third-party recovery tools. Some of these plug into SQL Server via a locally installed agent, and extract data using SQL Server's native techniques. They store the backup data elsewhere, usually on a backup server that uses a tape library. Some solutions perform *continuous backup*, meaning they grab every tiny change as it occurs and ship it off to a backup server.

Whatever tools and procedures you choose to follow, make sure you test them regularly. Some of my consulting customers will take their backups and try restoring them to a spare server in a lab. That way, they know their process works, and they also validate that the backup itself is usable. You certainly don't want to wait until you really, really need a backup to find out that you haven't been making them correctly!

Expert advice

Whatever backup and Recovery model you go with, I recommend you create a literal picture book of your restore procedures. Walk through the process and take screen shots each step of the way, showing and documenting whatever settings you'd select in your environment.

You will certainly appreciate having that picture book when the need to perform a real recovery, in production, finally arises. You'll be in a stressful situation, and you don't want to have to think about what you're doing. The picture book will help ensure you pick the right options and get your server back online as fast as possible, without errors.

5.5   Special procedures for system databases

I mentioned that the system databases require somewhat special treatment.

- TempDB doesn't require backing up, since it's never supposed to contain permanent data. If you delete TempDB, SQL Server will make a new one.

- Model doesn't require backing up unless you've made changes to it, which is unusual; if you have, grab a backup after making those changes and keep the backup handy in case you need it.

- MSDB can be treated the same as an ordinary database. If you need to recover it, you would temporarily stop the SQL Server Agent service during the recovery, and restart it when you're done.

- Master is the tricky one. As I wrote earlier, this database keeps track of SQL Server's configuration, meaning SQL Server can't start or run without it. To restore it, follow the steps at http://technet.microsoft.com/en-us/library/ms190190.aspx.

5.6   Backup and recovery using T-SQL or PowerShell

Thus far, I've shown you how to perform backups and restores using SQL Server Management Studio's GUI, but you can also use T-SQL commands. To create a full backup:

```
BACKUP DATABASE <database_name>
TO <backup_device>
WITH FORMAT,
  MEDIANAME = 'E:\Backups\Backup.bak'
  NAME = 'My backup name'
```

This command creates a new media set on the E: drive. If you're using SQL Server 2012 or later, you can also execute a Windows PowerShell Command:

```
Backup-SqlDatabase -ServerInstance SERVERA\SQLEXPRESS
  -Database MyDatabase
  -BackupAction Database
```

You'd substitute the correct server\instance name and the correct database name. You can use similar commands for differential and log backups; see http://technet.micro-soft.com/en-us/library/ms187510.aspx#TsqlProcedure for syntax and a list of those related procedures.

Transaction logs can also be backed up this way:

```
BACKUP LOG <database_name>
    TO <backup_device_name>
```

Or, using PowerShell:

```
Backup-SqlDatabase -ServerInstance SERVERA\SQLEXPRESS
    -Database MyDatabase
    -BackupAction Log
```

Again, provide the correct server\instance name and database name. Backing up the transaction log will truncate it; note that older versions of SQL Server offered a WITH TRUNCATE ONLY option that would truncate the log but not back it up. SQL Server 2012 discontinued that option.

5.7   *Hands-on lab*

Your lab for this chapter is to follow along with the backup and restore procedures I described in the chapter. If you've already done so, then you're done with today's lunch!

Authentication: who are you?

Security experts often refer to the "three As" of security: authentication, or who you are; authorization, or what you can do; and accounting, or auditing, which is what you've done. In this and the next two chapters we'll explore those concepts as they apply to SQL Server. We'll begin with authentication. Are you who you say you are? SQL Server uses a two-layer system of authentication—logins and database users—with lots of variations and options. Some of these options are in the product because they've always been there; some of them are new concepts for SQL Server that are designed to meet changing business and operational requirements.

6.1 Understanding logins

The first layer in traditional SQL Server Authentication is the *login*. A login lets you connect to the server itself, and can be used to assign certain server-wide permissions. A login doesn't have anything to do with a specific database.

Remember that SQL Server has two authentication modes. In Windows Authentication mode, all SQL Server logins are either local user or group accounts, or domain user or group accounts. In other words, SQL Server doesn't authenticate you. Instead, you're authenticated by Active Directory, or by the local computer's Security Accounts Manager (SAM). SQL Server merely believes whatever they say.

Let's say your Active Directory domain account belongs to the Domain Users domain user group. (By default, all users belong to that group, so this is a pretty common example.) Let's also say that you've added the Domain Users domain user group to SQL Server as a login. That means you—and every other member of the group—are now allowed to connect to the server. SQL Server knows who you are.

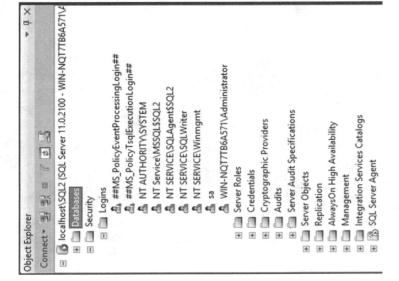

Figure 6.1   Logins are listed in the Object Explorer.

In fact, when you do connect, SQL Server will "see" your actual user account, so it will know very specifically who you are. Anything you do could potentially be audited, or logged, and your user account name will show up right next to that activity.

When it comes time to assign permissions, SQL Server can only assign permissions to every user in the Domain Users group, because it's the Domain Users group that's been created as a login. Logins are listed under the Security tab of the Object Explorer, as shown in figure 6.1. The icons don't differentiate Windows logins, but the login names make it pretty clear which ones come from Windows: they're preceded either by the domain name, the computer name, or something like "NT Service."

You can right-click the Logins folder to create a login. Notice that you have two options: Windows Authentication or SQL Server Authentication. Let's discuss each option.

6.1.1   *Windows Authentication*

As shown in figure 6.2, when you choose Windows Authentication you're only expected to provide a name. That would be the local computer or domain user or user group name. You don't provide a password; that's handled by Active Directory or by the local SAM.

The upside of Windows Authentication is that, once you've added the login, you don't have to worry about it. SQL Server doesn't have to worry about passwords being changed or anything else. If you add a group, then the folks who control that group in

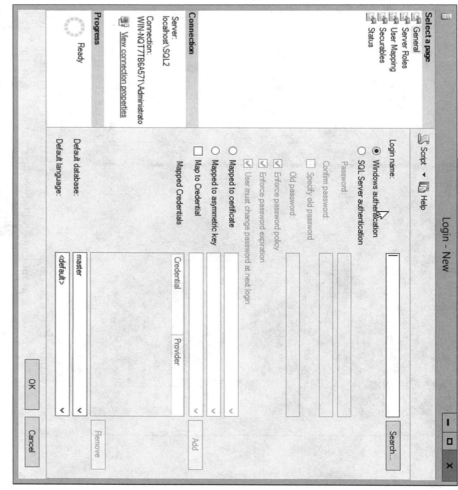

Figure 6.2   Specify a name to create a Windows login.

Active Directory will decide who needs to be in it—not you. Windows logins are generally lower overhead for whoever is managing SQL Server. However, applications have to be configured to use this kind of login. When an application connects to SQL Server, it must specify a *connection string* that specifies a *trusted connection*. That tells SQL Server to use the user's Windows logon credential, and to pass that through to SQL Server. If the application can't be configured to do that (and many can't), then Windows Authentication isn't an option.

6.1.2 *Mixed Mode Authentication*

The entire SQL Server instance must be configured to support the alternative, which is Mixed Mode Authentication. Mixed Mode is what makes SQL Server Authentication available (shown in figure 6.2). When you select that option, you then have to provide a password for the user, and decide if you'll enforce the SQL Server password policy (how complex the password must be), password expiration, and other options. With

SQL Authentication, SQL Server is entirely in charge of the authentication process. It prompts for the password when the user connects, and it checks to see if the password is correct. In an application, the user name and password are usually provided in the connection string, which means—and this is a security concern—the user name and password are built right into the application's source code, or stored elsewhere in clear text. Yes, clear text. No, it isn't a great idea, but that's what a lot of application developers do. More on that later in this chapter.

TRY IT NOW What logins are present in your SQL Server computer (or computers)? What Authentication mode—Windows only, or Mixed Mode—do your servers use?

When in Mixed Mode, SQL Server provides a default SQL Server login named sa, which stands for system administrator. By default, this login is given all-powerful server-wide permissions. Earlier versions of SQL Server allowed this login to exist without having a password (you can imagine what a horrible security idea that was) but newer versions require a complex password for this login. Because sa exists by default on nearly every SQL Server, it's often the most common target for attackers. One best practice is to disable the login entirely, and to manually create a new login to use in its place.

6.2 Understanding database users

A login only grants you some kind of access to the entire SQL Server instance. From there, you'll want to get into one or more databases. That happens by mapping a login to a *database user* inside each database that you'll be using. Figure 6.3 shows the relationship between logins and database users.

The idea here is that one person (or group) will manage the server itself, and so they get to control who will connect to it. They do that by managing logins. But SQL Server

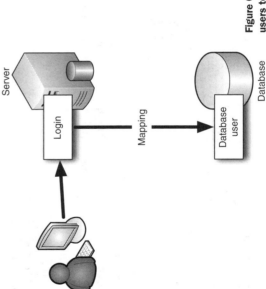

Figure 6.3 Mapping database users to logins

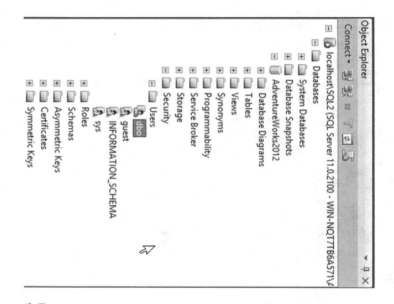

Figure 6.4 Use Object Explorer to view database users.

realizes that the people who own the actual databases might be different, such as when a departmental application database needs a SQL Server to live on. The SQL Server administrator wants to control access to the server, but the department manager wants to control who gets to his or her data. So logins don't grant any explicit access to databases. Instead, someone inside the database creates *database users*. Those don't come with their own password or anything (well, usually they don't). Instead, they reference an existing server-wide login. Permissions within the database can then be assigned to the database user, controlling what that login can do inside the database.

A single login might well be mapped to database users inside many different databases, and might well have different permissions assigned within each. This whole two-layer security design is designed to separate control. Unfortunately, the two-layer design is often redundant, because often as not the people controlling server access are *also* controlling database access, and so the login+user model can seem like unneeded complexity.

Database users are shown under the Security folder of an actual database, as shown in figure 6.4. You'll notice a couple of special database users in the list:

- *dbo*—A default database user, meaning it exists in every new database. It's mapped to the sysadmin fixed server role (which we'll discuss in the next chapter). That effectively gives all server administrators access to every database.

- *guest*—Another default database user. It's disabled by default, meaning it can't be used. If enabled, any login trying to use the database, but that hasn't been mapped to a database user, will be dynamically mapped to guest. The login will then receive whatever permissions have been assigned to guest. You shouldn't enable the guest user unless your application specifically requires it.

As shown in figure 6.5, when you create a database user you get to pick the login that the user maps to. Anyone who uses that login to connect to SQL Server will be represented by that database user when they use your database.

The login+user model can also make it more difficult to move databases around. Let's say you have a database that contains five database users. Each maps to a specific login on the server. You find, over time, that your database isn't performing well, and so you decide to move it to a different server in your organization. You detach the database, copy its files, and attach it to the new SQL Server instance. Right away, your database might not work, because the new instance might not have the same logins as the old instance. So you think, "No problem, I'll just create the logins I need. There are only five of them, so it's no big deal." Wrong. Internally, SQL Server keeps track of

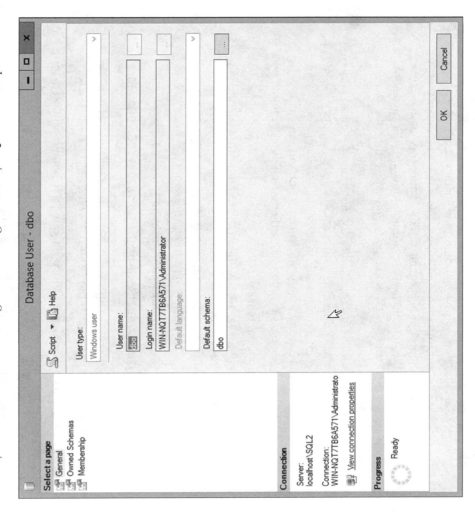

Figure 6.5   Creating a database user requires you to specify a login.

logins by a GUID, which is a long string of hexadecimal values. You can recreate logins with the same *names* as on the old server, but their GUIDs will be different, so they still won't match up to the logins your database users are mapped to. Now you've got even more work to do to fix the GUIDs! By the way, the problem and solution for these so-called *orphaned* logins are well-described at www.codeproject.com/Articles/594134/How-to-Fix-Orphaned-SQL-Users, should you ever need to perform that task yourself.

Anyway, Microsoft has started rethinking the whole authentication layer with the goal of making databases more self-contained. In fact, that's the word they're using: *contained*. The idea is to make a database user that has its own password, and that isn't mapped to a login at all. Essentially, you're bypassing the entire login layer, and letting users authenticate directly to the database. If all of your database users are created in that fashion, then you've created a *contained database*, which can be easily moved from server to server with no server-level dependencies to worry about. As Microsoft and private data centers start to think more about cloud-like management processes, this ability to quickly relocate a database becomes very valuable. Databases must be configured so that their Containment Type option is Partial, and they must be hosted in a SQL Server instance that has been configured to permit contained databases.

TRY IT NOW Take a moment to inventory the users in your database. Which ones map to logins? Do you have any that are contained within the database?

6.3 *How the real world often does authentication*

Here's how Microsoft thinks you should approach SQL Server security:

- Use only Windows Authentication mode.
- Create logins that represent domain user groups from Active Directory.
- Configure all applications to use a trusted connection when connecting to SQL Server, meaning they pass along the user's Windows logon identity.
- Map Windows logins in SQL Server to database users.

In most cases, this gives you the maximum amount of flexibility, the lowest operational overhead, and the best information about your server. You can easily see each user's identity, meaning monitoring, many performance-tuning tasks, and auditing all become easier. This model can work well for internal applications. Of course, when you're running a public application like a website, where your users aren't logging on to a domain, this model doesn't apply. Instead, you'll usually create an Active Directory user to represent your anonymous users (customers, partners, or whatever they are). You create a SQL Server login for that user account, and map it to a database user. Any *internal* users who connect to the database would still be uniquely identifiable, because you'd create a separate login and database user for them.

The problem is, many application developers don't like using this model. They get a little lazy. They don't want to have to troubleshoot all of those layers. Instead, they tend to adopt a different model:

- They create a single, non-Windows login for their application. Or, they use the built-in sa account, which is a horrible practice.

- They hardcode the login name and password into their application's connection string.

- They map the login to a single database user.

The downside here is that every user connected to the server is indistinguishable from the rest. They're all sharing the same credential, so you can't tell them apart. That single database user is given all-powerful permissions in the database, and the application implements its own security layer. A problem is that the login name and password isn't all that hard to retrieve—.NET Framework applications, for example, can be readily decompiled to reveal the login information. That would allow someone to connect directly to SQL Server, bypassing the application and its security, and enabling them to do whatever they wanted to your data. I've seen it happen.

So what can you do? It depends a bit on the application. If you can access the application's connection string (it may be stored in a configuration file, in the Windows registry, or somewhere else you can get to), you can potentially change it to use Windows Authentication instead. You'll have to work with the application developer or a knowledgeable consultant to set up the permissions that the application is expecting in SQL Server, but it's possible. For some applications, however, you won't be able to make that change, and you'll simply be stuck with whatever the developer did.

6.4 *Understanding application roles*

SQL Server offers a third authentication option that's designed to accommodate developers' laziness (or lack of understanding, or whatever it is that makes them do what they do in their applications) while preserving a higher level of security than the "let's just use a single login for everyone" approach. This third option is an *application role*. These are listed in Object Explorer, under the database's Security folder, within the Roles subfolder.

An application role isn't mapped to a login, nor does it require a database user. You assign permissions directly to it. The application itself either connects using Windows Authentication (meaning it uses the user's logon credentials), or by using a typical connection string. But then the application executes a couple of lines of code to *activate* the application role. Immediately, all permissions assigned to the login and/or database user are gone for that connection, and the permissions assigned to the application role take over for the duration of the connection. This lets someone connect to SQL Server with a relatively low-permission credential, and then have elevated permissions activated for use by the application. Application roles are much more difficult for a user to activate on their own, meaning the role can't be used as easily to bypass any in-application security by connecting directly to SQL Server. SQL Server's Books Online contains more information about using application roles, including code samples. Application roles are great, but as an administrator, you don't really get to decide whether or not to use them. You can recommend them to developers, but ultimately it's the application developer who has to implement them.

6.5   *Hands-on lab*

Your lab for this chapter is a bit complex.

First, I'd like you to change your lab SQL Server to Mixed Mode Authentication, if you haven't done so already. Ensure that the default sa account is given a password such as "P@ssw0rd." Do these tasks by using SQL Server Management Studio.

Then, create a new SQL Server login named testuser. Also assign it the password "P@ssw0rd". In the AdventureWorks database, create a new database user named testuser, and map it to the testuser login. The trick? Create the login and user by running T-SQL commands in a query window, not by using the GUI. That means you may have to look up the correct syntax in SQL Server's Books Online. I'll give you a hint: the commands you're looking for are CREATE LOGIN and CREATE USER, respectively.

Authorization: what are you allowed to do?

We're on the second "A" of security: after authenticating you so that it knows who you are, SQL Server needs to decide what you're allowed to do. By default, the answer is "Nothing." You have to be granted permission to do things, both at the server level and within individual databases, and that's what this chapter is all about.

7.1 Understanding SQL Server permissions

SQL Server has an extremely granular system of permissions that determines who is allowed to do what. Remember, the authentication process tells SQL Server who you are; these permissions then determine what you can do.

There are server-wide permissions that govern your ability to do things such as create new databases and logins, but most of the time you'll be more concerned with database-level permissions. These determine what a user can do from within a specific database, and there are a lot of options.

REMEMBER Server-level permissions are assigned to logins, and database-level permissions are assigned to database users.

To discuss permissions, it's often useful to use *views* as an example. A view is a type of virtual table. Views are a real database object that basically contains a SQL Server query, rather than containing data. When you access the new view, SQL Server runs the query and presents the results. You can use views to provide a convenient way of viewing data from multiple related tables at once, or use views to provide certain users with a subset of a table's data. SQL Server has some performance optimizations that can make a view faster to execute than simply running its query on demand.

7.1.1 Securing database objects

Inside a database you have a number of types of objects, including tables, stored procedures, views, and user-defined functions. These objects are called *securables*, meaning they are something that can have permissions assigned to them. Each kind of securable has different types of permissions. On a table you can give permission to alter the table, execute INSERT, DELETE, UPDATE, or SELECT queries, view the table's definition, and so on. Views have similar permission types, while stored procedures only have permissions for altering the procedure, executing it, and so on. Different object types = different permission types.

For each permission type, you can assign a GRANT or DENY permission. When you grant a permission, you also have the option to do a WITH GRANT. Here's how it all works:

- *Assigning a GRANT permission gives the user the ability to perform that task.* Assigning GRANT for the SELECT statement lets a user perform SELECT queries on the table.

- *WITH GRANT gives a user the ability to pass their permission on to other users.* You might do this with a manager who's allowed to read a table, and allowed to assign others the ability to read a table.

- *A DENY permission prevents a user from performing the given task.* A user could be granted permission to run UPDATE queries, but denied the ability to run DELETE queries. Would that make sense to do? Maybe not, but you can do it.

You can manage permissions in the SQL Server Management Studio GUI, or you can run TSQL commands. This command gives a user the ability to insert data into a table, and gives them the option to pass that permission on to other users:

```
GRANT INSERT ON [HumanResources].[Department] TO [testuser] WITH GRANT OPTION
```

This example gives them permission to delete data, but not to pass that permission on to others:

```
GRANT DELETE ON [HumanResources].[Department] TO [testuser]
```

This example shows how to deny someone the ability to select data from a table:

```
DENY SELECT ON [HumanResources].[Department] TO [testuser]
```

Each of these commands creates an entry in an internal SQL Server table, which is how SQL Server keeps track of the permissions. That's easier to imagine in the GUI, where, as shown in figure 7.1, you can also check boxes to assign these permissions. Note that the Permissions page shown in the figure will always be blank when you first open the dialog box; you have to use the Search button to find a specific user, then work with their permissions.

TRY IT NOW In SQL Server Management Studio, expand the AdventureWorks-2012 database. Under the Tables folder, right-click a table and choose Properties. On the Permissions page, click Search and enter the name of a user (use testuser if you completed the lab in the previous chapter, or dbo if you didn't).

Notice the permissions on the Explicit tab.

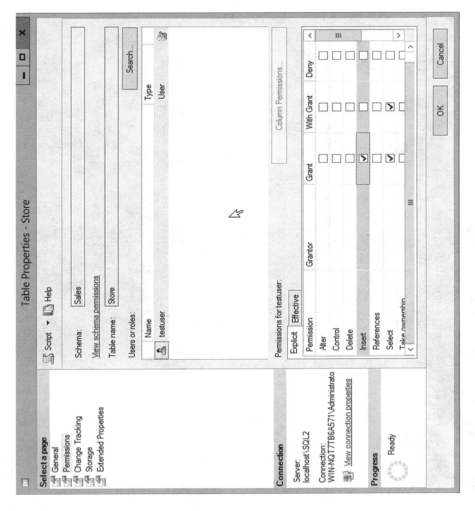

Figure 7.1 Assigning permissions is as easy as checking boxes.

7.1.2 *Revoking permissions*

REVOKE is used to remove a permissions entry from the table (in the GUI, you uncheck a checkbox to remove permissions). That can be a bit confusing, because "revoke" doesn't always mean "stop them from using this!"

If you revoke a DENY permission, then you may be granting someone access! How could that happen? Normally, a DENY permission means you can't do something, even if you have permission to do that task from somewhere else. Let's say you are given select permissions to your database user account, but that you're also in a group where select permission was denied. Normally, the DENY overrides everything, and you wouldn't be able to run SELECT queries. But if that DENY is revoked, your other GRANT permission would suddenly kick in, giving you the ability to run SELECT queries. Most DBAs try to avoid using DENY permissions, because it can get a bit tough to keep track of and troubleshoot.

7.1.3   *Column-level permissions*

Here's another wrinkle: while you can apply permissions to an entire table, you can also apply them to individual columns. That's right. You can give someone the ability to only select data from only a single column within a table!

In a default SQL Server configuration, a table-level DENY *will not override* a column-level GRANT. That is, the column-level permissions are seen as more specific, so even though there's a DENY in there, the person would have the specified permission on the column. That's for a *default* SQL Server configuration.

If SQL Server is configured to use the Common Criteria audit specification (available in Enterprise Edition only), then a column-level GRANT will be overridden by a table-level DENY. Confusing, right? The default behavior (where the table-level DENY doesn't override) is an inconsistency in the product. Microsoft's official statement is that the behavior has been left in for backward-compatibility, but that a future version of SQL Server will change the behavior.

> **NOTE**   For more information on Common Criteria in SQL Server, visit http://technet.microsoft.com/en-us/library/bb326650.aspx.

7.1.4   *The many sources of permissions*

Figure 7.1 also shows the existence of an Effective tab for permissions management. While the Explicit tab shows the permissions assigned to a given user right on that object, the Effective tab shows all of their permissions on that object, even permissions that come from their membership in a group or role. In other words, the Effective tab shows the permissions they're operating with, down to the individual column level. The tab is useful for troubleshooting: if someone thinks they should have permission to do something, but they're running into "access denied" errors, the Effective tab lets you check their actual permissions, and where those permissions came from.

7.2   *Using server roles*

Before we get further down the rabbit hole of permissions, let's look at the concept of *roles*. A role is a SQL Server object that bundles a set of permissions, so you can conveniently assign those permissions to one or more users by placing the user (or users) into that role.

Server roles, as the name implies, focus on server-level permissions. Prior to SQL Server 2012, these were officially called *fixed server roles*, because they came with SQL Server and couldn't be changed. You could put logins into the roles, but you couldn't change the roles' permissions. The dbcreator server role grants the ability to create new databases; the sysadmin role grants all server-wide privileges. As of SQL Server 2012, you can also create your own server roles, and assign them custom permissions. You still can't modify the permissions assigned to the built-in roles, but you can at least make up new roles as needed.

There's also a special server role called public. All users belong to this role, and you *can* modify its permissions. So this is basically the common set of permissions shared by all users of the server. By default, it grants the permission to connect to the server, meaning any user can connect to the server. That permission is granted to all of SQL Server's default connection mechanisms, include TCP, VIA, and named pipes. The public role is also given permission to see that all databases exist, meaning anyone can list all of the databases on the server. They can't necessarily do anything inside those databases, but they can see them.

Apart from the public role, most SQL Server users won't be in a server role. In a typical environment, only administrators, and perhaps developers, will have a place in a server role. To manage role memberships:

1 In SQL Server Management Studio, expand the Security folder in Object Explorer.
2 Expand the Roles folder.
3 Right-click a role and select Properties.
4 Add or remove role members as needed.

TRY IT NOW How many server roles are in your default configuration of SQL Server?

7.3   *Using database roles*

Database roles serve the same basic purpose as server roles: to bundle a set of permissions, making it easy to assign that set to one or more users. There are fixed database roles, whose permissions you can't change, and custom database roles, whose permissions you control. (Custom database roles have been in SQL Server since the concept of roles was introduced.) You'll find databases roles in SQL Server Management Studio by expanding the database, expanding Security, then expanding Roles.

The fixed database roles provide common permission sets:

■ *db_accessadmin*—Provides the ability to control database permissions.
■ *db_backupoperator*—Gives permission to run backup operations (although not to restore backed-up data).
■ *db_datareader and db_datawriter*—Grant permission to select data, and to update, insert, or delete data.
■ *db_denydatawriter and db_denydatareader*—Explicitly deny write and read permission.
■ *db_ddladmin*—Grants permission to run DDL commands, which control the database design and schema.
■ *db_owner*—Typically all-powerful within the database.

Again, there's a special public role, which controls the common permissions granted to anyone in the database. Its permissions can be modified, and by default only include the ability to access certain built-in common functions, stored procedures, and system views.

7.4   Schemas and owners

As you mess around with permissions in SQL Server Management Studio, you'll come across two important terms: *owner* and *schema*.

TRY IT NOW   What objects are included in the permissions for the public role in the AdventureWorks2012 database?

7.4.1   *Owners*

Every object in a SQL Server database has an owner. By default, that's usually the built-in dbo database user (dbo stands for database owner). Any object can, technically, be owned by any user. When an object is created, if the creating user is a member of the db_owner role, the owner is assigned as dbo rather than as the creating user. But if a user who *isn't* a member of db_owner creates an object, the object is owned by that user until someone changes the ownership. There are also situations where someone who belongs to db_owner can create an object and end up having it owned by themselves, rather than by dbo, but it's a bit unusual.

Owners have full control over their objects, and can modify them, assign permissions to them, and so on. Owners also play an important role in permission chains, which we'll discuss in a bit.

In older versions of SQL Server, you could refer to an object by a *fully qualified name*, which took the form server.database.owner.object. So a table named MyTable, owned by dbo, in the Corp database, on a server named SQL1, would be sql1.corp.dbo.mytable. You rarely need to use all of those naming components; SQL Server defaults to the current server, to the current database, and to dbo. Assuming we wanted to access MyTable on the current server and in the current database, you'd refer to it simply as mytable. But the fully qualified name lets you refer to objects in other databases, on other servers, or owned by users other than dbo.

Older versions of SQL Server wouldn't let you delete a user if they owned anything. So if you had created john.mytable, the user John couldn't be deleted until ownership of MyTable had been transferred to another user.

7.4.2   *Schemas*

Newer versions of SQL Server (2005 and later) introduced *schemas*. These broke the connection between naming and ownership, and they can be a bit tricky to understand. One reason they're confusing is that, for backward-compatibility, SQL Server has built-in schemas named after the most common owner user names of the past. That means a database will have, by default, both a user and a schema named dbo, guest, and so on. Confusing!

So what's a schema? Basically it's a container, like a box. The dbo schema is the default one, and all objects are placed into that schema unless you specify otherwise. The dbo schema itself is owned by the dbo database user. When you create new database users, they're given a *default schema*, which will also be dbo if you don't specify differently. So now, the fully qualified naming convention is server.database.schema.object, taking the owner out of the equation.

It's possible to have multiple objects with the same name, provided they're in different schemas. You could, for example, have a view named dbo.myview and one named barney.myview if you wanted to. When a user executes a query that refers to MyView, and doesn't use a fully qualified name, SQL Server will start by looking for the object *in the user's default schema*. If the object doesn't exist, SQL Server will look for it in the dbo schema. Let's say you create a database user named Fred, and set his default schema to be Barney. Fred then runs `SELECT * FROM MyView`. Fred will be querying from barney.myview. That means the same query could potentially work differently for different users, based on their schema. This can get mega-confusing, so it's something most developers try to avoid. Instead, they'll tend to use schemas strictly as a way of organizing tables and other objects. In the AdventureWorks2012 database, for example, you'll see schemas for HumanResources, Production, Sales, and so on, showing how the developer organized the database objects based on their role in the application.

It's possible to assign permissions to an entire schema, which can save a lot of time in permissions management. For example, if your Sales department needs uniform access to a set of objects, placing those objects in a Sales schema makes it easy to assign all of the needed permissions in one simple step. In SQL Server Management Studio, under the database's Security folder, you'll see a Schemas folder that contains all of the database's schemas. You can assign permissions right there.

TRY IT NOW Locate the Schemas folder in the AdventureWorks2012 database. Does anyone have special permissions in the HumanResources schema?

7.5 *Permission chains*

Permission chains are an important part of how SQL Server works, and they're connected to object ownership. The concept is pretty basic: when you access an object, SQL Server checks to see if you have permission to do whatever you're doing. If you do, SQL Server proceeds.

If the object you accessed has to access other objects behind the scenes, SQL Server *does not recheck your permissions* so long as the objects are all owned by the same user, including the object you initially accessed.

Let's say you try to query a view named MyView, which is built on a table named MyTable. Both are owned by dbo, and you have permission to query MyView, but you don't have any permissions on MyTable. The query will succeed: SQL Server will check your permissions on MyView, and because the underlying MyTable has the same owner, it won't recheck your permissions when the view accesses the table.

This behavior means you can grant people access to UI objects, but you don't have to grant them access to the underlying data. You can force users to access data only through views, functions, stored procedures, and other objects that may limit the users' functional capabilities. The users won't be able to bypass those objects, because the users won't have any permissions on the actual tables.

Permission chains are a big reason why most database developers leave all object ownership with the built-in dbo user. When ownership changes in an object access chain, SQL Server rechecks permissions. Let's say MyView is owned by dbo, but MyTable is owned by a user named Diane. You have permission on MyView, but not on MyTable. So you query MyView, and SQL Server is okay with that. But when the view tries to access the underlying table, SQL Server has to recheck permissions because the owner is different. SQL Server would realize that you don't have permission to the table, and the query would fail.

Why would you ever want to set up that kind of situation? Suppose you had a table that contained sensitive information such as employee salaries. Making that table owned by a separate user would ensure *nobody* would be able to query that data without having explicit permissions right on the table itself. Developers couldn't build views or stored procedures that bypassed that security requirement, unless those views or stored procedures were owned by that same, separate user.

TRY IT NOW Let's run through a permission chain example in the Adventure-Works2012 database. I'll assume you completed the hands-on lab in the previous chapter, so you have a testuser login, and a testuser database user in the database. If you don't, go back to the previous chapter and complete the "Try it Now" and hands-on lab sections.

Start by opening a new query window and making sure the AdventureWorks2012 database is selected: Click New Query in the toolbar, then press Ctrl+U, and select AdventureWorks2012. In the query window, type and execute this query:

```
EXECUTE AS USER = 'testuser'
SELECT * FROM HumanResources.Department
```

You should get an access denied error, because testuser hasn't been given permission on that table. Open a new query—this will reset your permissions back to whomever you're logged on as. In the new query window, run the following:

```
CREATE VIEW HumanResources.DeptTest
AS
SELECT * FROM HumanResources.Department;
GO
GRANT SELECT ON HumanResources.DeptTest
TO testuser;
GO
```

This creates a new view named DeptTest, and gives testuser permission on it. Because we didn't specify an owner, it should have the default owner. Back in your original query window, run this query:

```
SELECT * FROM HumanResources.DeptTest
```

That should work. Testuser doesn't have permission to the table, but that wasn't checked. Testuser has permission to DeptTest, and because it's owned by the same user as the underlying table, the permission was only checked on DeptTest.

7.6 How the real world often does authorization

In the real world, you won't always see the approaches outlined in this chapter used. It's unfortunate, but many software developers don't know much about SQL Server Authorization, and they don't take the time to learn. Instead, they program their applications to connect to SQL Server by means of a single SQL Server login, and they give that login full permissions within their application's database. Their application then decides what individual users are allowed to do. This approach has a number of downsides:

- SQL Server "sees" all users connecting as a single user. That means SQL Server can't tell them apart, which makes for difficult management and troubleshooting. If you need to disconnect a particular user, you can't, because you can't easily determine who is using what connection. Finding a user that's running a slow-running query is not easy.

- If someone discovers the login name and password that the application is using (something that's remarkably easy to do, even by a minimally experienced user) then they can bypass the application, connect directly to SQL Server, and do whatever they want. You'll have difficulty identifying those users, because they're logging in using the same credentials as legitimate users.

- Too often, the single user account selected by developers is the all-powerful sa account, giving applications and malicious users full access to the entire server.

- Changes to "who is allowed to do what" often mandate an update to the application, which may even mean deploying that update. That's significantly harder to do than if permissions were centrally managed at SQL Server.

So what can you do about these applications? Unfortunately, not always very much. If the application's connection string is available—if it's in a configuration file that you can change or in the Windows registry—you may be able to modify it to use Windows logins instead of hardcoded credentials. For example, if you see this connection string:

```
Server=myServerAddress;Database=myDataBase;User Id=myUsername;
Password=myPassword;
```

Changing it to this would probably work:

```
Server=myServerAddress;Database=myDataBase;Trusted_Connection=True;
```

The application won't necessarily know that you've made a change. Having done that, you do need to make sure your users' Windows logon credentials are passed through to SQL Server. That will be automatic if their client application is connecting directly to SQL Server, and if they're running the application on a Windows OS. It isn't automatic if they're connecting to some middle-tier application or running a non-Windows application. You'll also have to make sure that each user (or, more likely, a user group that they belong to) is assigned the needed permissions in SQL Server. If a user (or the application) attempts to do something that isn't authorized for the current logon, the application will receive an error from SQL Server. Given that the application probably *expected* to have full access, that error may crash the application, forcing the user to start over. It's pretty rare that you can switch an application over to another permissions model, but you can definitely communicate with vendors and developers and ask them to consider a switch in an upcoming release of the software.

7.7   *Hands-on lab*

This lab assumes that you completed the previous chapter's lab; if you haven't, go back and do that first.

For this lab, feel free to use the SQL Server Management Studio GUI. That said, to challenge yourself, see if you can identify the commands that will accomplish each task in this lab. I'll provide answers in the downloadable lab answer guide available at MoreLunches.com.

1 Create a database role in AdventureWorks2012. Name the role SalesReader.
2 Grant the Sales role SELECT permission over all tables in the Sales schema.
3 Add the testuser database user to the Sales role.
4 Confirm that testuser can query information from the Sales.Customer table.

HINT   In a query window, run EXECUTE AS USER = 'testuser' to have that query window run subsequent queries using the testuser database user.

Accounting: what did you do?

After authentication and authorization, many organizations have a need for the third "A" of security: accounting. Typically, the IT world refers to that as *auditing*, and there are a number of ways that SQL Server can help you keep track of who's doing what. I'll start by introducing you to three auditing mechanisms that you probably won't use, mainly so I can explain *why* you won't use them; I'll then introduce SQL Audit, which is the auditing technology you'll probably rely on the most.

8.1 Triggers

Triggers are one way that SQL Server can help log actions made in a database. I need to start by pointing out that these absolutely require custom programming, and they're far from foolproof: an administrator can easily disable triggers, bypassing them completely. They also come with a lot of design considerations and a few caveats. Because they're a programming element, I'm not going to cover them in depth, since this isn't a book about SQL Server programming, but I do want you to know what they are. If you want to learn a lot more about them, dive into the official documentation at http://msdn.microsoft.com/en-us/library/ms189799.aspx.

A *trigger* is a special kind of stored procedure, which is a script that lives inside a SQL Server database. Triggers can contain one or more T-SQL statements, and can in fact be quite complex (it's also possible to create them in a .NET Framework language like C# or Visual Basic). Triggers run automatically in response to specific things happening inside the database.

DML triggers run in response to UPDATE, DELETE, or INSERT statements being run. They can either run in lieu of whatever change a query was trying to make, or they can run after the change is made. In theory, you could program a trigger to log the change to a separate table, creating your own auditing system. Triggers don't run in response to SELECT statements, so there's no way to use a DML trigger to keep track of all access to data.

DDL triggers run in response to database schema modifications, such as removing columns from a table or creating a new table. Again, you could use these to log schema changes to another table to create a sort of audit log; DDL triggers don't run in response to *every* possible configuration change in a database, so they're not a catchall way of auditing all administrative activity.

8.2 SQL Server Profiler

In theory, SQL Server Profiler offers a way to track system activity, down to the query level. Profiler is a pretty heavy monitoring solution, meaning it creates its own performance impact and isn't designed for continual use. It also doesn't log its data in a way that facilitates using it as an audit log.

8.3 Event logs and C2 auditing

SQL Server has supported C2 auditing almost forever. C2 refers to a government standard for auditing, requiring the server to log every possible access *attempt*, whether failed or successful. SQL Server logs that information in to the Windows event logs. Unfortunately, pretty much nobody uses C2 auditing, and I don't recommend you even try it out, because it can generate an *enormous* level of log traffic—more than the Windows event log architecture was designed to handle. Turning on C2 auditing requires that you include logging overhead in your server capacity design. It's *that* intensive. And the results are barely usable: the native event logs aren't designed to be easily queried or used to generate auditing reports.

8.4 SQL Audit

SQL Audit, a built-in feature of newer versions of SQL Server (2008 and later), is specifically designed to provide a granular level of audit log-quality accounting. Enterprise editions of SQL Server provide a full range of audit capabilities; Standard editions provide only a basic subset.

8.4.1 SQL Audit architecture

SQL Audit uses SQL Server's native Extended Events engine (which you'll learn about in chapter 17). Extended Events, unlike SQL Server Profiler, is a *lightweight* monitoring engine, meaning it's designed to run continuously, in the background, without severely impacting SQL Server's performance. SQL Audit receives events from the engine and uses them to create an audit trail of *only the activity you specify,* meaning you can decide how much detail you need to capture.

A *server audit* is defined at the SQL Server instance level, meaning they're active for all databases, not just a single database. You start by creating an *audit* object, which contains the complete definition for what you'll be auditing, where the audit log will go, and so on. You can have multiple active audits simultaneously, although I tend to try to keep everything consolidated into a single audit, or at least as few as possible, just to keep them easier to manage. You can also define *database audits*, which as the name implies are active only for a specific database.

Within an audit, you create an *audit specification*. That defines *what* will be audited. Each audit object can contain one, and only one, audit specification. Specifications let you indicate what *actions*, or events, you want audited, such as failed logins, server role membership changes, and so on. Actions are organized into *action groups*, making it a bit easier to select an entire related set of actions. The actions available to a server audit are different than those in a database audit, because you can do different things at the server level (such as log in) and the database level (such as dropping a table).

Audits also include a *target*, which details where the audit log will go. These can be the Windows Security event log, the Application event log (which can be viewed by any authenticated user), or to a file. I generally use a file, since they're easier to collect, consolidate, and manage than the event logs.

Note that the SQL Server service account must have permission to write to the target; if it can't, then the SQL Server instance may not start. You can modify the service startup properties to include the –f command-line parameter to start the instance and bypass auditing. That lets you get in and modify the target, disable the audit, or further troubleshoot the access problem. Additionally, if SQL Server tries to write an event to the audit target and fails to do so, you can configure the audit so that the instance will shut down immediately. The idea is to ensure all specified activity is audited; if it can't be, then the instance isn't allowed to run.

Database audits are referred to by an internal GUID. The audit doesn't live in the database itself, but the database refers to the audit by that GUID. When you detach a database and move it to another instance, the audit doesn't go with it, but the database will still be trying to refer to it by that GUID. That's called an *orphaned audit*, and it's similar to orphaned logins, which we discussed in chapter 6. You have to fix this by running the T-SQL ALTER DATABASE AUDIT SPECIFICATION command; look up the command for more details on correcting the problem.

NOTE Technically, an audit is an audit is an audit; it's the audit *specification* that is either server- or database-specific. Specifications become detached from their audits when you move a database to another instance, and it's that relationship you'll have to fix, reconnecting the database audit specification to the instance-level audit object it goes with (or creating a new one for it to refer to).

8.4.2 Creating an audit

I'm going to walk you through the process of creating an audit object, a server audit specification, and selecting an audit target.

TRY IT NOW Please follow along! I'll be using an example that includes some of the more common server-level audit actions, so this is good practice for a production server.

Start in SQL Server Management Studio.

1 In Object Explorer, expand the Security folder.

2 Right-click Audits, and select New Audit....

3 Configure the General page as shown in figure 8.1. I've provided a name for the audit, as well as a file path. You don't provide a file name; that'll be generated automatically in the specified path. Notice that I haven't configured this to shut down the instance if an audit fails. Also notice how I've configured the file handling: there will be no more than two files, of no more than 20 MB apiece. The audit will reserve that space immediately, ensuring it will have space to write to those files. Once the second file fills up, the first will be deleted and a new one created. So I'll always have 40 MB in audit files.

4 The audit is disabled by default; you'll see that in its icon once you click OK. We'll enable it in a bit.

5 Right-click Server Audit Specifications and select New Server Audit Specification....

6 Configure the General page as shown in figure 8.2. I've attached this specification to the audit object I just created, and I've selected three login- and password-related action groups to include in the specification. Click OK. Notice that the specification is also disabled by default.

7 Enable both the specification and the audit by right-clicking them and selecting the Enable option; click Close on the status dialog box displayed by each.

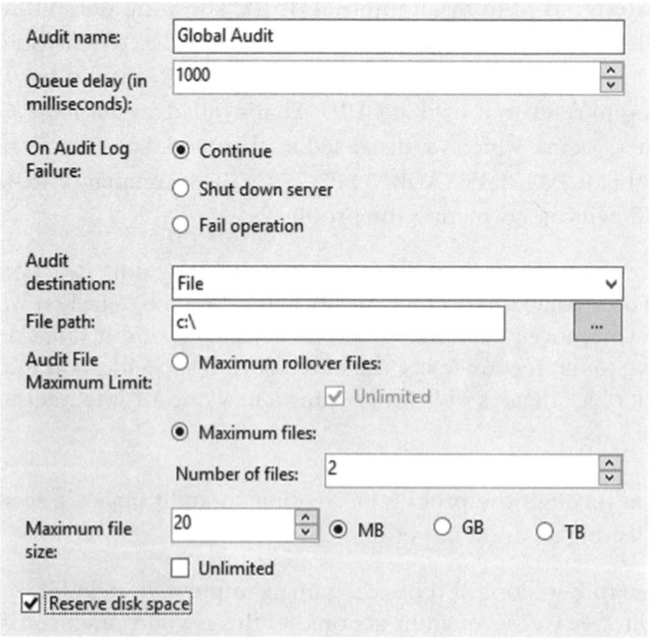

Audit name: [Global Audit]

Queue delay (in milliseconds): [1000] [⌄][⌃]

On Audit Log Failure:
- ⦿ Continue
- ○ Shut down server
- ○ Fail operation

Audit destination: [File] [⌄]

File path: [c:\] [...]

Audit File Maximum Limit:
- ○ Maximum rollover files: ☑ Unlimited
- ⦿ Maximum files: [2] [⌄][⌃]

Number of files: [2]

Maximum file size: [20] [⌄][⌃] ⦿ MB ○ GB ○ TB
☐ Unlimited

☑ Reserve disk space

Figure 8.1 Configure the General page for audit as shown.

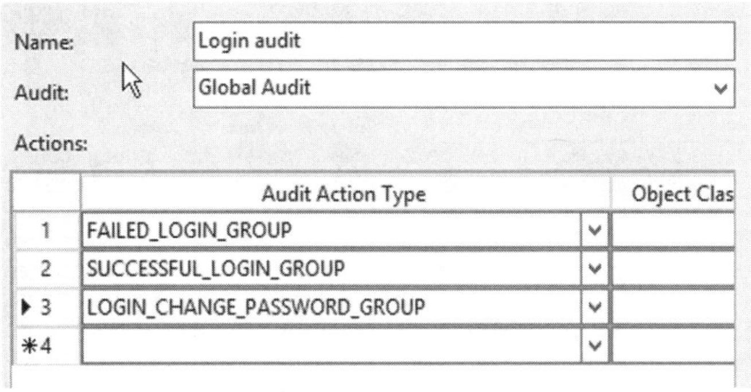

Name:	Login audit	
Audit:	Global Audit	∨

Actions:

	Audit Action Type	Object Clas
1	FAILED_LOGIN_GROUP	∨
2	SUCCESSFUL_LOGIN_GROUP	∨
▶ 3	LOGIN_CHANGE_PASSWORD_GROUP	∨
*4		∨

Figure 8.2 Configure the specification as shown.

TIP If the audit fails to enable, then it's likely the SQL Server instance's service account doesn't have read and write permissions to the file path you specified. I used C:\ in my example, and that *is* restricted on most server computers. You can fix the problem by creating a new path (such as C:\Audit) in Windows Explorer, and modifying its permissions to include SQL Server's service account (or something like Everyone:Full Control, which isn't awful for a lab environment). Then modify the audit to use that path instead.

Now let's test the audit. I'll launch a new copy of SQL Server Management Studio and connect to my instance. That should generate a login success audit, and your audit path should now contain a file with a .sqlaudit filename extension. The filename will include your audit's name (Global%5Audit, in my example, with the "%5" being an encoded representation of a space) followed by a long unique identifier.

Audit files are in a binary format; you can't simply open them in Notepad. Instead, in SQL Server Management Studio, right-click the audit and select View Audit Logs.… You'll see something like figure 8.3, which shows all of the audited events. Notice that the bottom pane shows details about the selected event, and that you can filter, search, and export the log using toolbar buttons at the top. Exporting provides the ability to write to a text-based log format, or to a comma-separated values (CSV) file, which can be opened in Excel or imported into a database.

NOTE Once you're done playing with auditing, you can disable the audit object by right-clicking it and choosing the Disable option.

8.4.3 *Using SQL Audit for security auditing*

Say "audit" and most folks' minds justifiably jump to "security." SQL Audit—particularly on Enterprise editions of SQL Server, where more granular auditing is available—is well suited to maintaining security in the organization. Heck, I have customers whose legal and industry requirements demand that they audit all *read* access to certain database tables (like those containing confidential customer information). SQL Audit can do it.

That said, you don't start auditing massive amounts of activity without first spending serious time thinking about it. Auditing all SELECT access to a busy database, for

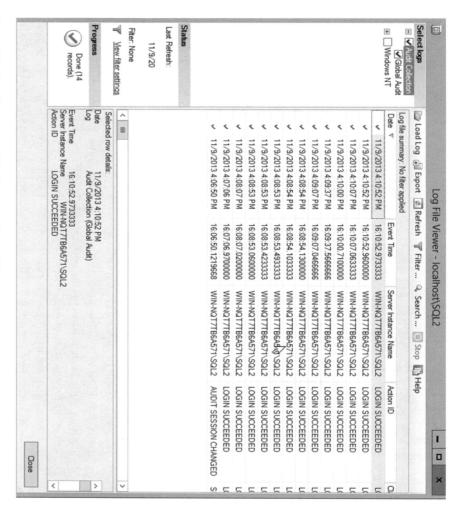

Figure 8.3 Use Management Studio to view the audit log.

example, generates a *lot* of audit traffic. A lot, lot, lot. You're going to have to set aside serious disk space to capture that information, and you're going to have to have a plan to maintain those logs, archiving them for however long you're required to do so. That level of auditing *is* going to impact SQL Server performance to some degree (although you'd have to run tests in a lab environment to determine exactly how much), so you might well have to upsize your SQL Server computer to handle it: more processor, more RAM, and certainly more disk controllers and faster disks. Point being, SQL Audit *can* do it, but you're not just going to flip the switch and be happy. It's going to require serious conversation and planning within your organization.

8.4.4 *Using SQL Audit for troubleshooting*

Folks tend to think of auditing as a security thing ("Make sure we know who accessed what, at all times!!!!") but it's equally useful as a troubleshooting tool. I'll often create an audit and a server audit specification that audits *failed* login attempts. I'll leave the audit disabled until a user calls in and says they're having trouble logging in. I can quickly enable the audit, ask the user to try again, and then examine the audit log to see what's going on. I can then disable the audit until I need it again.

Honestly, I find myself using SQL Audit a lot more for troubleshooting than for anything else. Yes, I have customers who need auditing for security purposes, but with such a wealth of information available, it's a powerful troubleshooting tool. I can even use it to capture specific queries for tuning, if needed, and it's a bit easier to turn on and off than it is to fire up SQL Server Profiler.

NOTE As you get started with SQL Server administration and maintenance, you probably won't use SQL Server Profiler much. It's a fairly advanced tool. However, we'll be using it to accomplish a few specific tasks, starting in chapter 11.

8.5 *Hands-on lab*

You don't have a mandatory hands-on lab in this chapter, but I do want to offer an optional one. This requires that you have an Enterprise edition of SQL Server, though; Standard and Express don't permit granular database audit specifications.

See if you can set up an audit specification in a database, to audit use of the SELECT statement by members of the db_owner database role on that database. *Don't* do this on a production server; perhaps download and install a trial of SQL Server Enterprise Edition to try this. In a production database this will likely create an *enormous* log *very* quickly. In fact, if you're able to set this up, try running a few SELECT statements to see just how fast a large number of events is created.

Analyzing indexes

Indexes, as I've mentioned in previous chapters, are hugely important to SQL Server. They also represent a complete compromise: every index has the potential to help certain types of query run faster, while slowing other types. It's extremely, extremely, extremely important that you understand what indexes are, how they work, and what you can do with them. This is also a good time to analyze an existing database to see what indexes it has. Becoming familiar with a database's indexing strategy is a real key to helping understand any performance issues that may crop up.

9.1 *Index basics*

Indexes in SQL Server apply to tables, not to entire databases, but when we talk about indexes we tend to think about their impact on overall database application performance. An index is, in a very real sense, a lot like an old-fashioned paper telephone book. Like a phone book, an index is designed to speed up queries, in this case, queries that need to find particular pieces of information, or put those pieces of information into a particular order.

Just like the data in a table, indexes are stored in 8 KB chunks called *pages*. These pages are stored in the database's files on disk, and they're moved into and out of the buffer cache in SQL Server's memory. SQL Server always reads and writes index pages in 8 KB increments, which becomes a key to understanding index performance.

In most real-world databases, you will find that every table has at least one index, although SQL Server doesn't require tables to have any indexes. Most tables will have multiple indexes, which are designed to help speed up specific different types of queries and cross-references.

9.2 Heaps

When a table lacks a clustered index, something I'll explain in the next section, it is referred to as a *heap*. Think of that as meaning something like, "a big old heap of data," because that phrase does a good job of conveying what you're dealing with: an unsorted, unordered, chaotic mess.

To understand what a heap does, let's start with a basic example of a few data pages in SQL Server. Remember, these data pages contain the data from the table. In this case, let's say that they're customer names. Each page can hold about 8 KB of data. Suppose, when we first create the table, we're loading customer names from a source that already has the names in alphabetical order. That means we'll be inserting the "A" customers first, then "B," and so on. So our initial data pages will be nicely in order, as shown in figure 9.1.

Because there's no index on this table, the data pages are not *linked*. That is, when SQL Server reads in the first page, it has no immediate idea which data page comes next. Even though they appear to be in order to our human eyes, SQL Server has no clue. So each time it needs another data page, SQL Server has to refer to the *Index Allocation Map*, or IAM. That's a special structure included with the table, also kept on 8 KB pages. Right there, we've halved our table's performance, because almost every time SQL Server needs to read an 8 KB data page, it must first backtrack and read through the IAM.

The problems begin to arise when you add data to the table. Suppose you add "Bentley" to our example table of customer names. Logically, the name goes after the "A" customers, but those data pages are already full. So SQL Server drops "Bentley" on the next available 8 KB chunk of disk space. The pages are now logically out of order, meaning SQL Server has to jump around the disk a lot in order to read the data. Figure 9.2 shows where we are now.

Even worse is when you change some data, and the changes no longer fit on the original page. For example, suppose we need to change "Charles" to "Charleston."

Able, Dan Abrams, Ann Adams, Keith Barstow, Ken Baden, Joe Bundt, Cathy	Carlton, Dana David, Dee Delgado, Don Earnhardt, Eric Francos, Barb Gooding, Ann	Hargrove, Chris Hart, Erin Jones, Don Kyling, Jeff Larson, Grace Lindly, John
1	2	3

Figure 9.1   The initial data pages in a table of customer names

1	2	3	4
Able, Dan Abrams, Ann Adams, Keith Barstow, Ken Baden, Joe Bundt, Cathy	Carlton, Dana David, Dee Delgado, Don Earnhardt, Eric Francos, Barb Gooding, Ann	Hargrove, Chris Hart, Erin Jones, Don Kyling, Jeff Larson, Grace Lindly, John	Bentley, Bob

Figure 9.2   Adding rows quickly causes the pages to become out of order.

The 8 KB page where "Charles" existed is full; there's no room for the additional three characters. So the entire data row gets moved to a new page, making the heap even more chaotic. Worse, the original page now has 7 empty bytes that won't get quickly reused. The result is a lot of wasted space as the table grows. Wasted space also means worse performance, because now a single 8 KB disk read operation won't be reading a full 8 KB of data—some of the read operation is wasted. As this *fragmentation* continues to occur, more space will be wasted, and performance will continue to slowly decline. There's no easy fix, either—except to index the table.

9.3   *Clustered indexes*

SQL Server builds indexes in a structure called a *B-Tree* (there's some debate about what the "B" stands for; it isn't "binary," but its origin seems to be lost in time). Figure 9.3 shows a simplified example. In order to locate a particular record, SQL Server starts at the top of the tree and works its way down, choosing between a small number of potential paths each time. Even with a large body of data, this structure makes it possible to locate a particular piece of data with relatively few read operations.

To find "Adams," SQL Server would start at the top. It knows the name it wants begins with "A," so it follows that path. It knows the name begins with "Ad," so it fol-

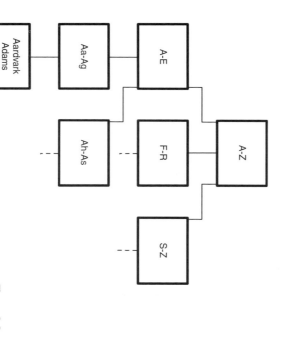

Figure 9.3   Indexes are built as B-tree structures.

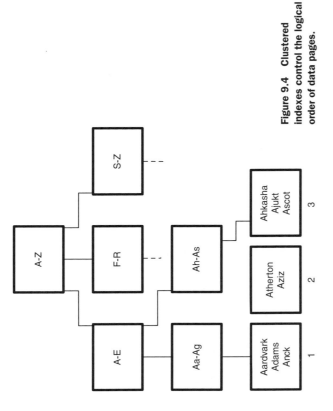

Figure 9.4   Clustered indexes control the logical order of data pages.

lows that path next. Each of these intermediate steps is referred to as a *node* within the index, and each is stored on the standard 8 KB page of disk space. The choices on each node point, or *link*, to a subsequent page, allowing SQL Server to scan the tree without having to refer back to an IAM. In a *clustered index*, the last nodes link to the data page containing the complete row of data that SQL Server was looking for. For that reason, clustered indexes are said to control the logical ordering of the data pages. Figure 9.4 illustrates the structure. Notice that the data pages, numbered 1 through 3, are not *physically* in order. But the index treats them as if they were *logically* in order, because the index has the data in order, and it points to the appropriate data pages.

Something to keep in mind: when you are putting the data pages in order, you can obviously only put them into *one kind of order.* In other words, suppose you took all the people in your office building and asked them to line up by last name. You probably couldn't also ask them to line up in order of height—they can only order themselves on one piece of data, or *key,* at a time. Therefore, SQL Server tables can have one, and only one, clustered index.

Clustered indexes are the fastest kind of index, so they're usually built on the key that is queried most frequently. They're fast because once SQL Server reaches the end of the index structure, it is *at* the actual data page. It doesn't have to go anywhere else to find the rest of the data it was looking for. It's as if you had a traditional paper phone book, which lists your city's residents in alphabetical order by last name, and as if you managed to get everyone to buy houses in exactly that same order—so that every person physically lived in alphabetical order. Once you found the person you were looking for, you'd have access to all of their information because you'd be standing right in front of the actual person.

ABOVE AND BEYOND

Some folks misunderstand clustered indexes, and mistakenly believe that they control the *physical* order of the pages on disk. That isn't true, but there's a grain of possible truth there.

In most table designs, a sequential number uniquely identifies each row. That is, rather than identifying a customer record by the customer's last name, since customers' names are hardly unique, there's an internal ID number of sorts that can be used instead. Database designers do this to ensure they have an absolutely unique value by which they can refer to any given row. Using an arbitrary, sequential number, something SQL Server calls an *identity column* and can create automatically for you, is extremely common.

Because each new identity value is larger than the one before it, the clustered index tends to keep the pages in the correct physical order as well as the correct logical order. That isn't the index's job, it's simply a byproduct of the fact that the index key is an arbitrary, sequential number. When you add a new row, it will always contain the largest key value in the table at that point in time, so when SQL Server writes the page to the end of the database file, it just happens to be in numeric order.

9.4 *Nonclustered indexes*

If a table can have only one clustered index, what happens if you need to sort the data, or search through it, using other criteria? That is, if we've built an index on a customer's last name, what if we need to search for customers in a particular city? This is where *nonclustered indexes* come in. You can have as many of these as you want on a given table, and they work exactly like a traditional paper phone book.

Using the phone book, you look up a resident by last name. Once you have their row in the index, you're given the person's physical address. If you need to know more about them, their age, their height, or something else, you have to make the "jump" to their house in order to obtain that information. As shown in figure 9.5, that's how nonclustered indexes work. When you reach the end of the index, the *leaf page*, you aren't looking at the complete row for the record you're after. Instead, you're given a reference to the data page. SQL Server then has to jump to that data page to read the information. Nonclustered indexes are therefore slightly slower than a clustered index, since a nonclustered index involves that extra jump.

The reference contained in a nonclustered index's leaf nodes depends on whether or not the table is a heap. When a table contains a clustered index, the nonclustered indexes all point to the clustered index key. Let's say you were searching for "Derby" in a customer list. You've built a clustered index on that table, using an arbitrary, sequential *identity column* as the clustered index key. A nonclustered index

NONCLUSTERED INDEX

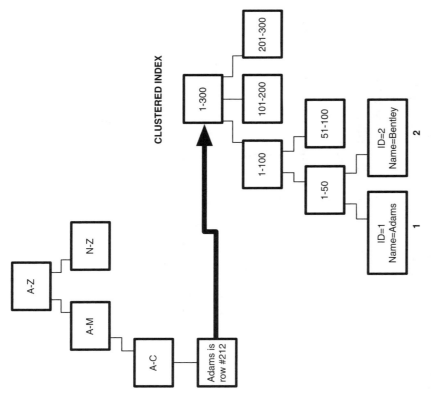

CLUSTERED INDEX

Figure 9.5 Nonclustered indexes require a jump to the actual data page.

on customers' names would end in a reference to that identity column, let's say "Derby" resolved to identity number 34726. SQL Server would then quickly seek through the clustered index to find key 34726, which would lead the server to the data row for that customer.

NOTE You read that right: using a nonclustered index necessarily involves two index operations. The first operation is the nonclustered index, and the second operation is the clustered index. That's why nonclustered indexes are a bit slower. They always involve that second operation.

You may be thinking, "Wow, that sounds like horrible performance," but it isn't that bad. Clustered index seeking is a super-quick operation in most cases, so it adds only a tiny bit of overhead. What's *really* awful is if the table doesn't have a clustered index, meaning the table is a heap.

In that case, the nonclustered index leaf nodes contain a reference to the internal SQL Server row ID number for the desired data page. You might think, "Wow, that's a

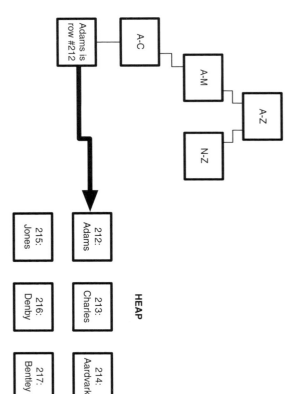

NONCLUSTERED INDEX

HEAP

Figure 9.6   From nonclustered index to data page in a heap

lot faster than doing a clustered index seek," right? After all, you go straight from the nonclustered index to the data page, as shown in figure 9.6.

Unfortunately, that great situation doesn't tend to exist in a heap for very long. Recall from the earlier explanation on heaps that changes to data rows tend to result in the row being moved to a new page, *fragmenting* the table's data pages. When that happens, nonclustered indexes *aren't updated* with the new location! Instead, a little pointer is left behind. So now, as shown in figure 9.7, SQL Server seeks through the nonclustered index, jumps to the data page, and finds a forwarding number. It has to jump to the new page, where there might be yet another forwarding number. Over time, this will massively reduce overall performance. Heaps are *terrible* (except for tiny tables that don't ever change). Had the table been given a clustered index, the clustered index would be continually tracking where the data page was, meaning you would *always* have that one extra clustered index lookup. With a heap, you might have zero to a bazillion additional operations, with no way to predict what it would be, and no real way to clean up and improve performance.

9.5   *Index inventory*

You can review the indexes on a table right within SQL Server Management Studio. As shown in figure 9.8, expanding a table reveals an Indexes folder, where all of the table's indexes are listed.

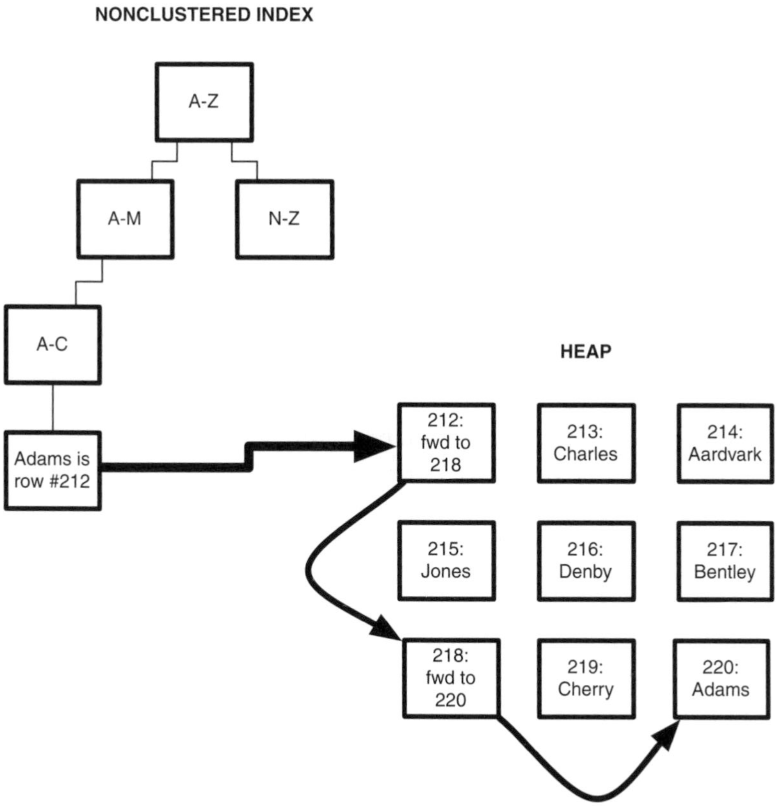

NONCLUSTERED INDEX

A-Z

A-M | N-Z

A-C

Adams is row #212

HEAP

212: fwd to 218 | 213: Charles | 214: Aardvark

215: Jones | 216: Denby | 217: Bentley

218: fwd to 220 | 219: Cherry | 220: Adams

Figure 9.7 Nonclustered indexes on a heap perform more poorly over time.

You can double-click any index to see the column or columns used to build the index, and obviously you can see right in the list which index is clustered, and which ones are nonclustered. Be skeptical of any table that shows nonclustered indexes, but no clustered indexes; those nonclustered indexes will be built on a heap, which as you've learned in this chapter can present serious performance problems over time.

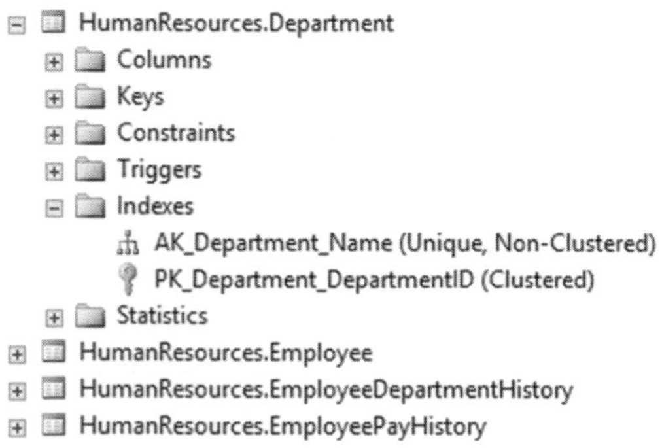

HumanResources.Department
    Columns
    Keys
    Constraints
    Triggers
    Indexes
        AK_Department_Name (Unique, Non-Clustered)
        PK_Department_DepartmentID (Clustered)
    Statistics
HumanResources.Employee
HumanResources.EmployeeDepartmentHistory
HumanResources.EmployeePayHistory

Figure 9.8 Indexes are listed in SQL Server Management Studio

9.6 *Constraints and indexes*

Most database tables have relationships with one another. In figure 9.9, you can see a table that contains customer information, and a second table that contains orders. Obviously, *customers* place *orders*, and so these two tables are related to one another.

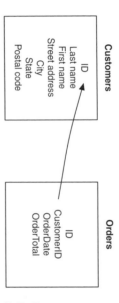

Customers

ID
Last name
First name
Street address
City
State
Postal code

Orders

ID
CustomerID
OrderDate
OrderTotal

Figure 9.9   Tables often relate to one another within a database.

SQL Server provides mechanisms, called *constraints*, that can help enforce these relationships. Specifically, a *foreign key constraint* (commonly called an *FK*) tells SQL Server that a particular table column can only contain values pulled from a specified column in the related table. In our example, the CustomerID column in the Orders table includes an FK to the ID column of the Customers table. Using this constraint, we're assured that orders can only relate to actual customers.

FKs typically point to a related table's *primary key*, or PK. When the database application needs to pull information from the related tables, perhaps displaying an order, which would also involve looking up the customer information, the application executes a special kind of query called a *join*. Joins can perform poorly if a good indexing strategy isn't employed. Usually, the join will execute well if the PK is also the key for the related table's clustered index. In our example from figure 9.8, the ID column of the Customers table would be the key column for that table's clustered index; any other indexes on the Customers table would be nonclustered indexes.

This relationship is another reason why:

- Database designers tend to add a column that is an identity column, meaning an arbitrary, sequential number. This column gives them an easy value to make into the PK, which is what other tables' FK-constrained columns will point to.

- Designers tend to build tables' clustered indexes on that PK column, to help speed up the join queries that will draw information from related tables.

While there are no specific technical rules that drive these decisions, the performance implications tend to make these rules almost universal in database design.

9.7 *More about indexes*

There are other tactics related to indexes that we'll cover in several upcoming chapters, including things like covering indexes, composite indexes, and more. Those kinds of indexes are still either clustered or nonclustered, but are designed to meet specific query performance needs.

We'll also, in several upcoming chapters, discuss the pros and cons of having indexes. Remember that while an index can speed up queries that need to find specific data or need to get the data into a specific order, indexes will *slow down* queries that add data, delete data, or make changes to data. That's because each modification to the table's data requires that one or more indexes also be updated, increasing the time it takes to execute those changes. The entire act of balancing those pros and cons is called *index tuning*, and chapter 11 covers that topic.

9.8 Hands-on lab

Let's practice what you've just read about in this chapter. Go to MoreLunches.com, click this book's cover image, and find the Index Inventory Sheet download. Complete one sheet for each of several tables on one of your SQL Server instances. You can pick which tables to inventory; if your database doesn't have a huge number, inventory them all. If you don't have a production environment to inventory, complete the worksheet for your AdventureWorks database instead.

Maintaining indexes 10

In the previous chapter, I explained how SQL Server indexes are built, and broadly hinted at how SQL Server uses them. Indexes will play a big part in many upcoming chapters, as they're one of the biggest performance-related items that an administrator can potentially play with. In keeping with this book's overall theme, though, I'm assuming that your databases are already indexed using whatever indexes the database application developer figured would work well.

But indexes, like cars, don't work very well, for very long, unless they're properly maintained.

10.1 Understanding index fragmentation

The biggest problem—the only operational problem—that indexes run into is *fragmentation*. Remember that an index is an ordered reference to a particular table's data. The index takes all the values from a designated *key column*, like customer name or product stock number, and lists those values in a specific order. The idea is that it's much easier to find a piece of data when it's already sorted: you can *seek* to the section of the index you need, and find the item you want. That's what an index's B-tree structure helps to facilitate.

NOTE   I use the word *seek* specifically because it's the term SQL Server uses to describe a quick lookup in a B-tree. Another term is *scan*, wherein SQL Server literally starts at the top of the list and reads its way through, one item at a time. Seeks are almost always faster than a scan, except on a very small table.

Andrews Bailey **Colby** Delgado	Huntington Istan Jackson Kilarney Loos Mounteblat	Niven Oppenheimer Prost Quincey Rush Soloman

Figure 10.1   Indexes that remain in proper physical sequence perform the best.

Indexes really only work well when they are listed in it are listed in perfect sequence, on sequential data pages, as shown in figure 10.1.

The problem with keeping an index in that perfect condition is that indexes, like the data they point to, change. Let's go back to the traditional paper phone book. What happens when someone new moves into town? Most phone book pages are completely full, so there's no room to write in a new arrival. In some cities, the phone company periodically issues a supplement, which contains new information: if the original directory doesn't have the person you're after, then you flip through the latest supplement to see if they're listed there instead. As you can imagine, this slows things down, and it's pretty much what happens when a SQL Server index becomes fragmented.

Imagine that we need to insert the name "Colby" into the index shown in figure 10.1. The value belongs on page 1 of the index, but page 1 is full. So SQL Server *splits* page 1, creating a new page 4. Half the information from page 1 is copied to page 4, and the new value is inserted. The result is a half-empty page 1, and a half-empty page 4. Also, the pages are no longer in *physical sequence*. If SQL Server needs to read the data in logical order, as shown in figure 10.2, it has to read page 1, then page 4, and then skip back to read pages 2 and 3. Over time, this back-and-forth skipping caused by the *fragmented* index can slow SQL Server down considerably.

In fact, SQL Server internally keeps track of how fragmented an index is, and at a certain point—which depends on a fairly large number of factors—SQL Server will figure out that it's faster to scan the table for desired values than to use the index. At that point, performance is totally trashed. You're still wasting time *updating* the index, meaning you get all the downsides of having the index in place, but

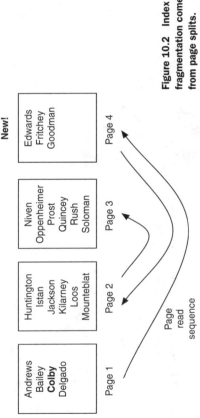

New!

Andrews Bailey **Colby** Delgado	Huntington Istan Jackson Kilarney Loos Mounteblat	Niven Oppenheimer Prost Quincey Rush Soloman	Edwards Fritchey Goodman
Page 1	Page 2	Page 3	Page 4

Page read sequence

Figure 10.2   Index fragmentation comes from page splits.

you're not using the index to speed up anything, so you get none of the index's intended benefits!

NOTE   If you have a specific query, and want to see if SQL Server is using indexes to execute that query, you can manually run the query in SQL Server Management Studio and look at the *execution plan* SQL Server came up with. I'll show you how to do that in chapter 12.

Fragmentation occurs to *all* indexes on tables where data is being added, deleted, or changed; the only time fragmentation isn't an issue is for a table that is entirely read-only. Not many databases have purely read-only tables, so index fragmentation is one of the biggest things that you, as a database maintenance person, need to worry about.

10.2   *Analyzing index fragmentation*

You can quickly check the fragmentation level of an index by opening the index's properties dialog. However, don't do it that way.

Checking fragmentation levels in the GUI is slow, and you're likely going to have to check dozens, if not hundreds, of indexes. This is where you definitely want to shift from the GUI to a query window, because SQL Server can deliver fragmentation information on multiple indexes all at once. Open the query window, and run the following:

```
SELECT *
FROM sys.dm_db_index_physical_stats(DB_ID('database_name'),
OBJECT_ID(N'schema.table_name'),
NULL,NULL,'Sampled')
```

You'll need to fill in the appropriate database_name, such as AdventureWorks2012. By specifying Sampled, you'll get a good tradeoff between speed of execution and accuracy; specify Limited for a faster but possibly less accurate scan; or specify Detailed for a slower, more accurate look at fragmentation.

You also need to replace schema.table_name with the appropriate table name, such as Person.Address (from the AdventureWorks2012 database). For example:

```
SELECT *
FROM sys.dm_db_index_physical_stats(DB_ID('AdventureWorks2012'),
OBJECT_ID(N'Person.Address'),
NULL,NULL,NULL,'Sampled')
```

You'll find a column named avg_fragmentation_in_percent that shows fragmentation percentage. Note that index names aren't shown in this output; instead, you get each index's unique numeric index ID. You'll also want to look at the page_count column, which shows how many pages the index occupies. For extremely small indexes (under a dozen pages or so), fragmentation percentage will never be zero, and will not be entirely accurate. For indexes that small, frankly, fragmentation isn't much of a concern.

TRY IT NOW Try analyzing the fragmentation in several tables in one of your databases. Keep in mind that, for especially small tables (which is almost all of them in the sample AdventureWorks database), the fragmentation percentage won't be accurate, and achieving 0% fragmentation may not be possible.

There are two kinds of fragmentation to worry about:

- *Internal fragmentation*—What I've described in this section. It's when the index's rows of information are out of order within the database.

- *External fragmentation*—A bit more complex. SQL Server groups 8 KB pages into sets of 8, called *extents*. When SQL Server needs to read a number of sequential pages, it's easier (and faster) to do so if they're all grouped into sequential extents. External fragmentation is when the pages of an index are spread across extents that are separated from each other by extents containing unrelated pages.

10.3 Indexes maintenance strategies

Once you've determined that an index is overly fragmented (as a rule, anything more than 30% is cause for concern) you need to defragment the index. You have several options, which become more and more flexible with newer versions of SQL Server.

- *Drop and rebuild the index.* This solves the problem, but introduces several of its own. For one, queries that depended upon the index will have poor performance until the index is online. In addition, building an index on a large table may lock the table, preventing changes from users. Here's the biggest downside if you do this with a clustered index: any nonclustered indexes will be automatically rebuilt on the resulting heap, and when you build the new index all the nonclustered indexes will be rebuilt *again*. Definitely don't do this during production hours!

- *Rebuild the index.* This is spiritually the same as dropping and recreating the index, but is done as a single operation in SQL Server. With a clustered index, you won't cause your nonclustered indexes to be rebuilt on a heap, and then rebuilt on the new clustered index. This can still be impactful in production: the index won't be available for use while it's being rebuilt, and queries may fail due to locking. There are two ways to perform this kind of rebuild:

  - CREATE INDEX with DROP_EXISTING uses the CREATE INDEX statement and its DROP_EXISTING option. Indexes that contain constraints (such as a UNIQUE constraint) can be rebuilt using this technique, although under the hood SQL Server has to drop and recreate the constraints, which can be time-consuming. A downside is that indexes have to be rebuilt one at a time, although as you'll see later in this chapter that isn't always a bad thing.
  - ALTER INDEX REBUILD uses the ALTER INDEX statement. Unlike the above option, this doesn't have to drop and re-create constraints in the index, so it can be faster to run. This is how I usually rebuild indexes.

- *Rebuild the index online.* An option in newer versions of SQL Server (2012 and later), this builds a new index behind the scenes, then uses some sleight-of-hand to swap in the new index and delete the old one. This has a performance impact, but it keeps everything functional and accessible. The big price is in disk space; you'll need enough to store that second copy of the index while it's being built.

- *Reorganize the index.* This can be accomplished while the index is still online and being used, because all it really does is rearrange the pages into the correct physical sequence. This process can be paused and restarted, although it may not always help you achieve 0% fragmentation. There's no impact on nonclustered indexes.

We'll cover how to rebuild and reorganize an index in a minute. But first, a couple of final notes before moving on.

10.3.1 *Fill factor*

There's an important concept called *fill factor* that comes into play when you rebuild (but not reorganize) a nonclustered index. The fill factor determines how full (or, if you're a pessimist, how empty) index leaf pages are in the rebuilt index. A fill factor of 50 means the page is half full (or half empty); a fill factor of 70 means the page is 70% full (30% empty).

Why leave empty space? Empty space allows for the addition of new rows to the index leaf pages without splitting pages, meaning the index lasts longer before it becomes too fragmented to be useful and needs to be rebuilt. But there's a downside to a low fill factor: while it helps avoid page splits for a period of time, it also slows down SQL Server. Keep in mind that SQL Server reads the entire index page from disk; if the page is half empty, then SQL Server just wasted time reading nothing! For best disk performance, always SQL Server's weakest spot, you want your index pages 100% full, so that each disk operation is completely useful. Full pages will result in page splits and fragmentation almost immediately, so coming up with the right fill factor is a balancing act. More on that in a moment.

10.3.2 *Databases that aren't yours*

How much of this maintenance stuff can you do for databases you don't "own," such as a database being used to support some line-of-business application?

It depends. You can *definitely* monitor fragmentation (keeping an eye on things never hurts). Some vendors build index maintenance routines into the application, and so you should see fragmentation go up and down as those routines run. On the other hand, many vendors don't do anything to maintain their database's indexes, so you'll see fragmentation go up . . . and up . . . and up . . . For those, you'll need to run index rebuilds and reorganizations on your own, probably on a regular basis. Doing so won't "hurt" the application. In fact, it'll help it perform much better.

10.4 *Performing the maintenance*

Although you can accomplish these maintenance tasks using the SQL Server Management Studio GUI, I much prefer to use T-SQL statements, since I can pop them into a SQL Server Agent job and have them run automatically. (You'll learn more about Agent in an upcoming chapter. Agent is somewhat like Windows Task Scheduler, only for SQL Server).

NOTE Because this maintenance is something you should perform regularly, try to get into the habit of using T-SQL to do it. Doing this in the GUI is going to be a bit tedious, and it's going to discourage you from doing this as often, and as well, as you should.

Note that I'm not offering command examples to drop and recreate an index. I don't ever recommend doing that as part of routine maintenance.

10.4.1 *Recreating an index with DROP_EXISTING*

As a quick reminder of what this will do:

- The index will be rebuilt.
- If it's a clustered index, there will be no impact on nonclustered indexes.
- Index constraints may be dropped and recreated automatically.
- You have to do one index at a time.
- For nonclustered indexes, you can specify a fill factor.
- SQL Server statistics on the index will be updated, so that SQL Server knows the index's new condition.

With that in mind, here's the command:

```
CREATE [UNIQUE] [CLUSTERED] INDEX index_name
ON schema.table_name(column_name)
WITH (DROP_EXISTING = ON);
```

There's a lot of information to fill in, so let me offer a concrete example. Suppose you want to rebuild an index named IDX1, on the Person.Address table, and it indexes on the table's AddrID column. It's a nonclustered index, but has a UNIQUE constraint, meaning every value in the column must be unique. Here's what you'd run:

```
CREATE UNIQUE INDEX IDX1
ON Person.Address(AddrID)
WITH (DROP_EXISTING = ON);
```

I never use this syntax. I always use ALTER INDEX instead, as it's easier and can do multiple indexes at once. It also offers the online-rebuild option, if I need it. But you may run into existing maintenance scripts that use this syntax, so you should be able to recognize it when you see it.

10.4.2   *Rebuilding an index by using ALTER INDEX*

As a reminder:

- The index will be rebuilt.
- If it's a clustered index, there will be no impact on nonclustered indexes.
- There will be no effect on index constraints.
- You can do multiple indexes with one command.
- You can specify a fill factor for nonclustered indexes.
- SQL Server statistics on the index will be updated, so that SQL Server knows the index's new condition.

Here's how to do it:

```
ALTER INDEX index_name ON schema.table_name REBUILD;
```

Provide the correct index name and schema.table name (for example, Person.Address) in the appropriate places. Or, to do all indexes on a table:

```
ALTER INDEX ALL ON schema.table_name REBUILD;
```

10.4.3   *Rebuild the index online*

In SQL Server 2012 Enterprise Edition (and later versions), you can also execute this as an online operation, which I described previously. Here's how:

```
ALTER INDEX index_name ON schema.table_name REBUILD
WITH (ONLINE = ON);
```

And, you can specify a new fill factor. If you don't, the last-used fill factor will be used for the rebuild. Here's how to specify a new one:

```
ALTER INDEX index_name ON schema.table_name REBUILD
WITH (FILLFACTOR = number);
```

Provide a number such as 70 for 70% and you're good to go. This can be used in combination with an online rebuild:

```
WITH (ONLINE = ON, FILLFACTOR = number
```

10.4.4   *Reorganizing an index*

As a reminder of what this will do:

- The index will be reorganized, but not completely defragmented.
- If it's a clustered index, there will be no impact on nonclustered indexes.
- Index constraints are not affected.
- You can do multiple indexes in one command.
- You cannot modify the fill factor.
- SQL Server statistics on the index will not be updated, so you typically want to run an UPDATE STATISTICS command after reorganizing.

Here's the command:

```
ALTER INDEX index_name ON schema.table_name REORGANIZE;
```

Provide the correct index name and schema.table name (e.g., Person.Address) in the appropriate places. Or, to do all indexes on a table:

```
ALTER INDEX ALL ON schema.table_name REORGANIZE;
```

10.5 Suggestions for index maintenance

I'm going to offer suggestions for coming up with the right index maintenance strategy, including the right fill factor for your nonclustered indexes. I have a few assumptions I make going into this, which are based entirely on my own experience with customers. These aren't hard-and-fast rules, but they're the guidelines I tend to follow:

- I don't like to rebuild indexes during production hours, so I try to identify a maintenance window where a rebuild can be conducted.

- When I'm on a version of SQL Server that supports it, I prefer to use online index rebuilds, even though that requires more disk space. Disk space is cheap these days, and online rebuilds avoid the chance that I'll disrupt some other user or process that's accessing the database, even during a declared maintenance window.

- I try to minimize rebuilds, just because they *do* create impact in the database.

- I come up with a maintenance strategy on a *per-index basis*. That's because each index on each table tends, in my experience, to be used somewhat differently. If I'm being a bit lazy, I'll use a one-size-fits-all strategy and choose a strategy that's good (if not great) for all the indexes, but I try not to be lazy.

- I try to find a good balance between index performance and disk performance.

With that in mind, here's what I do:

1 I start by rebuilding all of my indexes. For my nonclustered indexes, I choose a somewhat arbitrary fill factor. I grab a number out of the air, usually 70.

2 I monitor fragmentation daily. When I start approaching 30%, I execute a reorganization on the index. If I get to that point quickly— say, in the middle of the workday—I lower my target fill factor.

3 By the time I hit my next maintenance period for an index rebuild, I want to have fragmentation at about 20-30%. If I get to that period and fragmentation is higher than that, I lower my target fill factor; if fragmentation is lower, then I raise my target fill factor.

This often goes on for a few weeks, since in many cases I can only do rebuilds on the weekends. In other words, I want to hit Friday afternoon with 20-30% fragmentation, which means I'm filling up my index pages as much as possible without over-fragmenting. If I hit that 30% threshold midweek, I'll use a reorganization to buy some time. In scenarios where I have a short nightly maintenance window, I can often use a nightly index reorganization to keep fragmentation fairly low, but I always try to get that weekly rebuild (at least for busy indexes) to rebalance the fill factor for the upcoming week.

Again, *not every index is the same* because not every table gets used the same. For example, some databases have lookup tables that contain fairly static data. Because the tables don't change much, their indexes don't change much, and I might only run an index rebuild once a month, once a quarter, or something like that. Sometimes I just monitor the indexes and manually run a rebuild when it's needed, for that kind of table.

The point is to *watch what's happening* with fragmentation, and to keep in mind the balancing act between index fragmentation and disk performance.

Go automatic

SQL Server fan Michelle Ufford wrote a complete stored procedure that helps automate some of the index maintenance balancing act. You can find it at http://sqlfool.com/wp-content/uploads/2011/06/dba_indexDefrag_sp_v41.txt.

I want to call special attention to the 30% number that I've used a couple of times. That's just a kind of general rule that the SQL Server community uses; it does *not* mean that an index with less than 30% fragmentation is just fine. *Any* fragmentation slows things down; with an especially large index, 30% fragmentation may well be too high for the index to be useful. We ideally want 0% fragmentation, but we can't practically achieve that, so we learn to live with a little fragmentation, and we actively maintain the indexes to minimize how much fragmentation we have to live with. Nothing but experience will tell you what's acceptable for a given application in a given environment.

10.6   *Hands-on lab*

For this chapter's hands-on lab, try to perform an index reorganization and an index rebuild. The commands were provided in this chapter; if you're using the Adventure-Works sample database, then odds are you won't find much fragmentation or see your rebuild or reorganization have much effect. That's because AdventureWorks doesn't contain much data. But becoming comfortable with the maintenance commands is a good reason to try 'em out, anyway.

Because the command syntax is provided in this chapter, you won't find sample answers for this lab on MoreLunches.com.

Tuning index designs 11

By now, you should understand how indexes work, and how to maintain them. But what do you do if some of your indexes are no longer hitting the perfect balance of positive and negative performance impact? It may be time to tune those things!

We're about to embark on something that is traditionally collaboration between developers and DBAs, and we'll potentially be modifying portions of the overall database design (specifically, the index structure). Please follow along carefully, and be sure to follow the cautions and tips that I'll offer.

11.1 How indexes can become less useful

The indexes that a developer or DBA creates on a database are often put there as a best guess about what will provide the most balanced performance for the application. Keep in mind that indexes can both speed up and slow down queries, and finding the perfect balance requires a deep understanding of how the database is being used by real-world users in real-world conditions. Sometimes that "best guess" isn't 100% on the money.

Perhaps the database contains a lot more data than anticipated, and the nature of the data means that indexes aren't providing much of a performance boost, but they're still slowing down data inserts and updates. Or perhaps a database has become more read-only over time, and could benefit from having more indexes. Maybe users aren't searching for records the way someone had anticipated, and entirely different indexes would be useful.

Whatever the case, sometimes the initial index structure in a database isn't the perfect one anymore. *Tuning* is the process of figuring out where the best balance lies for *current* usage patterns.

Index tuning is as much art as science, and this book isn't going to go into every possible gory detail. Instead, I'm going to provide the best starting point I can, and help you understand the process. In most cases, what I'm giving you will help you validate that the current indexes *are* providing a good, balanced performance. In some cases, you'll get suggestions for index changes that can create a positive overall impact.

11.2 *Using Profiler to capture usage patterns*

The important thing here is to make sure we're not *guessing* at how the database is being used. Instead, we need to *observe* how the database *is* being used, right in the production environment, and use that data to see what indexes are offering the best balance of performance. We'll start by using SQL Server Profiler to capture representative, real-world traffic that shows us how the database is being used.

> **NOTE** Although it's fine in a lab environment, in production you should avoid running Profiler on the server from which you're planning to capture traffic. Profiler imposes a lot of overhead, and that can affect your results. Instead, install SQL Server's management tools on a client computer, and run Profiler there.

I'm going to assume you *don't* have the management tools from SQL Server 2012 or later, which means you'll need to build a trace template. If you *do* have SQL Server 2012 (or later) management tools, there's a built-in trace template already, so you can skip down to "11.2.2: Capturing the traffic." As a suggestion, try to get a copy of the SQL Server 2012 management tools. If you have any installations of SQL Server 2012, then you're licensed to use its tools, and they can be used with older versions of SQL Server, too.

> **TRY IT NOW** I suggest that you follow along with the next two sections. The trace template, in particular, is something you can easily reuse in your production environment. You might install SQL Server's management tools on your production client computer, so you can create the trace template right now.

11.2.1 *Creating a trace template*

You'll need to start by launching SQL Server Profiler. It'll ask you to connect to a server, but for now hit Cancel on that dialog.

Find and click a New Template button on the toolbar. Choose the appropriate server type, such as Microsoft SQL Server 2008, and name the template something like 2008 Tuning. I advise using "Tuning" somewhere in the name, to help clearly identify the template as being for tuning.

The Event Selection tab is where you'll need to carefully select the following (check all checkboxes that aren't grayed out in the UI):

- Under Stored Procedures, choose RPC:Completed and SP:StmtCompleted.
- Under TSQL, choose SQL:BatchCompleted.

Hit Save to save the template.

11.2.2 Capturing the traffic

Open SQL Server Profiler, and if you aren't prompted to connect to a server then hit the New Trace button in the toolbar. You'll connect to the SQL Server instance that contains the database you want to tune; again, *do not* run Profiler *on* that same server. Run it from your client computer, if possible.

Name your trace whatever you like—"AdventureWorks2012 trace 1" or something. Select the Tuning template (if you created a tuning template, select that). You also need to decide where you're going to save the trace data: I prefer using a file on my local computer. You can also save the information to a SQL Server database, but it needs to be a different server than the one you're profiling, so you don't overly impact performance. I'll often install SQL Server Express on my local computer, so I can save the trace data there.

Before you hit Run to start the trace, make sure that you're about to capture *representative traffic*. In other words, you need to run this trace during a period when users are using the database in a typical fashion. I like to try to capture traffic for an hour or so, provided I'm sure that's *representative* in terms of the activity users will be conducting. You can optionally enable an automatic stop time for the trace (useful when you need to run one overnight in order to catch that representative traffic). SQL Server not only needs to see the queries users are running, it also needs an idea of how often each query is run, so that it can help create balanced recommendations.

If you didn't configure an automatic trace stop time, click the Stop button in the toolbar of SQL Server Profiler when you've captured enough traffic. You can now close Profiler.

TRY IT NOW Go ahead and try running a capture. You'll notice that, until you run some queries, there won't be anything to capture. That's okay. In your hands-on lab for this chapter I'll help you capture some actual traffic.

11.3 Using the Database Engine Tuning Advisor

We're about to jump into a process that alters your database's index structure, so a warning is in order:

WARNING Don't make any changes to your indexes until you've backed up the existing index structure.

11.3.1 Backing up an index

To back up an existing index, and make it easy to recreate the index if needed, you can use SQL Server Management Studio:

1 Locate the index in the Object Explorer.
2 Right-click the index and select Script Index as, then choose CREATE To, then choose File....
3 Provide a filename (usually with a .sql filename extension), saving the file someplace safe.

The result will be a text file containing a CREATE INDEX statement that will completely recreate the index at need. If you have a lot of indexes, that's going to be a time-consuming process. Instead, consider grabbing the SQL script from http://sqlship .wordpress.com/2009/12/15/script-indexes-sql-server-2005-sql-server-2008/, which will script out all of your database's indexes as CREATE INDEX commands.

11.3.2   *Running the Advisor*

The Database Engine Tuning Advisor is a separate utility installed along with SQL Server's administrative tools; it isn't part of SQL Server Management Studio. That said, you can easily launch it from the Tools menu in SQL Server Management Studio. The Advisor is designed to analyze query traffic and help decide if you've got the right indexes in place to maximize performance for those queries.

NOTE Older versions of SQL Server (SQL Server 2005 and earlier) called this tool the Index Tuning Wizard, and it might not be accessible directly from older versions of SQL Server's management console. I always suggest using the latest management tools whenever you can practically (and legally) do so.

Start by connecting the Advisor to the SQL Server instance that contains the database you're trying to tune. Note that what you're about to do *will* create a performance impact on SQL Server; the Advisor is going to ask it to optimize all the queries you captured using Profiler, but to not actually run the queries. This is a process you should ideally do during a slow period in user activity, or during a maintenance window. Because some of SQL Server's query optimization decisions are based on current workload, the Advisor won't get 100% accurate optimizer results, but it's designed to work with "close enough."

As shown in figure 11.1, you'll come up with a name for this tuning session, point the Advisor to the trace file (or database) that you captured earlier, and give it a database in which to store its temporary work data. You'll also specify the database being tuned, which in the figure is AdventureWorks2012.

The Tuning Options tab is where all the fun happens:

- *You can choose to limit how long the Advisor tries to optimize the workload.* A large trace capture can take hours to process, so if you're running the Advisor during a maintenance window, the Limit tuning time option lets you ensure it'll quit working before the maintenance window ends and your users come back to work.

- *You can have the Advisor evaluate several different aspects of your Physical Design Structures, such as all indexes, nonclustered indexes only, and so on.* You can also have it evaluate the effectiveness of what's already in place, meaning it won't make suggestions about things you could potentially add.

- *You can specify existing items to keep.* This includes the option to consider discarding everything and starting from scratch.

Once you've dialed in the options you want, click Start Analysis in the toolbar, and go get a cup of coffee. No changes will be made at this time; you're only asking for

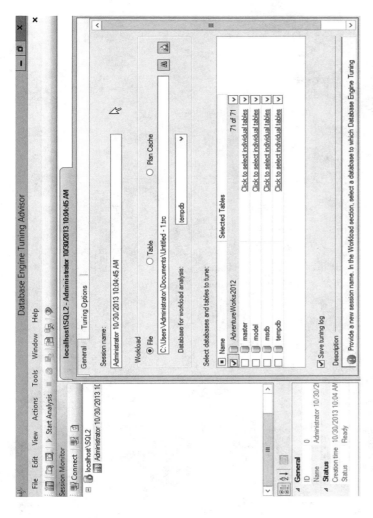

Figure 11.1   Set up the Advisor to tune your database.

recommendations. The final report will show an estimated improvement percent-age, along with recommendations, if any were generated. You can then choose to implement the suggestions, if desired. Figure 11.2 shows a portion of the completed report, and you'll notice in this case there were no suggestions for improvement. That's good! It means everything's already pretty well optimized for the workload you provided.

11.4   *What you can and can't do with indexes on someone else's database*

This is a tricky bit. Performing index tuning is pretty straightforward for databases where you own, or have access to, the application's code. You, or a developer who works with you, can easily verify that the application doesn't have any hard-coded internal dependencies on a specific index.

When you're working with a database that supports a third-party application (an application you don't have the source code for) things aren't so straightforward. *Most* applications don't know, or care, what indexes exist or don't exist. For the most part, indexes are entirely a SQL Server-side thing, and are invisible to the applica-tions that connect to SQL Server. There are exceptions. You can potentially break applications that:

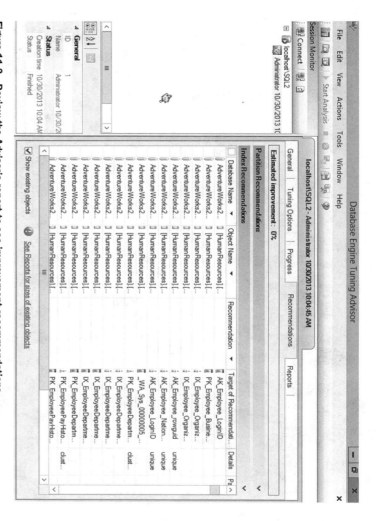

Figure 11.2   Review the Advisor's report to see improvement recommendations.

- *Have internal maintenance routines that explicitly rebuild, reorganize, or otherwise reference specific indexes.* This doesn't apply to *all* applications that run their own index maintenance routines; for example, an application that runs ALTER INDEX ALL doesn't refer to *specific* indexes.

- *Have queries that use index hints.* These are generally regarded as a poor practice, because they override SQL Server's built-in query optimization intelligence, but they exist.

How can you tell if an application falls into one (or both) of these scenarios? Well, without access to the source code, it's a bit difficult. I'll typically spin up a virtual machine that has a copy of the application's database, then run a copy of the application against that copy of the database. That way, I can remove or modify indexes and see if anything breaks. There are certainly more formal ways of getting SQL Server to tell you what indexes are being used, also, but I've tended to find the "try-it-to-see-if-anything-breaks" approach will keep me from potentially overlooking something.

If you're able to determine that an application *does not* explicitly refer to any specific indexes by name, you're pretty much free to modify the indexes in the database however you like. That's just the *technical* aspect of modifying the indexes. It's entirely possible that the application's vendor, if they discover you've been tampering with their indexing strategy, might not want to offer you technical support on the application. That's something you can discuss with them in advance.

You can—and absolutely should—also back up the original indexes, making it easy to put them back in place if needed.

11.5 Hands-on lab

I'd definitely like you to play with profiler and the Advisor a bit, with the understanding that the AdventureWorks database doesn't have a lot of data, and we don't have a way of generating a lot of traffic for you to capture. That said, it's still worth going through the process, so that you're familiar with it.

Start a tuning trace against your AdventureWorks2012 database. While the trace is running, go into SQL Server Management Studio, open a new query window, and run the following:

```
USE AdventureWorks2012;
GO

SELECT Name, StartTime FROM HumanResources.Shift
ORDER BY Name, StartTime

SELECT * FROM Person.Address

SELECT * FROM Person.Person
```

That will generate a bit of traffic for Profiler to capture. Stop the trace capture, and use the resulting trace data to run through the Database Engine Tuning Advisor. See what suggestions (if any) it offers. There's no right answer for this lab, so you won't find a solution on MoreLunches.com.

NOTE   As I mentioned earlier, it's likely you won't generate any Advisor results, because it won't have much to work with. It's important to see *how* to use this tool, though, because in order to see it in action you'll need to run it on a production network, and you certainly want to know what you're doing when that time comes!

11.6 Way above and way beyond

As an administrator, you don't necessarily *need* to know much more about index design tuning than I've presented in this chapter. But it's useful to know more, so if you'd like to get some deeper background on index design, keep reading the *extremely optional* remainder of this chapter.

I'm going to try to explain some of the more advanced index design choices that you might consider, that the Advisor might recommend, or that you just might want to be on the lookout for in your own databases.

11.6.1 Index key size

SQL Server works best with keys that are of a fairly limited size. There's no real hard-and-fast rule here, but in general you want to try to keep key sizes small. Indexing on a 20-character text field (like a name) tends to perform better than an index built on a 200-character field. Why? Mainly because when you have a smaller key, more values can fit on a single 8 KB index page. That means SQL Server needs fewer disk operations to read through the index, and fewer disk operations always helps performance. It also means SQL Server can cache more pages in memory, avoiding disk operations altogether for cached pages.

Obviously, you put your indexes where they need to be; you don't necessarily forgo indexing a column *just* because it's a big column. But some common-sense table design decisions can help decrease key size. Let's say you have a table that uses a SQL Server IDENTITY specification to create unique, numeric values for each row in the table. *Most* tables have a column like that, but what *data type* do you choose for it? SQL Server has numerous integer data types, all of which are usable, but all of which offer different key sizes. A TINYINT, for example, is just 1 byte long, making for a very small key size but it only offers 255 possible key values, so unless you know you'll never have more than 255 rows of data, TINYINT isn't a very good choice for a unique identifier. BIGINT can hold an enormous number of values (more than 9 quintillion), but each value takes 8 bytes. That's twice the storage needed than for a regular INT, which still offers more than 2 billion possible identifier values. So selecting an *appropriate* data type can help provide a good balance for index performance.

11.6.2   Index selectivity

Selectivity is a measurement of how unique the various values in an index are. Let's say you built an index on a column that holds U.S. state names: you'd have a bit more than 50 possible values (including places like Washington, D.C.). Now let's say that the table held a million data rows. Fifty or so values out of a million rows isn't very *selective*. In other words, the index doesn't let you narrow down the rows very much, since there are so few index values compared to the number of data rows.

SQL Server tracks, as part of its statistics, how selective an index is. Indexes with low selectivity may not wind up being used often, which means you'll be incurring overhead in keeping the indexes up-to-date, but not getting much actual benefit from the indexes.

11.6.3   Compound indexes

Although many indexes are built on a single column, SQL Server supports *compound indexes*, which are built on multiple columns. There's a trick to making these as effective as possible in terms of improving query performance, and it's to keep the *leading edge* of the index as selective as possible.

Let's say you have a table with a column for a customer's first name, and a second column for the customer's last name. You might well build a compound index that includes both columns. The leading edge of the index is the first column: would you put first name first, or last name first?

In most English-speaking cultures, there's a tendency to want to make the compound index "last name, first name," because when we think of looking up someone by name, we tend to start with the last (or family) name. But that won't necessarily make the performance of the index better. You need to know a bit more about *how* the data will be queried by users.

If users will *primarily* be looking up users by last name, then making the last name the leading edge of the index might make sense. You have to ask yourself why you're making a compound index that includes the first name, if the last name is what most queries will be focused on!

But if users will *primarily* be looking for *both* first name and last name, then putting the *first* name as the compound index's leading edge might make more sense. A lot of people share the same last name, which might make it *less* selective. Let's say you have a hundred customers with the last name Jones, but only two customers with the first name Don. Putting the first name as the leading edge of the index means SQL Server can immediately narrow down the results to those two rows containing Don, and then scan those two rows to match the requested last name. If you'd put the last name first, SQL Server would only be able to initially narrow down to 100 rows, which it would then have to scan in order to match the desired first name.

11.6.4 Covering indexes

The last index trick you should know about is a covering index. This isn't a special type of index that you explicitly create, but is rather any regular index—single-column or compound—that contains all of the data needed to satisfy a query.

You know from previous chapters that a nonclustered index provides a pointer to the actual data row you're after, which incurs a bit of a performance hit when SQL Server has to jump to the data row. Suppose you have a customer table that contains columns for first name, last name, and mailing address. Say that you built a compound index on the first name and last name columns. Now imagine that you execute a query like SELECT FirstName,LastName FROM Customers WHERE LastName = 'Jones'. You can expect SQL Server to use your compound index to help speed up that query, but because in this case the index itself contains the two values you asked for, SQL Server won't ever make the jump to the data row. Because you asked *only* for values that were already in the index, the index *covered* the query's data, so there was no need to jump to the data row to look up more information.

It can be tempting to try to build all kinds of covering indexes to help speed up queries, but you have to exercise restraint. Keeping those indexes maintained can cause an enormous negative performance impact in a database that has a lot of updates happening, and the performance bonus of a covering index won't offset that cost.

12

Reading query execution plans

When SQL Server is given a query to execute, it runs the query through an internal *query optimizer*. The optimizer looks at what the query is trying to do, what indexes are available to help, what condition those indexes are in, what load the server is currently handling, literally dozens of different factors. It considers all the ways it might execute the query—scanning a table, seeking in an index, and so on. There's a limit on how long it'll run through the permutations, because eventually it'll be wasting time instead of running the query! At some point it'll pick the best choice found by then, and that becomes the *execution plan* for that query. SQL Server then runs the plan, executing the query.

12.1 What's an execution plan?

Imagine that you need to drive to work. You probably have several different routes that you can use, and you might take into account several factors:

- *How much fuel do you have in the car?* If you're getting low, you might discard a longer or a more stop-and-start routing.
- *What condition are the roads in?* Watching the morning news or checking an online traffic report might make one route more attractive than another.
- *Do you have any additional stops along the way?* Those errands might dictate specific routes.

SQL Server goes through that process each time it needs to run a query. It won't spend forever contemplating every available option, any more than you'll spend an hour researching traffic reports before you jump into your car for a half-hour drive!

Just as you probably do, SQL Server can also *cache*, or save, execution plans for future reuse. That saves time when executing the same query over and over, since SQL Server won't have to go through the optimization process every time. Plans tend to be most easily cached for stored procedures and views, because those are persistent objects that SQL Server expects to see run again and again. An *ad-hoc query*, or a query that is handed to SQL Server instead of being placed into a stored procedure, won't benefit as much from cached execution plans. It isn't that ad-hoc queries' plans aren't cached; it's just that SQL Server's likelihood of reusing them before they're removed from the cache isn't as high.

NOTE   Although administrators can't do anything about it, *developers* can contribute to application performance by having their applications run stored procedures, rather than by sending ad-hoc queries to SQL Server.

You can use SQL Server Management Studio to see the execution plans that SQL Server comes up with. These are stored internally (and can be saved to disk) as XML-based data, but SQL Server also provides a graphical visualization of the execution plan.

TRY IT NOW   I'm going to walk you through executing an ad-hoc query in AdventureWorks2012; please follow along and make sure you're getting similar results.

Start by opening SQL Server Management Studio and connecting to your SQL Server instance. Open a new query window, and make sure it's focused on the Adventure-Works2012 database. In the query window, enter the following query:

```
SELECT p.Title,p.FirstName,p.LastName,
       ea.EmailAddress
FROM Person.Person AS p
INNER JOIN Person.EmailAddress AS ea
ON p.BusinessEntityID = ea.BusinessEntityID
WHERE Title IS NOT NULL
ORDER BY LastName ASC, FirstName DESC
```

Execute the query to make sure you don't have any typos; as you can see in figure 12.1, I got about 1,000 rows of data from the query.

Now let's see the execution plan SQL Server came up with. We'll start by asking SQL Server to display the *estimated* plan; this submits our query to the optimizer, but doesn't run the query. The estimated plan is usually close to the final plan, but there are a few things SQL Server doesn't take into account. We'll compare the actual plan in a bit. For now, in SQL Server Management Studio, click the Query menu and select Display Estimated Execution Plan (or press Ctrl+L). Figure 12.2 shows what you should see.

We'll spend some time interpreting this output in the next section; for now, let's see the actual execution plan, too. From the Query menu again, select Include Actual Execution Plan (or press Ctrl+M). This time, you'll also have to run the query to get

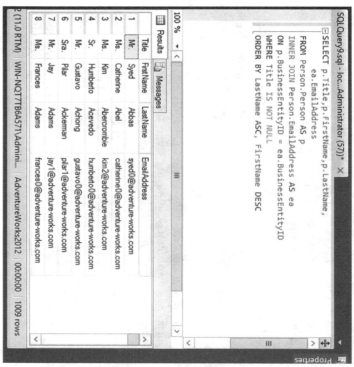

```
SQLQuery9.sql - loc...Administrator (57))*  ×

SELECT   p.Title,p.FirstName,p.LastName,
         ea.EmailAddress
FROM Person.Person AS p
INNER JOIN Person.EmailAddress AS ea
ON p.BusinessEntityID = ea.BusinessEntityID
WHERE Title IS NOT NULL
ORDER BY LastName ASC, FirstName DESC
```

100 %			
Results	Messages		

	Title	FirstName	LastName	EmailAddress
1	Mr.	Syed	Abbas	syed0@adventure-works.com
2	Ms.	Catherine	Abel	catherine0@adventure-works.com
3	Ms.	Kim	Abercrombie	kim2@adventure-works.com
4	Sr.	Humberto	Acevedo	humberto0@adventure-works.com
5	Mr.	Gustavo	Achong	gustavo0@adventure-works.com
6	Sra.	Pilar	Ackerman	pilar1@adventure-works.com
7	Mr.	Jay	Adams	jay1@adventure-works.com
8	Ms.	Frances	Adams	frances0@adventure-works.com

2 (11.0 RTM)   WIN-NQ1TT86A571\Admini...   AdventureWorks2012   00:00:00   1009 rows

Figure 12.1   Run this query to make sure you're getting results.

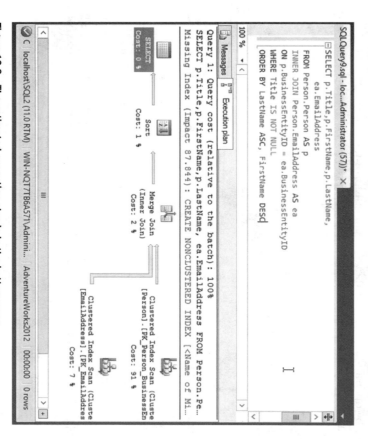

```
SQLQuery9.sql - loc...Administrator (57))*  ×

SELECT   p.Title,p.FirstName,p.LastName,
         ea.EmailAddress
FROM Person.Person AS p
INNER JOIN Person.EmailAddress AS ea
ON p.BusinessEntityID = ea.BusinessEntityID
WHERE Title IS NOT NULL
ORDER BY LastName ASC, FirstName DESC
```

100 %	
Messages	Execution plan

Query 1: Query cost (relative to the batch): 100%
SELECT p.Title,p.FirstName,p.LastName, ea.EmailAddress FROM Person.Pe...
Missing Index (Impact 87.844): CREATE NONCLUSTERED INDEX [<Name of Mi...

SELECT
Cost: 0 %

Sort
Cost: 1 %

Sort
(Inner Join)
Cost: 2 %

Merge Join
(Inner Join)
Cost: 2 %

Clustered Index Scan (Cluste
[Person].[PK_Person_BusinessEn
Cost: 91 %

Clustered Index Scan (Cluste
[EmailAddress].[PK_EmailAddres
Cost: 7 %

C   localhost\SQL2 (11.0 RTM)   WIN-NQ1TT86A571\Admini...   AdventureWorks2012   00:00:00   0 rows

Figure 12.2   The estimated execution plan is in the bottom pane.

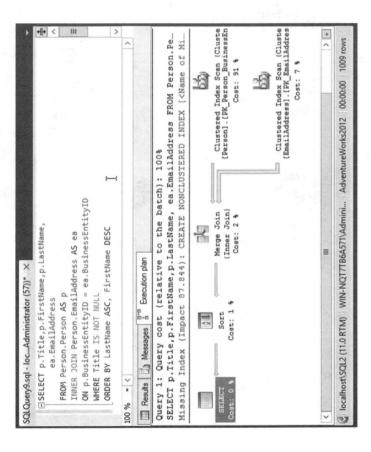

Figure 12.3 You have to run the query to get the actual execution plan.

the execution plan. Figure 12.3 shows what I got; your results should be similar if not identical.

You'll notice that the query results show up in their own tab, separate from the execution plan. This actual plan looks a lot like the estimated one, which is common, especially for simple queries running against a small set of tables. You'll also notice a textual hint above the graphical plan: Missing Index (Impact 87.844). That's SQL Server's way of saying, "Hey, I could have run this a lot faster—maybe 87% faster—if this other index had existed." Take those tips into consideration, but don't let them freak you out. An index that would speed up this particular query might slow down many, many others, so you have to put things into context. For example, this plan took a couple of milliseconds to run. A savings of 87% would still be a couple of milliseconds—87% seems like a big potential savings, but it's 87% of a tiny number, so any improvement will be pretty tiny, too.

12.2 *Common plan symbols and what they mean*

Let's run through some of the major symbols you'll see (refer to figures 12.2 and 12.3 as you're running through this list). I'm going to provide the icons used by SQL Server 2012; older versions have slightly different icons, and in some cases the operation names may even be slightly different.

Scan is usually a bad thing. This is like me giving you a huge list of names, which might not be in any particular order, and asking you to find one specific name. In anything but a very small table (maybe a dozen rows), this is an inefficient operation. You'll see this as table scan, clustered index scan, and nonclustered index scan.

NOTE In the icons, the little brackets are added to the clustered index operation; the nonclustered index operation doesn't have the little brackets.

 A seek is a good thing. This is when SQL Server uses a B-tree index, either in a clustered index seek or a nonclustered index seek.

 In conjunction with a seek, you'll often see a Bookmark Lookup. After seeking or scanning in a nonclustered index, SQL Server uses the Bookmark Lookup to jump to the actual data row. For a table that has a clustered index, it'll be a fast scan of that index; for a table that's only a heap, it'll be a jump to the row ID (RID) for the desired row (which may involve one or more forwarding hops, because it's a heap). Older versions of SQL Server call this a clustered index seek or RID Lookup, for clustered indexes and heaps, respectively.

 Next up is a Filter operation, which goes through the current result set one row at a time and removes rows that don't meet whatever criteria you've specified. This is less efficient than querying *only* the data you wanted in the first place, and often indicates that a suitable index wasn't available.

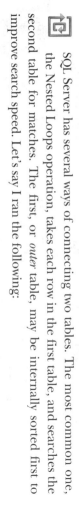 SQL Server has several ways of connecting two tables. The most common one, the Nested Loops operation, takes each row in the first table, and searches the second table for matches. The first, or *outer* table, may be internally sorted first to improve search speed. Let's say I ran the following:

```
SELECT One,Two FROM TableA INNER JOIN TableB ON Three = Four
```

TableA is the outer table, and I'm going to look at all the values in its Three column. For each value, I'll look in TableB's Four column to try to find matching values. Rows where I find a match are passed on to the next operation as my result.

A Hash Match is another way to join two tables. SQL Server will use this when keys are large, and for certain operations such as DISTINCT and UNION. SQL Server executes a quick cryptographic *hash* on each row in the first table, then looks for matching hashes in the second table.

A Merge Join is what you saw in the example execution plan that I ran earlier. This is an efficient way of matching two tables to each other. In my example, I matched the tables on their BusinessEntityID columns, both of which are the keys for the tables' respective clustered indexes. Imagine taking two stacks of papers, each of which has a person's name written on it. The stacks have been sorted into alphabetical order, so all you have to do is quickly merge them. This technique requires those stacks to be sorted first and in my earlier example the fact that I was doing this on an existing index made that possible.

 You'll see a Compute Scalar operation when SQL Server has been asked to do math (adding the value of two columns, for example).

 The Stream Aggregate operation comes up when you're grouping rows, perhaps grouping all of the sales orders for a particular region so that you can compute a regional total value. This operation will often sort the data if it hasn't already been sorted.

 The Sort operation does exactly what the name implies: sorts the data. This can be a bit slow for large data sets, and works better if the data is presorted, as would be the case if there were an index on the data being sorted.

There are a couple of other operations you can often expect to see. These have more to do with some fun bits of SQL Server internals, but it can be interesting to understand what they're doing:

- The Parallelism operator means that SQL Server is splitting some of the query operation across multiple threads of execution. These usually come in sets: Repartition Streams indicates that SQL Server is taking multiple streams of data and rearranging them into other multiple streams to facilitate parallel processing; Gather Streams is where SQL Server brings everything back together into a single output stream. The opposite of that is Distribute Streams, which engages parallelism by splitting a bunch of records into multiple streams for simultaneous processing.

- Index and Clustered Index modifications, including Update, Insert, and Delete, only occur in UPDATE, INSERT, and DELETE queries, and they can visually show you how much work SQL Server is doing to keep indexes updated when performing those queries.

With some of those in mind, let's look at how to interpret them in the context of a real execution plan.

12.3   *How to read an execution plan*

First, remember your goal when reading an execution plan: *you might not be able to fix anything!* You're trying to spot bad queries or operations that indicate there's an operational or design problem. You'll typically need to report these to a vendor or a developer. You're diagnosing the problem, even though you may not be able to fix the problem all by yourself.

Let's check out that execution plan again (figure 12.4).

These are read from right to left, so we start with two Clustered Index Scan operations. Wait, did I say a *scan*? Aren't those slow? Well, yes, but in this case it's because

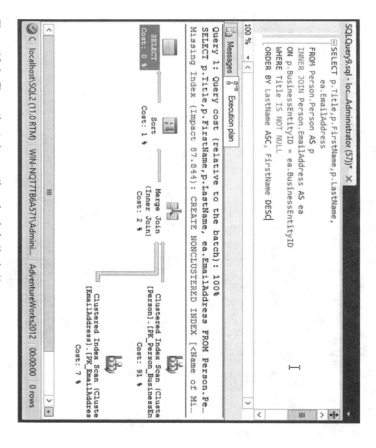

Figure 12.4   The estimated execution plan is in the bottom pane.

I'm asking for *all rows* in the table, rather than scanning for a specific value. But you'll notice that 91% of the query's execution time came from that scan. Retrieving data from disk is expensive.

Next, the two stacks of sorted rows are run through a Merge Join, giving a single result set. That's passed to a Sort, although I'm betting the data was at least partially in the right order already, because the Sort didn't take long. The last operation, SELECT, indicates that the query is over and the results are ready.

TIP   Hovering your cursor over any operation reveals additional details.

TRY IT NOW   I'd like you to look at the little hover-over details box on your own computer; I'll describe what you're seeing.

My "big three" pieces of additional information are:

- *Actual Number of Rows*—How many rows the operation returned.
- *Estimated I/O Cost*—The amount of disk time spent executing the operation. Reducing this number is usually the best way to improve performance.
- *Estimated CPU Cost*—Tells you how much processor time the operation took to complete.

Consider reading the fantastic article at www.simple-talk.com/sql/performance/execution-plan-basics/ for more details on how plans are cached, and how to interpret various kinds of plans. I'm focusing on graphical plans because they're the easiest to start with; that article also covers text-based plans and XML-based plans, which can make it easier to work through extremely complex queries.

12.4   What to look for in an execution plan

You're staring at a plan. Now what? Start by looking for low-hanging fruit, meaning the highest-cost operations in a query. If an operation contributed 80% to the overall query, then reducing the execution time of that operation can help the most in improving the overall query performance. The biggest single "win" can often be had by adding an index, but be *very* careful about over-improving one query at a cost to all the others. You can rarely look at just one query; you need to consider the entire system. That's where the Database Engine Tuning Advisor can help.

Some other major considerations—things I generally try to keep an eye out for—include:

- *Major differences between estimated and actual plans are often caused by stale statistics.* That's much like watching a traffic report in the morning and heading off to work hours later. Your actual commute will be different than what you'd estimated, because your statistics are old. To fix this in SQL Server, manually update statistics or allow automatic statistics updates to correct this problem. Note that you won't spot this unless you're checking queries for both their estimated and actual plans, which SQL Server Management Studio won't do by default.

- *Those "Missing Index" messages when displaying execution plans.* As I noted earlier, those aren't always a mandate to create the missing index, but they're definitely something that needs to be considered.

- *Table scans on anything other than very tiny tables.* That *always* indicates that a suitable index wasn't available. Adding the index isn't necessarily a foregone conclusion, because, as you know by now, indexes are all about compromise. Frequent table scans across a large table may also indicate that an index is missing (perhaps accidentally dropped) or other problem.

- *Bookmark lookups to a RID.* Because newer versions of SQL Server use the same icon for that as well as a clustered index seek, you'll need to dig into that details pop-up every time you see a bookmark lookup, especially one that has a high percentage of execution time. RID lookups indicate a hop from a nonclustered index to a heap, and heaps are almost always bad.

- *Hash joins aren't inherently bad, but they're not very efficient.* If you're seeing a lot of them across a large number of queries, there might be indexes that could be added to help drive a nested loop or, even better, a merge join.

- *Massive numbers of joins in a single query can be tough for SQL Server to execute efficiently.* I start paying close attention to queries with five or more tables being joined, although five tables isn't a danger zone for SQL Server. It's where I start checking to make sure the right indexes are in place to facilitate those joins. Start showing me queries with seven, nine, eleven, or more tables being joined, and I start wondering if maybe the database design hasn't been overnormalized. It's far from trivial to fix that, but it's worth a discussion with the developer or vendor.

At the end of the day, you're looking for long-running, high-percentage operations so you can report them to a vendor or developer. They might not be seeing the same execution plans in their development environments, and sharing your plans with them can help them improve their code, or make suggestions for tuning your particular system. Saving plans as XML (easily done from the File menu in SQL Server Management Studio when you're viewing a plan) is a great way to share plans, because the XML can be easily attached to an email.

12.5 *Hands-on lab*

Analyze the execution plan on the following query (which uses the AdventureWorks-2012 database):

```
SELECT  Sales.SalesOrderDetail.OrderQty ,
Sales.SalesOrderDetail.SpecialOfferID ,
Sales.SalesOrderDetail.UnitPrice ,
Sales.SalesOrderDetail.UnitPriceDiscount ,
Sales.SalesOrderHeader.Status ,
Sales.SalesOrderHeader.AccountNumber
FROM    Sales.SalesOrderDetail
INNER JOIN Sales.SalesOrderHeader ON Sales.SalesOrderDetail.SalesOrderID =
Sales.SalesOrderHeader.SalesOrderID
ORDER BY Sales.SalesOrderDetail.UnitPrice DESC
```

See if you can now answer a few questions about the execution plan:

1   There are two tables being joined, so you should expect to see at least two operations running on the right-hand side of the plan. What are the first two operations? Note that you may only get one operation if your SQL Server computer only has a single processor. In a virtual machine, you can try adding a second virtual CPU so that SQL Server can use parallelization.

2   What kind of partitioning type do the parallelism operators use? You'll need to look in the pop-up details box for this answer.

3   Given the type of partitioning, what kind of join operator might you expect to see next?

4   Do you notice anything unusual about the icons in this execution plan, compared to the icons you saw in previous examples in this chapter?

5   What's the most expensive operation in this execution plan?

You'll find answers at MoreLunches.com. Find this book's cover image, click it, and look for the file downloads section.

13
Block and deadlock analysis

If only one or two users needed to get to your data, then locking and blocking wouldn't be necessary, but there wouldn't be very much point to having SQL Server, either! As it is, concurrent-access database systems like SQL Server implement *locking* to help ensure individual users don't overly impact one another when they're all accessing the same data. In this chapter, we'll look at what locks do, how they work, and how they can negatively impact system performance. I'll be focusing on helping you gather evidence of poorly written or slow-running queries, so that you can work with a developer or vendor to help improve performance.

13.1 What's locking and blocking?

Imagine a bunch of people gathered around a bulletin board, all trying to read the posted information. As some are trying to read the list, others are erasing items and scribbling in new ones. Sometimes, people don't get to read an entire item before someone else is erasing it. Sometimes, two people are trying to rewrite the same item at the same time, getting into arguments, writing over each other's post, and generally creating chaos.

Locking is a SQL Server feature that helps manage that process. Whenever you access data in any way, SQL Server locks it. If you're trying to read data, for example, SQL Server quickly places a *shared lock* on the data, allowing others to read it (peering over your shoulder at the same list, as it were), but preventing anyone else from changing the data until you're done reading it. If you need to change data, SQL Server puts a stronger lock on the data, preventing anyone else from peeking at it until your change is complete.

119

Blocking is a natural outcome of locking. If you're changing something, and I'm trying to read it, my process gets *blocked* until you're done changing it, your lock is released, and I'm allowed to take my own lock. Because most queries execute so quickly, locks don't last for long (we're talking milliseconds, here), so nobody gets blocked for long. But in an extremely busy database application, particularly one with poorly designed or long-running queries, block times can start to add up. Users find themselves waiting for perceptible lengths of time, and although SQL Server isn't necessarily working all that hard, the overall application starts to feel sluggish.

Being able to monitor locking and blocking, and to spot problem areas, is a key to helping maintain SQL Server performance. Sometimes, performance doesn't always drag because SQL Server is out of memory or because the processor utilization is pegged; sometimes, blocking makes the application *feel* slow.

13.2   Understanding transactions

Transactions play a key role in the lifetime of a lock. A typical SQL query, like a SELECT query, is an implicit transaction. That is, any locks needed to execute the query will only last until the query is complete. That's pretty easy to understand, and in most applications you'll rarely run into blocking issues with those simple queries.

Sometimes, a developer needs several queries to execute together in a batch. Perhaps you need to create a customer order, and attach several items to it. You don't want to insert the rows representing just *some* order items, because then the order would be incomplete. A developer might take those several simple queries and attach them to each other in an *explicit transaction*.

With an explicit transaction, all of the statements in the transaction will either fail together, or succeed together. In their code, the developer can even abort the transaction, and SQL Server will magically undo everything that the transaction had done up to that point.

Unfortunately, that magic involves locking. The queries inside the transaction still need to lock data in the same way that they would if they were running individually, outside a transaction. But because SQL Server needs the ability to undo *everything* that happened in the transaction, each query's locks don't go away when that one query completes. Instead, the locks stay in place until the *entire transaction* is completed. The more queries that get jammed into the transaction, the longer those locks will live, and the longer they'll block others from accessing the same data. If the transaction happens to be accessing a lot of data—and therefore locking it—there's a good chance more people will be blocked, increasing the perception of poor application performance.

13.3   Types of locks

SQL Server thinks about locks in two ways: *what* is being locked, and *how* it is being locked. When choosing what to lock, SQL Server tries to lock the smallest bit of data possible, so that it can minimize the blocking impact on other users. Keeping track of a bunch of tiny locks can be memory- and processor-intensive, so sometimes SQL Server will *escalate* the lock, and lock a larger chunk of data.

Let's say you have a database table with 100 rows of data. You start a transaction that modifies a single row, so SQL Server locks that row. Your next query locks another row, and so on. At some point, say, 30 rows in, SQL Server decides it's tired of keeping track of all those single-row locks. It releases them, and instead acquires a lock on the entire table. Even though you're not technically modifying the entire table, you've now prevented anyone else from working with it. For this reason, lock escalation is something administrators have to keep a close eye on. That kind of "overlocking," as I call it, is almost always the result of poorly designed queries and transactions, which you'll have to report to a developer or vendor for analysis and correction.

What does SQL Server lock? Here's the list, more or less in order of increasing size:

- Single row of data
- A key (a row of data within an index)
- An entire 8 KB page of data
- An entire extent of 8 pages
- An entire heap or index
- An entire table
- An entire database file on disk
- An entire database

I've omitted a couple of the more rare lock types, because we're going to focus on locks that deal with user data. SQL Server more or less follows this list for escalations: it might start by locking a row, but might escalate to all of the rows on a page, and then to an entire table.

You'll notice that some of those lock types relate to tables, while others (such as a key lock) relate to indexes. That's because indexes change, and when updating them SQL Server has to get a lock on the data before the change can be made. You can start to imagine how many locks a single change might involve: if you modify a row in a table, and that table has 12 indexes, then you might have to have 13 locks! One lock will hold the row you're changing, while the other 12 will let the indexes be updated. That's how block times can start to add up, because now all 13 locks have to be held until both the table row and all 12 indexes are updated, something that might take a perceptible period of time.

The main types of locks SQL Server can hold are:

- *Shared*—Allows someone else to read, but not change, the data. SQL Server allows multiple Shared locks on the same data.
- *Update*—Allows someone else to read the data but tells SQL Server that the data is being read with the intent of updating it. SQL Server only allows one Update lock on a given piece of data, but it will allow multiple Shared locks at the same time. Update locks are eventually converted to an Exclusive lock when the

query makes the update. The idea here is that UPDATE queries are technically a two-step process, with the first step reading the existing data and the second step modifying it. An Update lock helps keep the data available for others to read for as long as possible.

- *Exclusive*—Used to change data. SQL Server will allow one and only one Exclusive lock on a given piece of data, and it won't allow any other locks on that same data. If you're trying to change data, and therefore trying to acquire an Exclusive lock on it, you'll be blocked until all other existing locks go away.

Thanks to escalation, SQL Server has to take a lot more locks than you might think. Let's say you get an Exclusive lock on a row. SQL Server doesn't know what your plans are for the entire transaction, so it has to reserve the right to escalate that lock to a page, extent, table, and so on. At the same time it gets your Exclusive lock on the row, it also gets an *Intent Exclusive* lock on the page, extent, table, and so on. Those intent locks are how the server enables itself to escalate your lock, if needed. SQL Server has to acquire the Intent locks *first*, meaning it starts from the largest object (say, the entire database) and works its way down until it reaches the data it wants the real lock on.

SQL Server also keeps track of a lock's *isolation level*. Isolation describes how well a transaction is protected from others. In a *Read Uncommitted* query, a SELECT statement is allowed to read data without first obtaining a Shared lock. That means other transactions might come along and obtain an Exclusive lock on the data, and that SELECT statement might be reading data that is actively being changed. That's called a *dirty read*, because the data being read might be *dirty*, or not fully committed. That level of isolation (technically it's nonisolation) helps improve concurrency, but the application has to be written to deal with potential data integrity problems. There are levels of isolation, but I'm not going to focus much on them because at a low level of administration you can't work with them. I'll mention them as appropriate in the upcoming discussion.

13.4   Lock and block analysis

How can you get your eyeballs on locks and blocks? One way to get an overall look at server-level locking is to use Performance Monitor. The SQLServer Locks object lets you look at granular lock activity, as shown in figure 13.1. You can see row-level locks, page-level locks, and so on, all in their own graph.

As you can see, you can get a pretty good overview of some key items:

- How many locks are being requested each second.
- How long, on average, queries are waiting before they get their locks. This isn't *exactly* the same as how long processes are being blocked, but this number tracks block time pretty closely.
- How many locks are timing out. You never want this to be a high number, as it indicates queries that weren't able to get their locks.

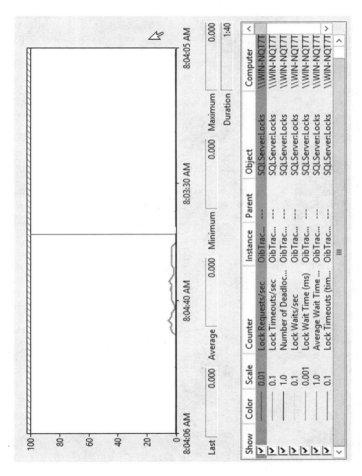

Figure 13.1 Use Performance Monitor to view system-level lock activity.

Each of these is available for specific data types, meaning you can see lock requests per second for rows, pages, extents, tables, and so on; there are _TOTAL instances that let you see aggregate values for the entire server instance.

Keep in mind that, using SQL Server Agent, you can configure alerts on these performance counters. That way, you can be notified when lock wait times exceed some threshold you've determined. I'll often do that when I'm troubleshooting an application that I know is having troubles; by receiving an alert when lock wait times start to go up, I can immediately start deeper level troubleshooting, knowing that the application is in fact having problems *right then*. I'll use a performance baseline from when the system is working well to determine a good lock wait time threshold.

TRY IT NOW You won't have a hands-on lab at the end of this chapter, but I urge you to follow along with the procedure I'll cover now.

One of those deeper troubleshooting steps is to configure a blocked process report, which runs from SQL Server's Extended Events system (introduced in SQL Server 2008, and expanded in subsequent versions). This will show you a list of processes that have been blocked for longer than the threshold you specify, so you need to decide on an acceptable length of time, in seconds, for a process to be blocked. Say you choose 5 seconds; you'd run the following command in SQL Server:

```
sp_configure 'show advanced options', 1 ;
GO
RECONFIGURE ;
GO
EXEC sp_configure 'blocked process threshold', 5;
RECONFIGURE;
```

NOTE   This is a "sticky" configuration setting, which means it will stay in effect after a server restart. All you're doing with this setting is generating an event, which doesn't impact server performance.

Now, when a process is blocked for more than 5 seconds, SQL Server can capture the event and generate a report for you. As I mentioned, that report is captured and viewed through SQL Server's Extended Events functionality, so we'll need to set that up:

1   In SQL Server Management Studio's Object Explorer, expand Management, then expand Extended Events. You should see a Sessions folder; right-click it and choose New Session....

2   Provide a Session name, such as My block report.

3   On the Events page, type block into the Event library; field, as I've done in figure 13.2. That should get you to the blocked_process_report; click that and then click the > (right-arrow) button to add it to the Selected events list.

Once you're done, click OK to close the window. You'll need to right-click the new session in SQL Server Management Studio, and select Start to start the session. When

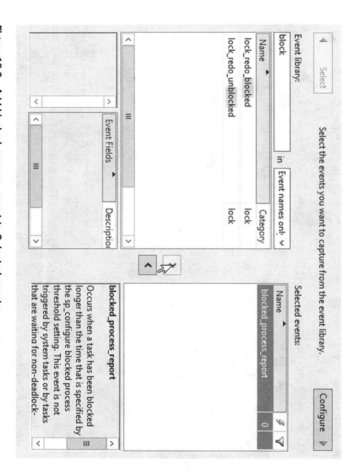

Figure 13.2   Add blocked_process_report to Selected events.

any new blocked process reports are generated, they'll be listed underneath that session. These reports show what processes are being blocked, what database they were trying to access, what kind of lock they were trying to obtain, and so on. This helps me figure out what exactly is happening, and to provide useful information to a developer or vendor.

ABOVE AND BEYOND

I won't get into Extended Events much in this chapter. I'll go into much more depth, and even repeat this example with a more detailed explanation, in chapter 17.

Extended Events is a lightweight way of monitoring key performance factors. By lightweight, I mean the system is designed to run continuously without impacting performance itself; that's different from, say, SQL Server Profiler, which can capture some of the same information but which imposes its own not-inconsiderable overhead.

Extended Events *sessions* are a persistent monitor for specific events. You set up a session to look for certain events, and run that session to begin capturing information about those events.

You can read more about Extended Events at http://technet.microsoft.com/en-us/library/bb630282(v=sql.110).aspx.

How do I use this blocked process report? For one, the actual report includes a big chunk of XML data that I can provide to a developer or vendor, telling them what was blocked, how long it was blocked, what query it was waiting on, and so forth. It even shows me what caused the block, so it's the first step in finding that information. We'll look more at that in chapter 17, when we dig deeper into Extended Events.

Your application users' experience will correlate with the blocked process report. That is, a user who is *being* blocked would show up, letting you match technical data (the report) to user complaints. From there, I'll typically rely on the developer or vendor to tell me what they need next in terms of diagnostic information.

13.5 Deadlocks

Deadlocks are an especially vicious kind of lock. They occur when two separate processes are each trying to obtain locks on two different resources. Let's say that Process A has obtained a lock on Resource 1, but it is waiting on a lock for Resource 2. Process B has a lock on Resource 2, and is waiting for a lock on Resource 1. The processes are said to be *deadlocked*, because unless one of them gives up pretty quickly, neither can "let go" of the locks they have, and they can't get the locks they want. SQL Server detects these situations automatically and selects one of the processes, at random, to be the *victim*. The victim process is then given an error, and all of its locks are released, allowing the nonvictim process to proceed.

NOTE   Technically, the victim isn't chosen randomly; SQL Server tries to figure out which deadlocked process will be the least expensive, meaning which one will involve the least rollback effort. The end result, though, usually appears to be pretty random. You can't control SQL Server's choice, although developers can (in their code) tag sessions as low- or high-priority to help steer SQL Server's decision. I don't run into many developers who do so.

You can't fix deadlocks, and they're not a massive problem if they don't happen too often. But poorly designed transactions, especially in a busy system, can start to increase the number of deadlocks you see. Because deadlocks result in a terminated process, they tend to crash applications and raise errors to users, making them visible and extremely annoying. The only resolution is to redesign the conflicting queries or transactions so that they don't deadlock anymore.

Another problem with deadlocks is that application developers don't always code their applications to deal well with being a deadlock victim. SQL Server returns a trappable error to the application, but it's up to the application to do something sensible with that error, like informing the user of the problem and asking them if they want to try their operation again. When not properly handled, the user may receive a generic error message, or the application may crash, or the application may not give any visible indication that anything went wrong—which means the user may think their operation succeeded. Again, you can't fix that as a SQL Server administrator. It's up to the developer or vendor to modify their code.

Performance Monitor is a good way to watch for deadlocks, as there's a specific counter that tracks terminated processes and deadlocks. You can also use another Extended Events session to watch for deadlock activity. SQL Server Profiler can also be used to view extended information about deadlocks, although it isn't a good idea to leave Profiler running all the time. I'll usually only use that tool once I know deadlocks are a problem, and I need to capture information for a developer or vendor to analyze. In those cases, they'll often tell me exactly what they need to see, so that I can set up the appropriate trace in Profiler.

On a routine basis, I'll monitor deadlock activity using Performance Monitor. I'll establish a baseline of acceptable deadlock level (it's often very low, or even "no deadlocks are acceptable"), then dig deeper if the system starts to exceed that threshold for any extended period of time. SQL Server Agent alerts on that performance counter, in fact, are a great idea, because you can get an immediate notification *right when* the problem is happening.

13.6 *Mitigating blocks and deadlocks*

While you, as an administrator, can't necessarily fix deadlocks or prevent long block times, you can certainly help reduce their frequency or impact. Keep in mind that blocks and deadlocks are, more or less, all about timing. If transactions can run quickly enough, it's much less likely that you'll get into a deadlock, and fast-running transactions won't hold locks for as long, which means they won't block other processes as long.

Improving disk performance is one of the best things you can do to speed up overall transaction throughput and reducing the likelihood of long block times or of deadlocks. Bear in mind that any given UPDATE, INSERT, or DELETE query is probably going to be updating not only table data, but also one or more indexes, all of which involves a lot of disk activity. The faster the disk throughput, the faster the query. We have a chapter coming up on performance, and I'll provide tips specific to the disk subsystem that should help a bit.

13.7 Hands-on lab

Because it can be so difficult to artificially create and observe locks and blocks, for this chapter I'd like you to become more familiar with the queries you'd run to do so. Go back through the chapter and make sure you're comfortable running the various queries. If you have a production SQL Server instance that you can monitor, use Performance Monitor to review some of the counters I pointed out in this chapter.

Automating management with SQL Server Agent

We've covered backups, index maintenance, and a number of other important maintenance tasks so far. You can perform all of those tasks manually, but wouldn't it be nicer if you could set them up once, and have them run on a regular basis? Of course! That's where SQL Server Agent becomes your very best friend.

14.1 What Is SQL Server Agent?

SQL Server Agent, Agent for short, is a separate service that installs along with SQL Server. It runs under its own service account, and it stores its configuration information in the built-in MSDB database. You can think of Agent as a kind of super-duper task scheduler: it runs tasks on whatever schedule you set. It can also do a lot to help automate certain aspects of SQL Server monitoring, and it can even provide a basic framework for automating certain kinds of reports.

Agent consists of three main elements: jobs, operators, and alerts. We'll cover each of those in this chapter, along with supporting mechanisms like Database Mail, Agent security, and Database Maintenance Plans. I'll even give you some ideas for putting Agent straight to use in your environment.

NOTE   I won't be covering 100% of what Agent can do, but I'll try to touch on the stuff that's most immediately usable in most environments. Still, it's worth spending some time later reading up on what else Agent can do for you. SQL Server Books Online is the place to start.

Start by finding Agent in SQL Server Management Studio. It has its own folder in the Object Explorer, as shown in figure 14.1. You'll need to make sure it's actually started, because some installations of SQL Server will *install* Agent, but not configure it to start automatically. You can use the separate SQL Server Configuration Manager console to modify the properties of the Agent service so that it starts automatically. Remember that if Agent is not running, nothing you set up will work!

On a server that has multiple instances of SQL Server, you'll also have multiple instances of Agent. Each SQL Server instance has its own Agent service; in figure 14.2, you can see that my SQL Server Configuration Manager shows two instances. The default is MSSQLSERVER, and my second instance is SQL2. Each instance has a SQL Server service and a SQL Server Agent service. At the edge of my Configuration Manager display, you can see that only one Agent instance (the one belonging to SQL2) is running. It's also the only instance set to start automatically.

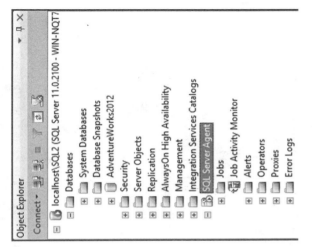

Figure 14.1　Agent can be found in Object Explorer.

14.2　Jobs

The real heart of Agent is its job system. A *job* is a unit of automation that you can either kick off manually, or schedule to run automatically. A job consists of one or more *job steps*, which can run SQL queries, run external commands, or perform any of a number of other tasks. Jobs can incorporate some very simple execution logic: after completing a job step, for example, you can have Agent quit the job (reporting the job as successful or failed, whichever makes sense), or proceed to the next step. Job steps can write their output to a file (useful if you're running a query that returns rows

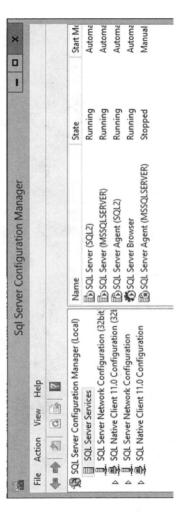

Figure 14.2　Each SQL Server instance also comes with an instance of Agent.

of data), and they can be configured to run as a specific user account, if needed (more on that later in this chapter).

Let's create a basic job that kicks off a reorganization of every index in one of the AdventureWorks2012 database tables:

TRY IT NOW   In the following list, I'm going to walk you through the process of setting up a basic job. Follow along in your own SQL Server instance; this will constitute the hands-on portion of this chapter.

1   In SQL Server Management Studio, expand SQL Server Agent.
2   Right-click the Jobs folder and select New Job....
3   On the General page, name the job Reorg AW2012.
4   Notice that the job's Enabled checkbox is checked by default; you can uncheck this to disable a job. Doing so prevents the job from running, but leaves it configured for later enablement.
5   On the Steps page, click New....
6   Name the step Run reorg. Leave the Type set to T-SQL.
7   For Database, choose AdventureWorks2012 from the drop-down list (this assumes you installed the AdventureWorks2012 database when you set up your SQL Server lab instance).
8   In the Command text box, type:

```
ALTER INDEX ALL ON Person.Address REORGANIZE;
```

9   Review the options on the Advanced tab, but don't make any changes at this time.
10 Click OK.
11 Notice that the Schedules page allows you to define one or more schedules, which would run the job automatically. We won't be setting one up right now.
12 Click OK.
13 Notice that your job now appears under Agent's Jobs folder in SQL Server Management Studio. (If it doesn't, press F5 to refresh the display.)
14 Right-click the new job and choose Start job at step....
15 The job should run successfully, as shown in figure 14.3.

Congratulations! You just made your first SQL Server Agent job.

14.3   *Operators*

Agent allows you to define *operators*, which represent an email address that SQL Server can use to send notifications. You might set up operators for actual people (like you) in your organization, or you might set up an operator that represents some kind of shared mailbox, like a help desk inbox.

Operators are targets for outgoing notifications, and SQL Server offers two, well, technically three, ways of sending those notifications:

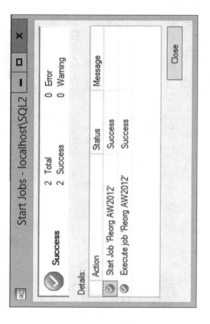

Figure 14.3   A status dialog shows the job's success or failure.

- Email
- Pager email
- NET SEND, which is a deprecated feature, unused by pretty much everybody, and won't work with any version of Windows you probably have in use today.

The difference between email and pager email is actually kind of cool. The intent is that a regular email is going to someone's inbox, which they probably aren't looking at 24 hours a day. A pager is intended to be an email address that perhaps goes to a cell phone as a text message (since pretty much nobody uses *pagers* anymore). SQL Server will send notifications to an email at any time, because it's assumed it won't be interrupting anyone's sleep, dinner, vacation, and so on. A pager email is assumed to be interruptive. Perhaps the recipient's cell phone will chime, for example, waking them up. Therefore, SQL Server lets you configure an *on-duty schedule* for the pager email, and notifications will be sent only during that schedule. You can define one schedule for weekdays, and separate schedules for Saturdays and Sundays.

TRY IT NOW   Go ahead and set up an operator using the steps that follow. Use a bogus email address, if you like. We'll need to set this up in order to do some other stuff later in the chapter.

Let's set up an operator:

1   Under SQL Server Agent, right-click Operators and select New Operator….

2   Name the new operator Help Desk.

3   For both Email name and Pager email name, enter an email address.

4   Click OK.

That's it! Because we didn't enable a pager schedule, only the Email name will be used, and any notifications sent to this operator will be allowed on any day, at any hour. We haven't actually configured SQL Server to be able to send email. That will happen in an upcoming section of this chapter.

14.4   Alerts

An *alert* is a configuration setting in Agent that tells it to notify an operator when a particular condition, usually an error, occurs. It's easiest to set one up to see what the options are, and to see how they work.

TRY IT NOW   Follow along to set up a sample alert; you'll need to have configured an operator in the previous section. We won't test the alert, but this is a good way to see what options are available.

1   In the Object Explorer of SQL Server Management Studio, expand SQL Server Agent and right-click Alerts. Choose New Alert....

2   Name the alert. I'll use AW2012 Problems as the name.

3   Leave the Type set to SQL Server event alert, but notice that you can also have alerts triggered by SQL Server performance conditions or WMI events (which we won't be covering here).

4   Select AdventureWorks2012 for Database name.

5   For alert severity, choose 019—Fatal Error in Resource. This will cause alerts to be sent for any errors that have this severity or higher. You do *not* want to set the alert severity too low, or SQL Server will start spewing notifications like you wouldn't believe. Typically, severity level 11 and higher is considered a problem condition, and severity levels 11 through 16 are usually developer- or query-related errors.

6   On the Response page, notice that you can have a job run in response to the alert. We won't do that, but go ahead and enable Notify operators. Select the operator you created earlier, and select E-mail.

7   On the Options page, notice the options you can choose. A nice one is the Delay between responses. For alerts that happen a lot, this can throttle the response frequency by making Agent wait for several minutes before re-responding to a recurrence of the same problem. This helps your inbox from getting flooded by something that happens a lot in a short period of time!

8   Click OK to save the alert.

Done! I suggest giving alerts descriptive names, so that you can easily figure out from Object Explorer what an alert is doing.

14.5   Database Mail

Before SQL Server can send email, it has to know *how* to send it. In older versions of SQL Server (think pre-2005), setting up outgoing email capability was a massive pain in the neck. You had to install an email client like Microsoft Outlook, log in as whatever user account ran SQL Server Agent . . . it was tragic. I mention this in case you have an old version of SQL Server still running; if it hasn't already been set up for email, it's almost not worth the bother to set it up. In fact, modern versions of Outlook might not even work to get the feature configured.

Newer versions of SQL Server (2005 and later) have a feature called Database Mail that's *much* easier to set up. You'll find this in SQL Server Management Studio's Object Explorer, under the Management folder. Right-click Database Mail and select Configure Database Mail... to set it up; the option won't be available if Database Mail is already configured. Figure 14.4 shows where it's located in Object Explorer.

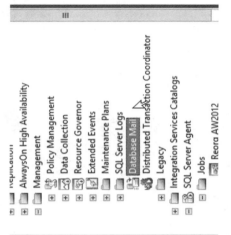

Figure 14.4 Database Mail is set up in SQL Server Management Studio.

DO NOT TRY IT NOW I'm not going to ask you to configure Database Mail, although you're welcome to do so if you like. You'll probably need some assistance and information from whoever runs your organization's mail server or services.

Database Mail is built around one or more *profiles;* you need at least one in order to have SQL Server send email. Each profile can have one or more Simple Mail Transport Protocol (SMTP) accounts associated with it, and Database Mail will try them in whatever order you list them. Each account specifies an email address, user name, password, SMTP server address, and other details—information you'll need to get from whoever runs email in your organization. Most of the time, you'll just have one profile, and it'll have just one SMTP account.

One reason you'll need help from your email administrator is most mail servers are pretty locked-down these days, meaning they'll only accept email from authenticated users. Most organizations I work with take one of two approaches:

- *They'll set up an actual email user account so that SQL Server can authenticate.* This can happen using Windows Authentication (which is safest), or using Basic Authentication. The latter transmits a username and password in clear text, so if you use that it's typically coupled with Secure Socket Layer (SSL) encryption to protect the credential. The mail server has to be set up to support all that.
- *They'll configure the mail server to allow anonymous relaying from the IP address used by the SQL Server computer.* This is the easiest to set up from the SQL Server side of things, because technically SQL Server isn't authenticating. Some organizations' security policies don't permit this kind of email setup, though.

Database Mail is pretty much set-it-and-forget-it; once it's configured, you won't mess with it much. However, be sure it's working! You can right-click Database Mail in SQL

Server Management Studio to send a test message, which helps verify that your configuration is working properly.

14.6   SQL Server Agent security

I'm going to be honest with you: Agent security can be a total pain in the neck. Security comes into play whenever a job runs, because obviously the job needs to access resources. The simple approach to security is to have jobs owned by a member of the sysadmin fixed server role; those jobs automatically execute under full administrative privileges. If that's not what you want, or if the job needs to be owned by someone else, things will get a little more complicated.

NOTE   This is an area of SQL Server that has evolved considerably through its various versions. I'm describing how SQL Server 2012 operates; newer versions may be a tiny bit different, and older versions will differ increasingly as you go back in time.

We'll begin with *credentials*, which you'll find in SQL Server Management Studio under the Security folder. A credential has a name so that you can identify it, and it includes an identity (a user name) and a password. Credentials can be encrypted to help protect the password from being discovered.

Let's move on to *proxies*, something you'll find under SQL Server Agent's section of SQL Server Management Studio. A proxy is because a user account that can be used to perform specific tasks, and you'll notice folders for several different kinds of tasks.

A proxy uses one of the credentials that you set up at the server level. You define the *principals* (users, user groups, server roles, and so on) that are allowed to use the proxy, and you define which Agent task types the proxy can be used for.

When you create a job step, you can use the Run as drop-down to choose a proxy. You'll only be able to choose proxies that are enabled for the type of job step you're creating, and that you have permission to use.

The purpose of this multipart security system is to allow top-level administrators to control the actual credentials, and to then make those available to other administrators or users for use in job steps. The person creating the job step doesn't need to know the credential password, because it's known to SQL Server. If you happen to be the *only* administrator of SQL Server, then this can all seem needlessly complex, but it's useful in larger environments that involve many different layers of administration.

Credentials and proxies are useful when you need to create a job step that runs an external command, like a command-line utility or Windows PowerShell command. Because those execute outside SQL Server, they can't make use of your SQL Server login. Credentials and proxies let you give those job steps the authority they need to run properly.

14.7   *A quick cheat: Database Maintenance Plans*

Database Maintenance Plans, or just Maintenance Plans, are an all-in-one way of automating the most common maintenance tasks, including backups and index maintenance.

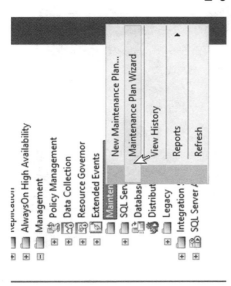

Figure 14.5   Use the wizard to create a new Maintenance Plan.

These are configured under the Management folder in SQL Server Management Studio, although they use some Agent functionality to actually execute. I'm mentioning Maintenance Plans in this chapter because they automate many of the common tasks that you might otherwise have to set up manually in Agent.

Maintenance Plans can be managed manually, although when I set them up I prefer to do so using the convenient built-in wizard. The wizard lets you select the databases that will be included in the Maintenance Plan, as well as the actual maintenance tasks that'll be run. Figure 14.5 shows how you can start the wizard by right-clicking Maintenance Plans in SQL Server Management Studio.

TRY IT NOW   Go ahead and run through the Maintenance Plan Wizard. I won't walk you through the steps, because that's what the wizard does, but I want you to see what a Maintenance Plan can include. Target the Maintenance Plan to your AdventureWorks database.

14.8   Ideas for using SQL Server Agent

What do I see people using SQL Server Agent to automate? Lots. Here are a few ideas:

- Running queries that return results, writing those results to a file, and attaching that file to an email. It's a simple way of automating basic reports. The output isn't fancy, but in some cases it gets the job done regardless.
- Obviously, running maintenance tasks like database maintenance plans, backups, and so on. This is what Agent was made for!
- Sending alerts when critical performance measurements, such as free disk space, pass some specified threshold.
- Automatically running data-loading or importing tasks, such as SSIS packages.

Another thing to keep in mind is Agent's support for centralized multiserver management. Agent lets you create a job that is sent to, and run on, multiple other servers all in parallel. We'll cover that in the next chapter.

14.9   *Hands-on lab*

As I mentioned earlier, your lab in this chapter was to follow along with the Try it Now sections, so you should have a Job, an Operator, and an Alert already configured. If you haven't done so, go back and do those steps now. And, now that you're using Agent, be sure you're backing up its database (MSDB) so that your Agent configuration is safe!

15
Multiserver management

Multiserver management is one of the cooler things you can do with SQL Server. The idea is to use SQL Server Agent to "push" a given job to one or more other SQL Server instances, running that job in parallel on all of them. It's a great way to automate the administration of multiple servers, helping to improve consistency and helping to save you time.

15.1 What is multiserver management?

Multiserver management is a feature of SQL Server Agent, which means every SQL Server instance that you want to participate needs to have its SQL Server Agent service running. You'll designate one SQL Server instance as your master server, and enroll one or more other instances as targets. When you run multiserver jobs, Agent will coordinate their execution on each target, and even track job progress for you, all in one central location.

15.2 Creating a multiserver management hierarchy

You have to have a master instance in order to use multiserver management, so let's start by creating one. Right-click SQL Server Agent in Object Explorer, select Multi Server Administration, and select Make this a Master.... Figure 15.1 shows where to find those options.

TRY IT NOW Follow along if you have two instances of SQL Server installed on your lab computer. If you don't, consider installing a second instance now, then proceeding with the rest of this chapter.

137

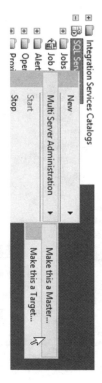

Figure 15.1　Make the instance a Master to get started.

You'll run through a little wizard, which will start by prompting you for the email address of a "multiserver operator." As you learned in the previous chapter, SQL Server Agent jobs can send notifications to operators; with multiserver jobs, only the operator you designate here can receive notifications. Whatever contact information you provide will be used to create an operator on the master and on any target instances that you later enroll. That way, they all have the same operator to send notifications to.

Figure 15.2 shows the next screen, where you can start enrolling targets. I'm setting up my SQL2 instance as the master instance, but my lab computer also has a default instance installed, and you can see that I've decided to enroll it as a target.

The next screen, shown in figure 15.3, may differ a bit depending on your server configuration. It's asking you what authentication the target servers should use; technically, targets *pull* (or download) jobs from the master, so the targets need a way to authenticate.

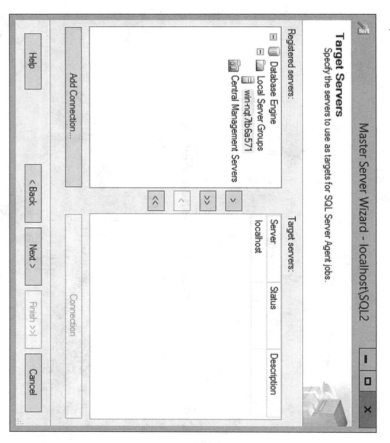

Figure 15.2　Specify target instances for this master.

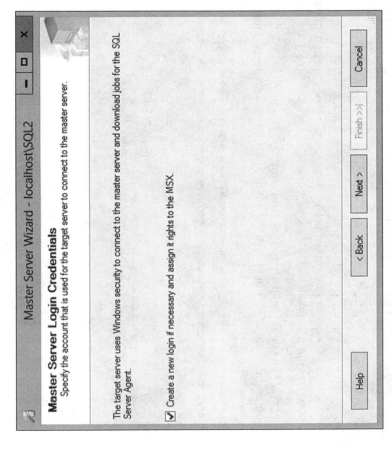

Figure 15.3   Tell the targets how to authenticate to the master.

You might run into an error, like the one shown in figure 15.4, which indicates that SQL Server's default security configuration doesn't allow the extended stored procedures needed to enable multiserver administration.

This is a common error, and usually indicates that SQL Server Agent has never been started on the target instance by using SQL Server Management Studio.

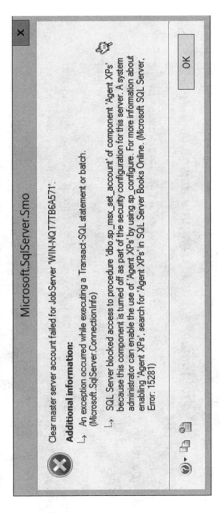

Figure 15.4   This is a common error when enrolling a target.

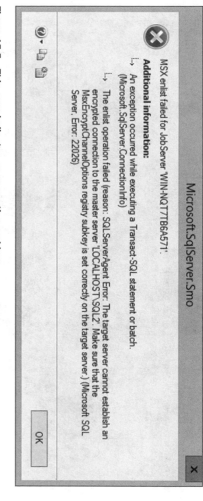

Figure 15.5   This error indicates an encryption problem.

NOTE   You can read more about the Agent XPs, and the security implications of XPs in general, at http://technet.microsoft.com/en-us/library/ms178127.aspx.

You can fix the problem by using SQL Server Management Studio to connect to the instance in question, right-clicking SQL Server Agent in Object Explorer, and choosing Start. If the service is already started, stop and restart it by using SQL Server Management Studio. That'll both start the SQL Server Agent service and enable the Agent XPs.

Another common error is shown in figure 15.5, and indicates that the multiserver administration components on the target weren't able to establish a secure connection to the master.

This is documented at http://technet.microsoft.com/en-us/library/ms365379.aspx, where you're directed to edit a specific registry key. This has some security implications, so I'd prefer you to read through that article and understand the ups and downs, rather than me telling you to make a change. You have the option to have SQL Server Agent *not* use encrypted communications between the target and master, which should only be done when you're certain that the network connection between them can't be compromised by an attacker.

Once you've done all that, you'll need to rerun the wizard to make your instance a master. This time, it should succeed. You'll have a master, and you'll have enrolled whatever targets you specified. It's entirely possible to enroll additional targets in the future. I usually do so by connecting to the target, right-clicking SQL Server Agent, choosing Multi Server Administration, and then selecting Make Target.... All you have to do then is specify the name of the master instance. Always make sure those Agent XPs are enabled on the target before you try doing that.

15.3   *Creating and using multiserver management jobs*

Let's set up a multiserver job that runs a simple T-SQL command. Start in SQL Server Management Studio on your master instance:

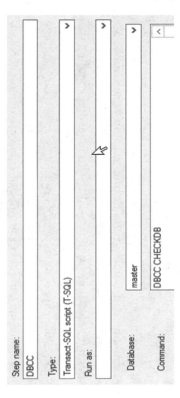

**Figure 15.6
Configure the job
step as shown.**

1   Expand SQL Server Agent.

2   Right-click Jobs and choose New Job....

3   On the General page, give the job a name. I used Multi Test.

4   On the Steps page, add a new job step. Configure the step as shown in figure 15.6. I'm having it run the DBCC CHECKDB command on the master database (because my second instance doesn't have any other database for me to play with). Click OK on the job step.

5   On the Targets page, select Target multiple servers and check the available target, as shown in figure 15.7.

6   Click OK to create the job.

7   To test the job, expand Jobs so that you can see the new job. Right-click the job and select Start job at step....

Figure 15.7   Target multiple instances with a single job.

This posts a request to the targets, asking them to connect to the master, download the job definition, and execute the job. It doesn't happen instantly, though, so you can use the Job Activity Monitor to keep an eye on it, and the job's history will show you when it was last run (along with its results). Jobs that are given a schedule will run more reliably, because the targets can check in, get the job, and run it on that schedule.

15.4   *Ideas for multiserver jobs*

I use multiserver jobs in a couple of different ways. One way is when I need to make a one-time configuration change across a large number of SQL Server instances. For that reason, I tend to have one instance of SQL Server that's my "personal" instance;

I'll use it to host small databases that I use to track computer inventory information and other operational tasks. That instance becomes my master for multiserver jobs, and I enroll all of my "real" SQL Server instances as targets. That way, when I need to make some configuration change, I can write the necessary T-SQL statements into a job and then assign that job to all of the targets. Bam! Mission accomplished.

Another way to use multiserver jobs is for routine maintenance, such as updating index statistics, reorganizing indexes, and so on. I'll admit that, although I've seen some administrators use a centralized multiserver job for those tasks, I don't do it much myself. I tend to want those kinds of things customized on a per-instance or per-database basis, which eliminates multiserver jobs as a good option. But, they're certainly an option for some kinds of routine maintenance, and you should keep them in mind as a possibility.

15.5   *Hands-on lab*

Because multiserver management necessarily requires multiple servers, I'm not going to ask you to do a hands-on lab for this chapter. However, if you have the ability to install multiple SQL Server instances on your lab computer, do so, and walk through the examples in this chapter as your hands-on experience.

Windows PowerShell and SQL Server

Windows PowerShell was introduced in 2007, and it has since become a standard platform for administrative automation across Microsoft business and server products. It's a command-line shell, and product teams (like SQL Server's team) extend the shell so it can help manage their products. In this chapter, we'll look at how to use PowerShell with SQL Server.

16.1 Windows PowerShell overview

Windows PowerShell is a command-line shell, not unlike Unix-style shells like Bash or the old Windows Command Prompt (Cmd.exe). What's different about Power-Shell is that it's a modern shell, designed around modern needs and with the Windows OS in mind. The shell itself contains minimal functionality; feature and product teams write *modules* (or snap-ins) that give the shell additional capabilities. For example, the SQL Server team created a module that lets the shell connect to, and manage, SQL Server. It's important to keep in mind that the ability to manage a product by using PowerShell is dependent upon the specific product version providing that module. SQL Server 2012 provided SQL Server's first fully functional module, making it the oldest version of SQL Server that can be extensively managed by using PowerShell. SQL Server 2008 R2 shipped with a less-complete snap-in for PowerShell.

NOTE This chapter assumes that you have a basic familiarity with Windows PowerShell; if you don't, consider reading *Learn Windows PowerShell 3 in a Month of Lunches, Second Edition* (Manning, 2012), which provides a beginner-level introduction, or *Learn PowerShell Toolmaking in a Month of Lunches* (Manning 2012), which gets into the scripting and toolmaking aspects of the shell. Jeffrey Hicks and I are the authors of both. *PowerShell In Depth* by Jeffrey Hicks, Richard Siddaway and me (Manning 2013) provides a comprehensive administrator's reference to shell functionality.

To get PowerShell running on any version of Windows where it's installed, hold the Windows key on your keyboard and press R. That brings up a Run dialog; type `powershell` and hit Enter (or click OK). If you're doing this for the first time on a computer, I suggest immediately typing `$PSVersionTable` into the shell and then pressing Enter. Doing so will reveal the shell's version information. (If nothing shows up, you're on v1.0.) Table 16.1 details the versions of PowerShell that ship with various versions of Windows, and the versions that can be installed.

Table 16.1 PowerShell and Windows versions

Windows version	Comes with PowerShell version	Supports PowerShell version
Windows XP / Windows Server 2003	None	1.0, 2.0
Windows Vista, Windows Server 2008	1.0	2.0, 3.0 (Windows Vista supports only 2.0)
Windows 7, Windows Server 2008 R2	2.0	3.0, 4.0
Windows 8, Windows Server 2012	3.0	3.0, 4.0
Windows 8.1, Windows Server 2012 R2	4.0	4.0

SQL Server 2012's PowerShell module requires at least PowerShell 2.0, and also works on PowerShell 3.0 (and later). If you want a later version of PowerShell than what comes with your version of Windows, you can download the Windows Management Framework (WMF) from http://download.microsoft.com. The WMF version corresponds to the PowerShell version (WMF 2.0 contains PowerShell 2.0), and the WMF includes supporting technologies, including Windows Remote Management and Background Intelligent Transfer Service.

NOTE   When Microsoft releases a new version of PowerShell, it typically is released as part of the latest version of Windows. A short time after that release, Microsoft typically makes the corresponding WMF download available for the two most recent versions of Windows. Avoid installing the latest WMF on servers until you've verified that the products running on that server are compatible with that version of the WMF and PowerShell.

One reason PowerShell has been well accepted by administrators is that, with a little bit of jump-start instruction, the shell is pretty easy to learn. It offers a number of discoverability features that help you find the commands you need to accomplish given tasks, and the command syntax is very straightforward and noncryptic. Commands typically come with extensive built-in help, including usage examples and explanations. Unfortunately, most of those features only apply to one of two ways that a product team can choose to implement PowerShell support—and unfortunately, the SQL Server team chose the *other* way.

16.2 *SQL Server and PowerShell*

There are a couple of ways to launch PowerShell and have SQL Server support preloaded for you. Note that launching PowerShell as I described earlier in this chapter will *not* automatically preload SQL Server's module; you'd have to do so manually.

In SQL Server Management Studio, you can right-click nearly anywhere and find a Start PowerShell menu option. That will open a shell with several SQL Server modules preloaded. If you only launch a plain copy of the shell, run Import-Module SQLPS to load up the main SQL Server module.

> **NOTE** Additional modules provide functionality for other SQL Server components, such as SQLASCMDLETS and Microsoft.AnalysisServices.PowerShell .Cmdlets. You can import those if needed. If you've installed SQL Server Management Studio on your client computer, then the PowerShell modules should also be installed and available.

If you get a list of commands implemented by the core SQL Server module, you won't be impressed:

```
PS SQLSERVER:\> get-command -module sqlps | select name

Name
----
Add-SqlAvailabilityDatabase
Add-SqlAvailabilityGroupListenerStaticIp
Backup-SqlDatabase
Convert-UrnToPath
Decode-SqlName
Disable-SqlAlwaysOn
Enable-SqlAlwaysOn
Encode-SqlName
Invoke-PolicyEvaluation
Invoke-Sqlcmd
Join-SqlAvailabilityGroup
New-SqlAvailabilityGroup
New-SqlAvailabilityGroupListener
New-SqlAvailabilityReplica
New-SqlHADREndpoint
Remove-SqlAvailabilityDatabase
Remove-SqlAvailabilityGroup
Remove-SqlAvailabilityReplica
Restore-SqlDatabase
Resume-SqlAvailabilityDatabase
Set-SqlAvailabilityGroup
Set-SqlAvailabilityGroupListener
```

```
Set-SqlAvailabilityReplica
Set-SqlHADREndpoint
SQLSERVER:
Suspend-SqlAvailabilityDatabase
Switch-SqlAvailabilityGroup
Test-SqlAvailabilityGroup
Test-SqlAvailabilityReplica
Test-SqlDatabaseReplicaState
```

Looking at the list, it doesn't seem like SQL Server's module can do much, does it? The awesome Invoke-SqlCmd command can do a lot, because it lets you execute any T-SQL command you like, and since most of SQL Server can be managed by running T-SQL commands. But that seems like cheating, right? Using PowerShell just to run T-SQL?

16.2.1 Meet the SQLSERVER provider

The trick is that much of SQL Server's PowerShell support is implemented by something called a PowerShell Provider, or PSProvider. These work a bit like a disk drive, with the root of the drive providing core functionality, and the folders beneath that root pointing to different SQL Server components. When the SQLPS module is loaded, it automatically maps to the local instance, if one exists; you can then add more connections to other instances that you want to manage.

For example, in the default SQLSERVER: drive, I can get a directory listing by running Dir or Ls, and see the following:

```
Name           Root                  Description
----           ----                  -----------
SQL            SQLSERVER:\SQL        SQL Server Database E...
SQLPolicy      SQLSERVER:\SQLPolicy  SQL Server Policy Man...
SQLRegistration SQLSERVER:\SQLRegistr... SQL Server Registrations
DataCollection SQLSERVER:\DataCollec... SQL Server Data Colle...
XEvent         SQLSERVER:\XEvent     SQL Server Extended E...
Utility        SQLSERVER:\Utility    SQL Server Utility
DAC            SQLSERVER:\DAC        SQL Server Data-Tier ...
SSIS           SQLSERVER:\SSIS       SQL Server Integratio...
SQLAS          SQLSERVER:\SQLAS      SQL Server Analysis S...
```

As you can see, the subfolders of the drive each represent a major SQL Server component: SQL is the main database engine, SSIS is SQL Server Integration Services (SSIS), and so on. Underneath each component is a connection to a specific computer, and under those are folders for connections to instances on those computers. For example:

```
PS SQLSERVER:\> cd sql
PS SQLSERVER:\sql> ls


MachineName
-----------
WIN-NQT7TB6A571


PS SQLSERVER:\> cd .\WIN-NQT7TB6A571
PS SQLSERVER:\sql> ls
PS SQLSERVER:\sql\WIN-NQT7TB6A571> ls
```

```
Instance Name
-------------
DEFAULT
SQL2
```

Figure 16.1 illustrates the basic hierarchy to that point.

This hierarchy can get a bit cumbersome, because to do anything you've got a long path just to get started. If I want to manage something in the Database Engine on my computer, which is named WIN-NQT7TB6A571, and in my instance named SQL2, my command-line path starts with SQLSERVER:\SQL\WIN-NQT7TB6A571\SQL2.

A problem with this provider-based approach is that PowerShell doesn't have a way to provide help files, or to help you discover what you can do or how to do it. You just kinda have to know. That's good for book authors like me, but it makes it hard to get started.

NOTE By the way, in support of my fellow book authors, I'll recommend *SQL Server 2012 with PowerShell V3 Cookbook* (Pact Publishing, 2012) by Donabel Santos. It's one I keep handy when I'm working with PowerShell and SQL Server.

Why did the SQL Server team elect to go down the provider path, rather than providing a set of more traditional commands? Possibly because the provider model made it easier for them to delegate their programming work across the many subteams that comprise the overall group. By having each major component (such as SSIS) plug in to a top-level SQL Server provider, they created something that probably looked elegant in the planning stages. Providers also have the benefit of being more

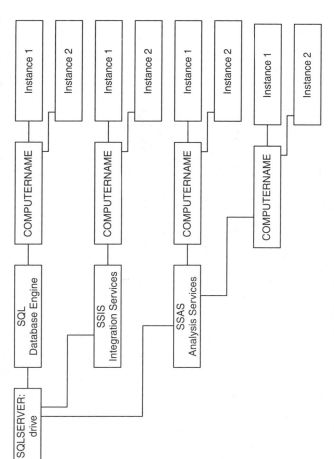

Figure 16.1 Exploring the SQLSERVER provider hierarchy

dynamic. You can add something to the hierarchy without necessarily having to program a whole new set of commands; the built-in PowerShell commands used to work within a provider will work. That said, the provider model has been criticized by some as being difficult to learn. Regardless, it's what we have to work with, so let's see what it can do.

16.2.2 *Doing something useful*

One common thing that administrators are asked for in SQL Server is a list of logins that, perhaps, have nonexpiring passwords. That's certainly a security concern for many organizations, but clicking through SQL Server Management Studio to find all of those accounts can be time-consuming. It's pretty easy information to get with a T-SQL query, but you can also do it with PowerShell:

TRY IT NOW By all means, follow along with these examples. I'll provide the commands I type in boldface, so that you can pick them out of the example more easily.

```
PS SQLSERVER:\sql\WIN-NQT7TB6A571\sql2\logins> Get-ChildItem | Where { -not
$_.PasswordExpirationEnabled } | Select Name,LoginType

Name                                    LoginType
----                                    ---------
##MS_PolicyEventProcessingLogin##       SqlLogin
##MS_PolicyTsqlExecutionLogin##         SqlLogin
NT AUTHORITY\SYSTEM                      WindowsUser
NT Service\MSSQL$SQL2                    WindowsUser
NT SERVICE\SQLAgent$SQL2                 WindowsUser
NT SERVICE\SQLWriter                     WindowsUser
NT SERVICE\Winmgmt                       WindowsUser
testuser                                 SqlLogin
WIN-NQT7TB6A571\Administrator            WindowsUser
```

I boldfaced the command to make it easier to read. You can see that I changed to the Logins folder of my SQL2 instance, running on the computer named WIN-NQT7TB6A571, under the SQL (Database Engine) component of the SQLSERVER: drive. I asked for a list of all items within that Logins folder, keeping only those whose PasswordExpirationEnabled property was False, and selecting just the Name and LoginType properties of those logins.

NOTE If all that seems clear as mud, keep in mind that most of the syntax is basic PowerShell stuff that I haven't covered. Again, a good beginner-level book in PowerShell will teach you those things pretty quickly.

Let's do another example. This one's useful: generating a list of blocking processes, meaning processes that are currently blocking other processes. This example shows that the provider model—and even the handful of commands provided in the SQLPS module—often aren't enough to do what you want. (This time, I'm using boldface to highlight the information you'll need to insert.)

```
$server = New-Object -TypeName Microsoft.SqlServer.Management.Smo.Server
    -ArgumentList "INSTANCE_NAME"
$server.EnumProcesses() |
Select Name,Spid,Command,Status,Login,Database,BlockingSpid |
Format-Table -Auto
```

That should be a list of all processes running on the given instance; to see blocking processes:

```
$server.EnumProcesses() |
Where { $_.BlockingSpid -ne 0 } |
Select Name,Spid,Command,Status,Login,Database,BlockingSpid |
Format-Table -Auto
```

This example used SQL Management Objects, or SMO (pronounced, "smoe"). That's a .NET Framework API provided by SQL Server for management purposes. If it looks a bit like programming. . .it is. It was originally designed as a Visual Basic or C# API, but it's accessible from within PowerShell. There's a *lot* to it, far more than I can cover in this one chapter, although the cookbook I referenced earlier provides a lot of SMO examples.

I wanted to show you these two examples as a way of helping you understand how PowerShell works with SQL Server. Yes, it's possibly more complex than it needs to be, given how other products (like Exchange Server) have managed to simplify their interfaces into sets of more easily discoverable and well-documented commands. But it's what we have to work with. So what can it help you automate?

- Inventory SQL Server configuration settings
- Alter database properties
- Change object ownership
- Maintain indexes
- Bulk-load data
- Kill blocking processes
- Check disk space usage
- Set up Database Mail
- List failed login attempts

The list is huge. Anything you have to do more than once is going to become cumbersome in the graphical SQL Server Management Studio, and although some things can be automated by using T-SQL, other tasks will require you to use SMO, and PowerShell is perhaps the easiest way to do that.

16.3 *SQL Server Agent and PowerShell*

SQL Server Agent, being an automation tool itself, works fine with Windows PowerShell. In fact, one of the cooler things you can do with it is running PowerShell scripts. This is useful for tasks that can't be handled by the Database Maintenance Plan functionality, or that can't easily be accomplished by using T-SQL. Agent pops open a background PowerShell process that has all the SQL Server modules preloaded, and then runs whatever commands you give it.

Name: | Blocked Process List

Owner: | WIN-NQT7TB6A571\Administrator | ...

Category: | [Uncategorized (Local)] | ∨ | ...

Description: | Sends a list of blocked processes. Will be triggered by an alert.

☑ Enabled

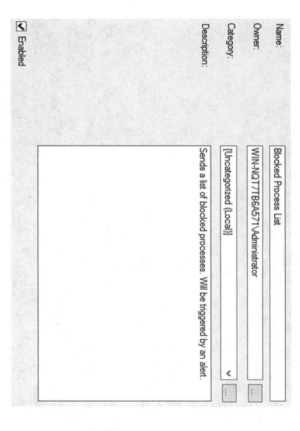

Figure 16.2   Configure the job's General page.

TRY IT NOW   This is another good example to follow along on, as there are a couple of easy-to-miss details that I'll point out.

To begin, I'm going to create a job that lists blocked processes, using the example code from the previous section of this chapter. Beginning in SQL Server Management Studio, with Management and SQL Server Agent expanded:

1   Right-click Jobs and select New Job....

2   Configure the General page as shown in figure 16.2.

3   On the Steps page, click New....

4   Configure the page as shown in figure 16.3. The command code I used is below; notice that I used boldface for items that you must change:

```
$server = New-Object -TypeName Microsoft.SqlServer.Management.Smo.Server
    -ArgumentList "INSTANCE_NAME"
$procs = $server.EnumProcesses() |
Where { $_.BlockingSpid -ne 0 } |
Select Name,Spid,Command,Status,Login,Database,BlockingSpid |
Format-Table -Auto

Send-MailMessage -To "who@company.com" -From "someone@company.com"
    -Body $procs -Subject "SQL blocked processes"
    -SmtpServer mail.company.com
```

5   Click OK twice.

Step name:

Generate blocked process list

Type:

PowerShell

Run as:

SQL Server Agent Service Account

Command:

```
$server = New-Object -TypeName Microsoft.SqlServer.Management.Sm
$procs = $server.EnumProcesses() |
Where { $_.BlockingSpid -ne 0 } |
Select Name,Spid,Command,Status,Login,Database,BlockingSpid |
Format-Table -Auto

Send-MailMessage -To "who@company.com" -From "someone@compa
```

Open...

Select All

Copy

Paste

Figure 16.3 Configure the Steps page.

This creates a job, but doesn't have it run on a schedule. Instead, we're going to run this as the result of an alert. Staying in SQL Server Management Studio:

1 Right-click Alerts and select New Alert....

2 Configure the General page as shown in figure 16.4. Note that I set the blocked process threshold to 5; you can adjust that how ever you like. Your report will be sent whenever the number of blocked processes rises above the specified number.

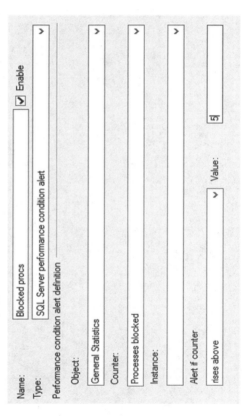

Name: Blocked procs

Type: SQL Server performance condition alert

☑ Enable

Performance condition alert definition

Object: General Statistics

Counter:

Instance: Processes blocked

Alert if counter

rises above   **Value:**   5

Figure 16.4 Configure the alert's General page.

Figure 16.5 Configure the alert's Response page.

3   Configure the Response page as shown in figure 16.5.

4   Click OK.

You're done! Go back to chapter 13 for an example of how I created a process that can block others; repeat that experiment if you'd like to test that your blocked process report. Note that the job I created depends upon the SQL Server Agent account being able to send email anonymously through the specified email server; that depends on the mail server being willing to do so. In your lab environment, without an SMTP mail server, the message won't be sent.

16.4   *Hands-on lab*

This lab may seem a little unfair, because I'm going to ask you to do something I haven't shown you how to do. But that's very real-world! You'll probably need to start using a search engine, including keywords like PowerShell, "SQL Server" (in quotes), and SMO to help limit the results to the most useful ones. I'll provide an answer on MoreLunches.com: find this book's cover image, click it, and find the Downloads section to get the sample solutions ZIP file.

Write a PowerShell command that will list all indexes with fragmentation of more than 10% (on your sample AdventureWorks2012 database, this may produce no output, because it's unlikely those indexes are that fragmented). Then, write a second command that will reorganize all indexes with more than 10% fragmentation.

Using Extended Events

I introduced you to Extended Events in chapter 13, where we used them to capture information on blocked processes. Now, I'd like to dig deeper into Extended Events with some very specific (and super-useful) scenarios. We'll walk through how the technology works, get it set up for various purposes, and look at what it can provide you.

17.1 What are Extended Events?

As I described earlier, Extended Events is a native SQL Server technology that allows for continuous monitoring and capturing of specific things happening on the server. You create a *session* that monitors for whatever events you're interested in, and it logs information from those events when they occur. You can then review those logs at your leisure.

In Windows (and SQL Server) terminology, an *event* is something like a log message sent from one piece of software to another. A piece of software has to be programmed to produce the event, and another piece of software registers to be notified when the event happens. With Extended Events, different pieces of SQL Server produce events, while the actual Extended Events system registers to receive those events.

There are a number of ways to work with Extended Events, but we'll use the GUI. Start in SQL Server Management Studio, in the Management folder of the Object Explorer. You should see an Extended Events item, which you can expand to reveal a Sessions folder. Each session can be stopped or started (you'll notice the icon change for each state), and each session is set up to capture specific information.

Sometimes, you'll set up sessions that you want running all of the time, and I'll show you how to do that. You'll often configure those to rotate data automatically, so that you always have a certain amount of running data available, but so that the data doesn't fill up local storage and explode or something. Other times, you'll set up sessions meant to help you troubleshoot specific problems; those may not rotate the data, and you'll typically start them on-demand when you're ready to use them. I'll walk you through examples of both kinds of session.

TRY IT NOW   Setting up and using sessions can be a bit complex, so I recommend that you follow along with all of the examples in this chapter. These examples also serve as your hands-on lab for this chapter.

17.2   *Creating and using a session*

Because sessions can be a little hard to set up, SQL Server includes the New Session Wizard, which helps create a new session based on predefined templates provided by Microsoft. I'll walk you through an example that tracks query batch information, and then discuss some of the permutations offered by the Wizard.

17.2.1   *Using the New Session Wizard*

Make sure you're in SQL Server Management Studio, looking at the Sessions folder under Extended Events, and then follow these steps:

1   Right-click Sessions and select New Session Wizard.
2   As shown in figure 17.1, provide a unique, descriptive name for your session, ideally describing what it will capture. You can check the Schedule checkbox to have this session begin capturing events each time the SQL Server instance starts. For this example, I'll leave that checkbox cleared.

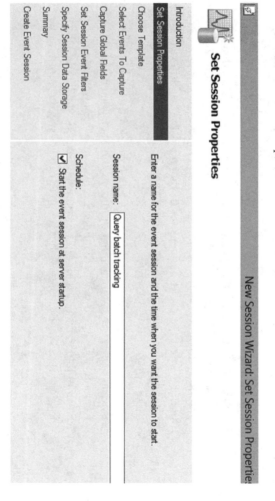

Figure 17.1   Provide a unique name for each session.

Figure 17.2   Start with a Microsoft-provided template.

3   As shown in figure 17.2, you can choose one of the existing session templates as a starting point, including connection tracking, activity tracking, counting query locks, and several templates related to query execution. These are all useful for performance monitoring, but for this example I'll start with the Query Batch Tracking template. You may notice that a lot of what Extended Events captures overlaps with what SQL Server Profiler can capture. We'll discuss that more in a bit.

4   If you start with a template, the next screen will show all of the preselected events. If you start without a template, you choose your own events. Each event captures specific data, which you can analyze later. For this example, I'm not going to specify any events beyond what the template preselected for me. Figure 17.3 shows how complex this screen is. You can type text into the Event library field, and the list of events will filter to only include those whose names (by default) match what you've typed (a quick way to search for events). The left and right arrow buttons move events from the library side to the Selected events side, meaning those events will be captured in the final session.

5   The next screen, a portion of which I show in figure 17.4, lets you specify the information you want to capture about each event. I'll often add database_name, which isn't usually selected by default but which I find easier to use than the numeric database ID. Note that not every event produces all of the same information; if you select a field that isn't included in whatever events you're capturing, then that data will be blank when you go to look at it.

6   On the next screen you can set filters, and only events that meet your filter criteria will be captured. This lets you eliminate noise from the captured logs, such as filtering so that only events for a specific database are captured. You can see in figure 17.5 that I've added a filter to capture only events relating to the AdventureWorks2012 database. You have to be careful when doing this: if I'm looking for events that don't populate the database_name field, then I might not capture anything because none of those will meet my filter criteria.

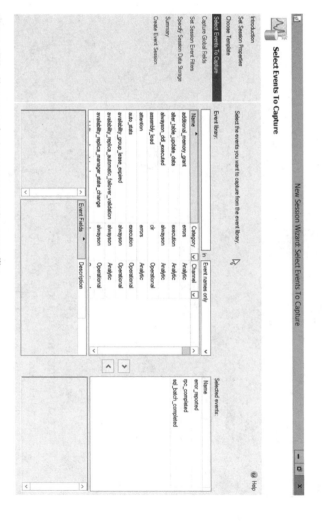

Figure 17.3 You can select as many events as you like.

7 The last screen asks where you want to store the data. As shown in figure 17.6, I've decided to store the events in memory, keeping only the 1,000 most recent events. You can also choose to save them to a local file, which is more appropriate if you plan to capture a large amount of information.

8 Finish the Wizard. I'm going to choose the option to start the session automatically, although you can also right-click any session to start or stop it. You can also choose to have the Wizard open a new results pane in SQL Server Management Studio, and to start displaying live information as it's captured. Figure 17.7 shows what that looks like.

Name ▲	Description
callstack	Collect the current call stack
client_app_name	Collect client application name
client_connection_id	Collects the optional identifier provided
client_hostname	Collect client hostname
client_pid	Collect client process ID
collect_cpu_cycle_time	Collect the current CPU's cycle count
collect_current_thread_id	Collect the current Windows thread ID
collect_system_time	Collect the current system time with 10(
context_info	Collect the same value as the CONTE>
cpu_id	Collect current CPU ID
database_id	Collect database ID
database_name	Collect current database name
event_sequence	Collect event sequence number

Figure 17.4 Add additional information to capture from each event.

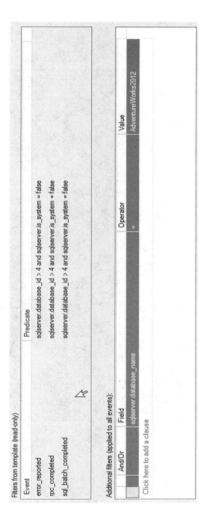

Figure 17.5   Add filters to help reduce the data captured.

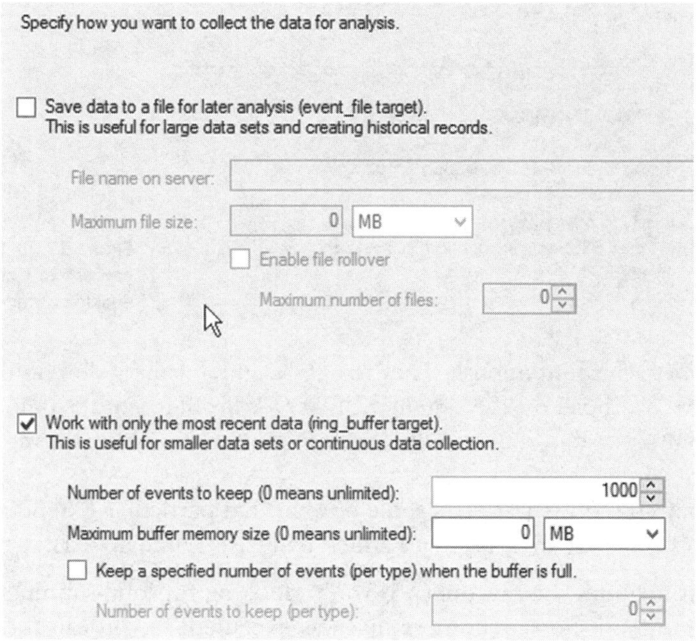

Specify how you want to collect the data for analysis.

☐ Save data to a file for later analysis (event_file target).
This is useful for large data sets and creating historical records.

File name on server

Maximum file size: 0   MB ⌄

☐ Enable file rollover

Maximum number of files: 0 ⌃⌄

☑ Work with only the most recent data (ring_buffer target).
This is useful for smaller data sets or continuous data collection.

Number of events to keep (0 means unlimited):   1000 ⌃⌄

Maximum buffer memory size (0 means unlimited):   0   MB ⌄

☐ Keep a specified number of events (per type) when the buffer is full.

Number of events to keep (per type)   0 ⌃⌄

Figure 17.6   Decide where event data will be stored.

NOTE   I executed a query, SELECT * FROM Person.Person, in a separate query window so that Extended Events would have a SQL batch to capture and display. That's what you're seeing in figure 17.7: the event data produced by that SQL query.

17.2.2 Viewing live session data

Obviously, the data you get from an event depends on the event itself. In my running example, I'm capturing basic information about executing queries. I could capture the same information by using SQL Server Profiler, but here's the difference: Extended

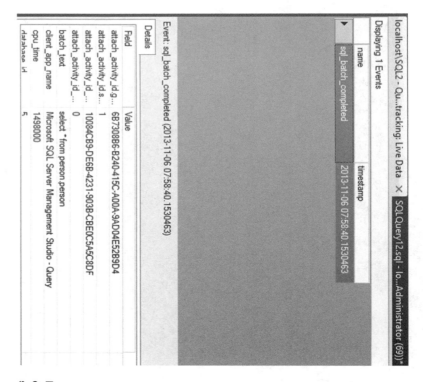

Figure 17.7 You can opt to view live session data.

Events are *designed* to run continuously. They're lightweight, meaning they don't impose their own massive overhead on the system. SQL Server Profiler. . .not so much. It's a pretty heavy monitoring tool that isn't designed to run continuously during production hours.

What information did I get? Here's some of what that particular Extended Events template captures (keeping in mind that I added database_name myself):

- Batch_text includes the raw query. If you're looking for long-running queries, this will show you the actual query that was executed, so you can then take it offline and test or tweak it.

- Client_app_name is the name of the application that executed the query batch.

- Cpu_time shows you how much processor effort was used to execute the query.

- Duration is the total time the query took to execute.

- Logical_reads is the number of reads SQL Server executed; some of these may have been served from buffer cache, so physical_reads shows you how many read operations went to physical storage. Writes shows the number of logical write operations, which will always, eventually, become a physical write.

- Row_count shows the number of rows returned by the query.

Keep in mind that you can always right-click a started session and select Watch Live Data to return to that live data screen.

17.2.3 Working with session logs

Live data isn't always what you want; sometimes you want to run a session all day, or overnight, and analyze what was captured at some later time. No problem. Take a look at figure 17.8.

You can see that my session expands to show the ring buffer being used to store event information. That's because, when I created the session, I elected to keep the most recent 1,000 events in memory, remember? The *ring buffer* is where those live. The buffer stores captured information in XML, and you can click the buffer data to display the XML, as shown in figure 17.9.

You can easily share this XML file with someone else via email or whatever, and as you can see it includes the same query batch information that I listed earlier. The problem with XML is that, although it's portable and kind of human-readable, you can't query it easily using SQL Server's native tools. If we

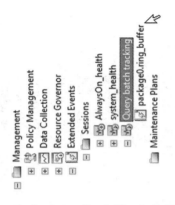

- Management
  - Policy Management
  - Data Collection
  - Resource Governor
  - Extended Events
    - Sessions
      - AlwaysOn_health
      - system_health
      - Query batch tracking
        - package0.ring_buffer
  - Maintenance Plans

Figure 17.8 Expand the session to access its logs or buffer.

Query batch tracking,ring_buffer2.xml ✕ localhostSQL2 - Qu...acking: ring_buffer

```
<RingBufferTarget truncated="0" processingTime="0" totalEventsProcessed="6" event
<event name="sql_batch_completed" package="sqlserver" timestamp="2013-11-06T15:
  <data name="cpu_time">
    <type name="uint64" package="package0"></type>
    <value>1498000</value>
  </data>
  <data name="duration">
    <type name="uint64" package="package0"></type>
    <value>2579229</value>
  </data>
  <data name="physical_reads">
    <type name="uint64" package="package0"></type>
    <value>25</value>
  </data>
  <data name="logical_reads">
    <type name="uint64" package="package0"></type>
    <value>4162</value>
  </data>
  <data name="writes">
    <type name="uint64" package="package0"></type>
    <value>0</value>
  </data>
  <data name="row_count">
    <type name="uint64" package="package0"></type>
    <value>19972</value>
  </data>
```

Figure 17.9 Viewing event data as XML

wanted to extract the longest-running queries from that XML log, it'd be a pain in the neck to do manually. Fortunately, we don't have to!

TRY IT NOW   The trick I'm going to show you next assumes that you've been logging event information to a file, rather than (or in addition to) a memory buffer. If you'd like to keep following along, you'll need to modify your session configuration, and remember the filename it logs to.

Start by extracting the event data into a temporary table, keeping it as XML for the moment:

```
SELECT CAST(event_data AS XML) AS event_data_XML
INTO #Events
FROM sys.fn_xe_file_target_read_file('filename*.xel', null, null, null)
AS F;
```

Notice where the filename goes in that command. This created a temporary table named #Events (all temporary table names are prefixed by a #; that's how SQL Server knows they're meant to be temporary). Next, you'll need to turn that XML into relational data that SQL Server can query easily:

```
SELECT
event_data_XML.value ('(/event/action[@name=''query_hash'']/value)[1]',
     'BINARY(8)'     ) AS query_hash,
event_data_XML.value ('(/event/data          [@name=''duration''
     'BIGINT'        ) AS duration,
event_data_XML.value ('(/event/data          [@name=''cpu_time''
     'BIGINT'        ) AS cpu_time,
event_data_XML.value ('(/event/data          [@name=''physical_reads'']/value)[1]',
     'BIGINT'        ) AS physical_reads,
event_data_XML.value ('(/event/data          [@name=''logical_reads''
     'BIGINT'        ) AS logical_reads,
event_data_XML.value ('(/event/data          [@name=''writes''
     'BIGINT'        ) AS writes,
event_data_XML.value ('(/event/data          [@name=''row_count''
     'BIGINT'        ) AS row_count,
event_data_XML.value ('(/event/data          [@name=''statement''
     'NVARCHAR(4000)') AS statement
INTO #Queries
FROM #Events;
```

```
CREATE CLUSTERED INDEX idx_cl_query_hash ON #Queries(query_hash);
```

This creates a temp table named #Queries, translating the XML into a normal SQL Server table. You can see at the end that I queried them all in descending order of duration, meaning my most expensive queries will be at the top of the list.

```
SELECT * FROM #Queries ORDER BY duration DESC;
```

NOTE   There's a great tutorial at www.solidq.com/sqj/Pages/Relational/Tracing-Query-Performance-with-Extended-Events.aspx that not only walks through this entire process, but gives you example queries to play with as well. I highly recommend you take the time to go through it.

17.3 Creating a custom session

Back in our discussion on lock and block analysis, I walked you through setting up an Extended Events report to capture blocked process information. I'd like to repeat that example, expanding on some of the explanations to help you better understand Extended Events.

As you recall, this report will show you a list of processes that have been blocked for longer than the threshold you specify, so you need to decide on an acceptable length of time, in seconds, for a process to be blocked. Say you choose 1 second; you'd run the following command in SQL Server:

```
sp_configure 'show advanced options', 1 ;
GO
RECONFIGURE ;
GO
EXEC sp_configure 'blocked process threshold', 1;
RECONFIGURE;
```

CAUTION I'd never actually configure 1 second. When we did this example earlier, I suggested 5 seconds. A 1-second threshold is going to generate a lot more data, which for this example is what I want. A short threshold will make it easier to generate something for us to look at in the lab environment.

Now SQL Server can produce the event, which can be captured by Extended Events, and used to generate a report for you. We need to set up a session to capture the event data:

1 In SQL Server Management Studio's Object Explorer, expand Management, and then expand Extended Events. You should see a Sessions folder; right-click it and choose New Session.... Notice that we're not using the Wizard this time.

2 Provide a Session name, such as My block report.

3 On the Events page, type block into the Event library: field. That should get you to the blocked_process_report; click that and then click the > (right-arrow) button to add it to the Selected events list. The only big difference between this example and the previous one, where we used the Wizard, is that we didn't get a preselected list of events by using a template. Figure 17.10 shows what your event should look like at this point.

4 Add database_name to the list of captured fields.

5 Don't include any filters.

6 Save the data to a file, as shown in figure 17.11, and make a note of the filename for later reference. I'm configuring the file to have a max size of 1 GB, and configuring SQL Server to automatically create up to 5 new files. At that point, the oldest file will be deleted automatically to make room for a new one, so I'll need to ensure I can spare 5 GB of local disk space.

Once you're done, ensure that the session is started. (If you still have a blocked process report session from chapter 13, stop that session. You can even delete it if you like.)

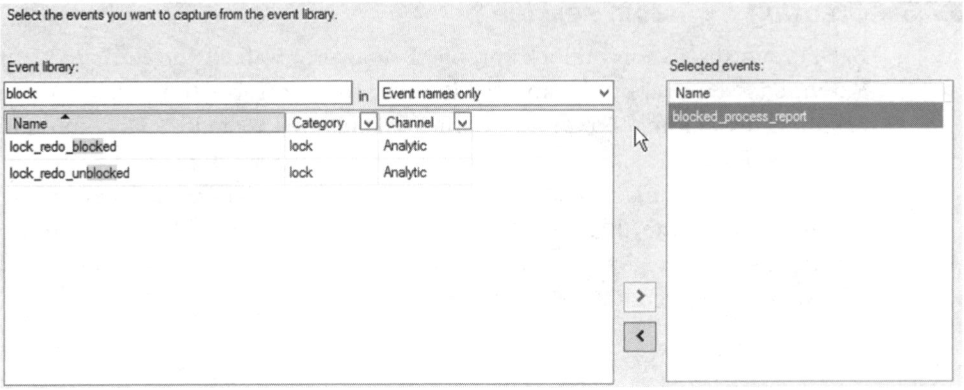

Select the events you want to capture from the event library.

Event library:

block

Name		Category	in	Event names only	✓
block	▲		in	Channel	✓
lock_redo_blocked		lock		Analytic	
lock_redo_unblocked		lock		Analytic	

[^] [∨]

Selected events:

Name
blocked_process_report

Figure 17.10   Capture the blocked_process_report event.

To try to create a blocked process, I'm going to open a new query window and run the following:

```
DECLARE @x INT = 0;

WHILE @x < 200
BEGIN

UPDATE Person.Person
    SET Title = NULL
    WHERE Title IS NULL;
SELECT @x = @x + 1;

END
```

This is making a meaningless set of changes to a table, but it's doing it 200 times. The idea is to put some locks in place that will exist for a long time. I then open a new SQL Server Management Studio window (I did this on a separate computer; you could also create a new connection to the same SQL Server instance right in the same Studio window) so that I'd have a separate process to work from. In that window, I ran the same

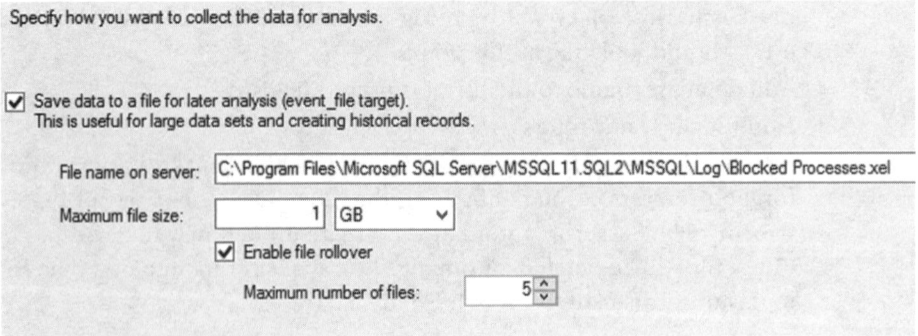

Specify how you want to collect the data for analysis.

☑ Save data to a file for later analysis (event_file target).
This is useful for large data sets and creating historical records.

File name on server: C:\Program Files\Microsoft SQL Server\MSSQL11.SQL2\MSSQL\Log\Blocked Processes.xel

Maximum file size: [1] [GB ✓]

☑ Enable file rollover

Maximum number of files: [5 ∧∨]

Figure 17.11   Capture the events to a file on disk.

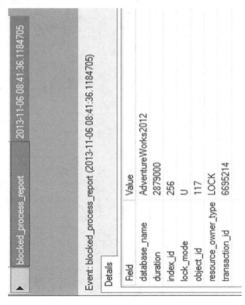

Figure 17.12 You can see the blocked process!

query. Again, the idea is to get it waiting for long enough to trigger my blocked process threshold.

TRY IT NOW If you're playing along, it's important to get both of these queries started at more or less the same time. I used a second computer because it was easier for me to run the first query, then immediately switch keyboards and get the second one running.

I've run one query that's going to put Exclusive locks on a bunch of database rows—possibly escalating to block entire pages or even the entire table—for several seconds. I then ran a second query that wanted to do exactly the same thing; it would remain blocked and hopefully generated a blocked process report.

After ensuring that the queries ran long enough to pass my blocked process threshold, I expanded the blocked process Extended Events session and double-clicked its target (which in my example, remember, is coming from a file on disk, not from a memory buffer). As shown in figure 17.12, I can see that a process was indeed blocked attempting to gain an Update lock (remember, UPDATE queries first grab an Update lock, which later becomes Exclusive). That means the second process I was running couldn't get a lock to read the data, because the first process already had an Exclusive lock.

The event data also includes a field named blocked_process, which contains a lot more data in XML format. Here's what I saw:

```
<blocked-process-report>
<blocked-process>
<process id="processc937b498" taskpriority="0" logused="0"
 waitresource="KEY: 5:72057594045599648 (819443284a0)" waittime="2879"
 ownerId="695214" transactionname="UPDATE" lasttranstarted="2013-11-
 06T08:41:33.210" XDES="0xff04f208" lockMode="U" schedulerid="2"
 kpid="3312" status="suspended" spid="71" sbid="0" ecid="0" priority="0"
 trancount="2" lastbatchstarted="2013-11-06T08:40:04.453"
```

```
lastbatchcompleted="2013-11-06T08:39:43.430" lastattention="1900-01-
01T00:00:00.430" clientapp="Microsoft SQL Server Management Studio -
Query" hostname="WIN-NQT7TB6A571" hostpid="1736" loginname="WIN-
NQT7TB6A571\Administrator" isolationlevel="read committed (2)"
xactid="6695214" currentdb="5" lockTimeout="4294967295"
clientoption1="671090784" clientoption2="390200">
```

This information is a treasure chest! It tells me what computer (hostname) was blocked, when this happened, how long the process waited for a lock before timing out, pretty much everything. What follows next is the query it was trying to run:

```
<executionStack>
<frame line="6" stmtstart="96" stmtend="222"
sqlhandle="0x02000000051b03e00e63acce39eea91553449dfe88852f55530000000000
0000000000000000000000000000" />
</executionStack>
<inputbuf>

DECLARE @x INT = 0;

BEGIN

WHILE @x < 200

SELECT @x = @x + 1;

UPDATE Person.Person
  SET Title = NULL
  WHERE Title IS NULL;

END   </inputbuf>
      </process>
    </blocked-process>
```

That's the *blocked* process; I also get a whole section on the *blocking* process, so I can see who and what was causing the problem:

```
<blocking-process>
<process status="suspended" spid="69" sbid="0" ecid="0" priority="0"
trancount="2" lastbatchstarted="2013-11-06T08:39:47.360"
lastbatchcompleted="2013-11-06T08:40:05.580" lastattention="1900-01-
01T00:00:360" clientapp="Microsoft SQL Server Management Studio -
Query" hostname="WIN-NQT7TB6A571" hostpid="704" loginname="WIN-
NQT7TB6A571\Administrator" isolationlevel="read committed (2)"
xactid="6694253" currentdb="5" lockTimeout="4294967295"
clientoption1="671090784" clientoption2="390200">
<executionStack>
<frame line="6" stmtstart="96" stmtend="222"
sqlhandle="0x020000000051b03e00e63acce39eea91553449dfe88852f55530000000000
0000000000000000000000000000" />
</executionStack>
<inputbuf>

DECLARE @x INT = 0;

BEGIN

WHILE @x < 200

UPDATE Person.Person
  SET Title = NULL
  WHERE Title IS NULL;

SELECT @x = @x + 1;
```

```
END    </inputbuf>
    </process>
    </blocking-process>
    </blocked-process-report>
```

That's a real wealth of information.

17.4 Tips for Extended Events

Extended Events provide a great deal of really useful information. It's worth exploring the templates in the New Session Wizard, because those represent predefined sets of events that most administrators will find useful at some point.

Additional tips:

- Avoid running sessions unnecessarily, to cut down on the amount of data you have to pore through. I tend to run sessions when I'm actively troubleshooting a problem.

- Document what you have each session capturing, ideally in some shared document that other administrators can get to as well.

- Be aware that Extended Events is actively under development by Microsoft, so older versions of SQL Server might not support as much variety, whereas newer versions will be able to capture much more.

17.5 Hands-on lab

I'm hoping you took the time to follow along with the examples in this chapter; if you didn't, at least run through that blocked process report, as it's a crazy-useful technique. That'll be your hands-on lab for this chapter.

18

Monitoring and analyzing performance

This is one of the most important chapters in this book. Aside from index maintenance and monitoring, performance monitoring is one of the most impactful things you can do as a SQL Server administrator. In this chapter, I'll focus on some of the easiest ways to monitor SQL Server performance, particularly from the perspective of SQL Server 2012 and later.

This chapter is, I'll admit, a wee bit on the long side. You may need a couple of days' lunches to go through everything.

18.1 Key Performance Monitor counters

Windows' built-in Performance Monitor tool remains one of the best ways to get a quick look at performance, and for compiling long-term performance information. It isn't an enterprise monitoring system as System Center Operations Manager, but it does let you dig in to see a snapshot at what's happening.

When using Performance Monitor, always run it on a machine *other* than the one you're analyzing. The tool works fine remotely and runs on all Windows computers. It can display information in a real-time chart, or save performance information to a log, called a *data collector set*. Those logs can be opened later and viewed in a non-real-time graph.

TIP To run Performance Monitor on nearly any Windows computer, hold the Windows key and press R. Then, type Perfmon and hit Enter.

ABOVE AND BEYOND

Newer versions of SQL Server, including SQL Server 2012, provide a new, native way of viewing bulk performance information. Called *Dynamic Management Objects*, or DMOs, they consist of two distinct elements: *Dynamic Management Views*, or DMVs, and *Dynamic Management Functions*, or DMFs.

To keep this book as version-neutral as possible, I'm going to focus primarily on Performance Monitor rather than on the DMOs. If you're using versions of SQL Server that support DMOs, it's worth your time to read up on them for they can make it easier, for example, to collect information into a spreadsheet or database for long-term trend analysis.

Performance Monitor breaks things down into *objects*, which are broad categories of performance items, and *counters*, which measure a specific performance metric. In many cases, counters are available in multiple instances. On a multiprocessor computer there will be an instance of the processor counters for each logical processor. In those cases, you'll also often find a _TOTAL instance that aggregates all of the individual instances.

Each of the next sections will focus on a particular performance object. I'll try to provide recommendations about what represents good and bad values, but in many cases I'll suggest you refer to a *baseline* value. That's an observed value on a system that you feel is working well, meaning it's handling its workload acceptably. In other words, you need to start analyzing performance when a system is working *well*, so that you know what "good" looks like. You then recapture and reanalyze periodically as your workload changes and evolves.

18.1.1 *Setting up Performance Monitor*

Once you have Performance Monitor (or PerfMon, to its friends), adding objects and counters is easy. Click the big + icon in the toolbar, or press Ctrl+N. Select your object, then the counters, and click OK. Note in figure 18.1 that you can pull objects from remote computers or the local machine.

Once you have all your counters, they'll display in a real-time graph, shown in figure 18.2.

You may need to adjust the line style, color, and weight to make it easier to differentiate each counter. You'll notice that clicking a counter in the list near the bottom of the graph will highlight that counter in the graph itself; double-clicking lets you configure the graph line appearance, as shown in figure 18.3.

TIP If you aren't getting the highlight effect when selecting a counter in the list, press Ctrl+H. That toggles the highlighting behavior. You can then use the arrow keys on your keyboard to move between counters, and each will be highlighted with a bolder, darker line to make it easier to pick out of the bunch.

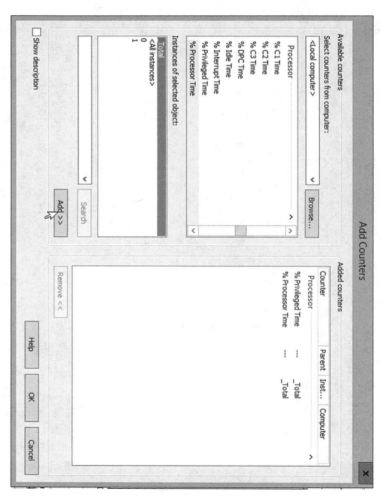

Figure 18.1   I prefer to set up one computer's counters in a single graph.

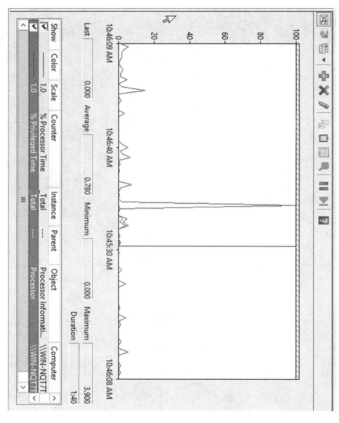

**Figure 18.2
Adding too
many lines
can make the
graph hard
to read.**

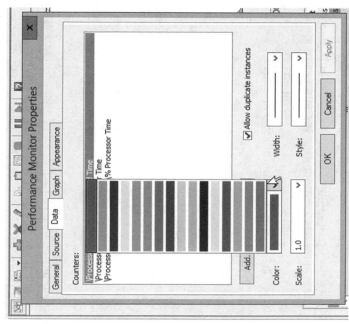

Figure 18.3　Customizing line appearance can restore sanity to the graph.

18.1.2　Memory

Within this object, consider the following counters:

- Pages/sec tracks how many pages of memory (not quite the same as SQL Server's 8 KB data pages) are being swapped between active RAM and the system page file. Lower numbers are better, but look for something under 50 on most systems.

- Page faults/sec measures how many times the OS looked for a page in memory, but had to go to the disk-based swap file for it instead. Lower numbers are better, but match this against your baseline.

TIP　Keep in mind that SQL Server can be configured, on a per-instance basis, with minimum and maximum memory values. If you're experiencing memory-related problems, don't forget to check the instance configuration.

18.1.3　SQLServer:Buffer Manager

This object lets you see how well SQL Server's in-memory caches are working. Since these a key to reducing disk I/O, it's important to keep track of these counters:

- *Buffer cache hit ratio*—Measures the percentage of data requests being served from SQL Server's cache, rather than from disk. Higher is better, and you ideally want around 90% or better in most transaction-based systems.

- *Page life expectancy*—Tells you how long a page of data can be expected to live in the cache before being flushed. Higher is better, but compare to your baseline for analysis.

- *Checkpoint pages/sec*—Tracks how many pages are being written to disk per second by the checkpoint process. You should see this stay under 30 on most systems.

- *Lazy writes/sec*—Tells you how many pages are being flushed from the cache. This should be under 20.

18.1.4 SQLServer:Memory Manager

There are three things to look at on this object:

- *Memory grants pending*—Tells you how many processes are waiting to be assigned memory. You want this at zero.

- *Target server memory and total server memory)*—These go together. The first should be close to the amount of RAM available in the computer, and the second should be close to the first.

18.1.5 PhysicalDisk

You'll want to watch instances of this object for any disks storing SQL Server data or log files. Focus on the following counters:

- *% disk time*—The amount of time the disk was busy; continuous readings over 85% indicate a system that has poor disk throughput. This is an urgent and immediate problem that will create significant impact on SQL Server.

- *Current disk queue length*—The number of disk requests waiting for the disk system to catch up. You want this under two per disk.

- *Avg. disk queue length*—The average number of items waiting for the disk system to catch up. It should also be under two per disk.

- *Disk transfers/sec*—Measures overall read/write operations on disk, and should be under 400 per disk.

- *Disk Bytes/sec*—Measures the amount of data moving back and forth to disk. You typically want this under 800 MB per second.

- *Avg. disk sec/read and avg. disk sec/write*—Measure the length of time read and write operations are taking. Each should be under 10 ms on average.

Note that this is one of the few objects that is absolutely reliable even inside a VM; we'll talk about the caveats of VM performance in chapter 20.

18.1.6 Processor (_Total) %

It's important to focus on *all* processors, hence the use of the special _Total aggregate instance, unless you've configured SQL Server to use something other than all available processors. Counters to watch:

- *Processor time*—Measures the amount of time the processor was busy. This should have an average value under 80%. I start to get worried when this averages above 50% under normal workloads, and that's my signal to start looking for other performance issues that might be contributing to the problem.

■ *% privileged*—Measures the amount of time the processor spent in privileged mode, typically servicing device drivers and kernel-level requests. You want this under 10% on average.

Keep in mind that overloaded processors can often be the result of the processor making up for some other bottleneck. Slow disk systems will require more disk queue and buffer management, which will eat up processor cycles.

18.1.7 System

This object measures a couple of important core counters:

■ *Processor queue length*—Measures the number of instructions waiting on the processor to get to them. This should be under 2.

■ *Context switches/sec*—Measures the number of times per second that the processor switches from one thread of execution to another. An average value under 2,000 is typically acceptable.

18.1.8 SQL Server:SQL Statistics

This object measures additional SQL Server-specific statistics. There are no firm recommendations for these, but you want to know what they look like on a system that's functioning well. Continue to monitor them for significant changes, as those will indicate increasing workload and potentially declining performance.

■ *Batch requests/sec*—The number of SQL command batches being handled each second.

■ *SQL compilations/sec and SQL recompilations/sec*—Measure the number of SQL statements being compiled for execution.

18.1.9 Network interface and network segment

People often forget that the network is a big part of how SQL Server works. These two objects (both of which tend to be reliable inside of a VM, by the way) help you understand how SQL Server is utilizing the network.

■ *Network Interface: Bytes total/sec*—Should be under 50% of the network card's capacity. Yes, 50%. Ethernet network performance degrades sharply after 50% saturation.

■ *Network segment: % net utilization*—Should stay under 80% of the network's bandwidth, the point at which Ethernet performance falls off most drastically.

Keep in mind that the network *segment* is being used by every computer connected to it; it can be saturated even before SQL Server starts using it! The network interface is specific to the computer.

18.2 Using Data Collectors and reports

A cool feature of newer versions (since 2008) of SQL Server is Data Collectors. These are designed to run continuously in the background, logging performance data to a centralized data warehouse (which is a specialized SQL Server database). You can therefore have several SQL Server instances reporting data to a single spot, and there are a ton of built-in, interactive reports you can use to summarize and monitor key performance metrics.

18.2.1 Setting up the data warehouse

Before you start collecting all that performance data, you need someplace to put it, so we'll start by creating a data warehouse. This can go on any SQL Server you like (that has some free capacity—obviously don't load up an already-busy server with this), and a single data warehouse can handle data from multiple SQL Server instances. A lot of my customers tend to set up a SQL Server instance for internal administrative stuff, little applications they create internally, or databases they create to store information collected by their administrative scripts. That's a perfect place to put the data warehouse. You probably do need to put it on a regular edition of SQL Server, as opposed to the free Express editions, because the Express edition isn't designed to accept numerous incoming connections all the time.

To get started, go to SQL Server Management Studio, expand the Management folder, and right-click Data Collection. You'll see an option to configure the data warehouse, as shown in figure 18.4.

The wizard will walk you through the process. You'll be setting up a new database, so you'll have to think about where it's going: you'll need to have adequate disk space, consider how you'll back up and maintain the database, and so on. This obviously isn't something you should drop onto any old SQL Server instance without forethought and planning. Part of the setup process also creates three database roles inside the new database, and lets you map specific logins into those, giving people permission within the database.

18.2.2 Configuring data collection

After the management data warehouse is set up, you'll need to run the wizard a second time, this time selecting the option to set up data collection. I've done that in figure 18.5.

Now that your data warehouse is set up, you'll only need to run the wizard once per SQL Server instance, selecting the Set up data collection option and pointing each instance to that data warehouse.

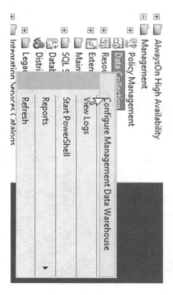

Figure 18.4   You must configure a data warehouse to use data collection.

Select configuration task
Select a task to configure a management data warehouse or a data collection set.

Select a task to perform:

○ Create or upgrade a management data warehouse

Creates or upgrades a management data warehouse for storing data collection set results. To configure data collection for this instance, run this wizard again and select "Set up data collection".

● Set up data collection

Configures this instance to start collecting data to an existing management data warehouse.

Figure 18.5   Run the wizard a second time to set up data collection.

One setup consideration is where the local data collector will cache its data before uploading it to the data warehouse. Typically, you can use the system TEMP directory, but if you need a specific SQL Server instance to use a different disk path, you specify that during data collection setup.

You'll know that data collection is set up by looking in Object Explorer in SQL Server Management Studio. As shown in figure 18.6, the default System Data Collection Sets folder will exist, with the default collectors underneath.

⊞ 🗀 Management
  ⊞ 🗀 Policy Management
  ⊞ ☒ Data Collection
    ⊟ 🗀 System Data Collection Sets
      🔲 Disk Usage
      🔲 Query Statistics
      🔲 Server Activity
      🔲 Utility Information

Figure 18.6   Use Object Explorer to verify data collection setup.

18.2.3   Configuring a data collection set

Data collection sets have a pretty reasonable default configuration, but you can double-click one to modify its settings if needed. Figure 18.7 shows what you'll see.

You can change the collection interval, modify the data warehouse location, and so on. You can even have data collected on one schedule and cached locally, with a less-frequent upload to the data warehouse. I have customers who'll use fairly regular collection, but only upload to the data warehouse in the evenings, so that the next day's reports are ready to go. You can also configure the data retention period (the default is 730 days).

NOTE   Data collection and upload is handled by a set of SQL Server Agent jobs, which you can see in Object Explorer after setting up data collection. Ensure that SQL Server Agent is running on the instance, or data collection won't happen.

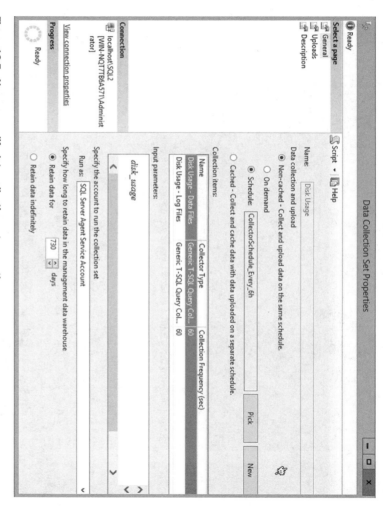

Figure 18.7   You can modify data collection set properties.

18.2.4   *Working with data collection reports*

Right-clicking Data Collection again will provide access to the available reports, as shown in figure 18.8. You can access built-in reports, or create your own custom reports.

The reports are somewhat interactive, offering the ability to drill down using hyperlinks. I find the query statistics history to be useful, since it highlights the most frequently run and most long-running queries on the system, giving me a place to start looking for potential query problems.

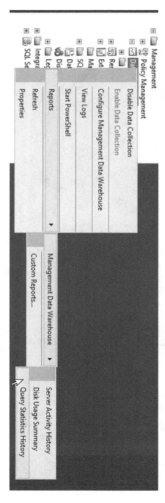

Figure 18.8   Choose from custom or built-in reports.

NOTE There's a great article on Microsoft's MSDN website that discusses the data collector architecture, going into more detail on the available reports and so forth. I heartily recommend that you read it. It's at http://msdn.microsoft.com/en-us/library/dd939169(v=sql.100).aspx. The article was written for SQL Server 2008, but it's applicable to later versions as well.

18.3 Watching for performance trends

Make no mistake: managing SQL Server performance is all about knowing what's normal on a given instance, and watching for deviations from normal. That's one reason the data collectors are so cool—they give you a built-in 2-year trend line to start with. But you should make sure that your regular performance monitoring of SQL Server includes building a trend line, and regularly comparing current performance to the trend.

Sadly, none of the native tools (aside from data collection) are designed for trend collection; you have to get into additional tools, such as System Center Operations Manager, to gain that capability. And you *do* need that capability.

I have a few specific kinds of trends that I like to watch for:

- *Increasing memory churn.* I like to see if SQL Server is generating a decreasing cache hit ratio in the OS, a sign that SQL Server isn't getting the memory it needs from physical RAM, and is instead swapping to the OS page file—a slower operation.
- *Increasing lock wait times in SQL Server.* This suggests that queries are taking longer to run, and more queries are waiting longer to access the data they need. This is *generally* traceable to a disk bottleneck, although memory or CPU starvation can contribute. Chapter 13 went into more detail on this problem.
- *Increasing network bandwidth utilization.* This is a good measure of steadily increasing workload, and although not alarming in and of itself, it does put me on the lookout for bottlenecks as the workload goes up.
- *Steadily increasing CPU utilization.* I look at long-term averages over an hour or so, because CPU activity naturally spikes a lot in the short term. Steadily increasing CPU utilization is another sign of increasing workload, and it means I have to be very careful to look for memory and disk bottlenecks.

18.4 The big performance killers

Let's look at some of the bigger performance-killers that you, as an administrator, can help mitigate.

18.4.1 Memory

Giving SQL Server as much memory as possible is almost never the wrong answer, although, depending on the way SQL Server is being used, a lot of memory won't necessarily help in every situation.

Try to run SQL Server on a 64-bit machine, using a 64-bit OS, and of course use a 64-bit edition of SQL Server. 64-bit doesn't inherently speed up anything, but 64-bit processors are more modern and do run faster than older processors. More importantly,

64-bit processors don't have a 4 GB limit on memory. Look carefully at the hard page faults performance monitor counters, and if they're getting high, SQL Server is likely starved for memory.

Also consider enabling data compression in SQL Server (not provided in every edition; generally, Enterprise Edition will have it). This helps increase both disk I/O and memory utilization, because data pages are stored on disk and in memory as compressed objects. There's a bit of extra CPU load in handling the compression, but the payoff is usually worth it.

18.4.2 *Disk*

Disk is the ultimate bottleneck for SQL Server. There's a lot you can do to speed things up, all of which primarily revolve around the theme of get more spindles on the job. That is, the more physical disks involved in SQL Server's disk I/O, the less likely you are to run into hard bottlenecks. Some suggestions:

- *SSD can have a tremendous impact.* FlashSoft (www.sandisk.com/products/flash-soft/), for example, relies on a local SSD for caching SQL Server data, and it can double or even triple performance.

- *Use large disk arrays comprised of many, many physical disks.* Most SANs are built this way, making them ideal for storing SQL Server databases.

- *Try to eliminate contention as much as possible.* Putting log files and data files on separate disks or arrays, for example, helps parallelize activity and reduce wait times. Parallelization is key: even having multiple disk controllers helps SQL Server do more things simultaneously, with each controller handling a separate array.

- *Go faster.* While Fibre Channel was once the platinum standard for SANs, iSCSI and other technologies have caught up and are, in some measures, pulling ahead. Faster is better.

- *Add RAM.* To a degree, more memory, meaning larger page cache buffers, can help mitigate slow disk I/O.

- *Spread out.* If you can spread database objects across multiple files, and move those files to separate storage, you'll help reduce contention and speed things up. Separate intelligently, moving your most active tables and objects to different files so that they can be accessed more simultaneously.

18.4.3 *Processor*

Add more processors. Use faster processors. Both are difficult resolutions in a physical machine, but they become easier in a VM. Processors having larger L2/L3 caches tend to work better with SQL Server, too.

One overlooked thing I try to focus on is whether or not my system's processors are being used efficiently. After all, if you can't add more or use faster CPUs, getting the most from what you have is key, right? Look at how much time the processor is spent in privileged mode, a counter I mentioned earlier in this chapter. Most privileged mode time comes from device drivers, so more efficient device drivers can help a lot. Also consider running SQL Server on Windows Server Core (in Windows Server 2012 and later, with SQL Server 2012 and later), since Server Core doesn't need fancy video drivers. Video is where a lot of privileged time gets eaten up. Manage your servers remotely, rather than by running management tools right on the server, because remote management helps reduce privileged time, too.

18.5 *Hands-on lab*

There's no specific hands-on lab for this chapter, but if you have access to a production SQL Server instance, fire up Performance Monitor and check out some of the key counters I listed in this chapter. Start getting a feel for what your production servers look like. You can also set up Data Collectors on your lab instance of SQL Server, if you like, and get a feel for what that process looks like. Be aware, of course, that because your lab instance isn't doing much of anything, the performance reports won't be very interesting.

Options for high availability

19.1 What is high availability?

High availability, or HA, involves building redundancy into your SQL Server platform. The idea is to have at least two of everything, so that if one fails, you've got a backup in place. SQL Server offers a number of different HA options, and you can implement HA practices that sit outside of SQL Server, too.

Make no mistake: HA costs. Take an extreme example, where you want to make sure SQL Server can keep running *absolutely, no matter what*. Even if a meteor hits your datacenter. The entire building needs to be redundant! You're going to have to build a new datacenter, either across town or across the country—you can see where this HA thing can get expensive really quickly.

That's why you have to start by setting goals for HA. What, exactly, do you need to be able to survive? You're going to need to have a budget, too, and the business

Most organizations using SQL Server depend on it pretty heavily. It's *mission critical*, as they say. The problem with mission critical is that computers and software break down from time to time. Hardware fails. A data file gets corrupted on disk. Or maybe you just need to maintain the server, applying a patch or two. What's that? Mission critical means it has to be running 24/7, with no downtime for maintenance? That's where *high availability* comes in.

This chapter is going to be mainly descriptive, meaning I'm going to explain how these technologies work and what they can do for you. We won't be getting into their setup, because in some cases that can require a significant amount of server hardware. SQL Server Books Online provides step-by-step details for setting these up, if you need instructions.

is going to have to come up with that number. It should be based on what downtime costs, not on some random figure pulled out of the air. If you know the company will lose a million dollars a day when SQL Server is offline, it's reasonable to have a budget based on that number. A million bucks could build a datacenter across town. Just saying.

19.2 *Log shipping*

SQL Server's easiest HA technique is called *log shipping.* This involves two servers: your main production server, and a *hot spare.* Normally, the hot spare does nothing but act as a redundant server, either a physical or a virtual machine. If it's doing no other work, Microsoft doesn't make you pay for the SQL Server license. It doesn't need to be the same kind of computer as your production server, meaning it could be a smaller, less expensive rig. (Of course, if you need to actually use it, performance may suffer if it's not up to snuff.)

Log shipping starts with a *snapshot* of your database, which is a complete backup of the entire database from that moment. From then on, the production server's transaction log is periodically bundled up and sent, or *shipped,* to the hot spare. The hot spare *replays* the transactions in the log against its copy of the database, bringing that copy up to current. This technique always involves a certain amount of data being at-risk, meaning the hot spare isn't being updated in real-time; if the production server fails you'll lose some data.

In the event of a production server failure, nothing happens automatically. You have to manually bring the hot spare online, and figure out a way to have clients talk to it instead of to the production server. Most folks do that with some DNS trickery: you have your clients all talking to a DNS CNAME alias, which normally points to the production server. In a failure, you modify DNS so that the CNAME points to the hot spare. Client computers may take as long as 10 minutes to adapt to that change, since they tend to cache DNS records locally for about that long. Some organizations will lower the time-to-live, or TTL, of the CNAME record so that clients cache it for shorter periods. A lower TTL does mean more DNS traffic, so you have to architect for that.

NOTE As of SQL Server 2012, log shipping is *deprecated.* That means Microsoft plans to get rid of the feature in the future, and is only including it for backward compatibility. It's good to know what log shipping is and how it works, because it serves as a kind of functional baseline, but you shouldn't start using it in new projects.

19.3 *Database mirroring*

Database mirroring is similar to log shipping, in that you have a production server and a hot spare. The hot spare can absolutely be doing production work for another database, meaning you can pair mirror servers to split workload. For example, Server A can be the main server for Database 1, while Server B is the main server for Database 2.

Each mirrors the other's databases, so Server A has a mirror of Database 2, and Server B has a mirror of Database 1. That way, both servers are being useful, meaning you're wasting less money on standby resources. In a failure, one server would be doing *all* the work, so you might have to accept a lower-than-normal level of performance from it during the failure period.

The big difference between log shipping and database mirroring is that mirroring happens more often, sending small groups of transactions rather than entire log files. That means your backup server is always a bit more up-to-date. That's the up side; the down side is that mirroring requires more processing power. Standard editions of SQL Server run mirroring in a single-threaded process, which means it's only effective for mirroring a single database. Enterprise Edition uses a multithreaded process that can, when backed by sufficient computing power, mirror multiple databases for you. As with log shipping, mirroring involves two—and only two—servers.

NOTE You have to mirror between the same editions: Enterprise to Enterprise, or Standard to Standard. You can read more about this and other requirements at http://technet.microsoft.com/en-us/library/bb934127(v=SQL.105).aspx.

As of SQL Server 2008, Enterprise Edition, the principal copy of the database—the production server—can use the mirror as a form of backup. In the event that a single 8 KB page of data gets corrupted on the principal, and the server is unable to read it, it will automatically request a fresh copy from the mirror server, which usually resolves the problem. It's a kind of invisible, low-level repair operation made possible by mirroring.

19.3.1 Mirroring modes

Mirroring can operate in one of two main modes, *synchronous* and *asynchronous*. Synchronous mode is also called the high-safety mode, because it tries harder to make sure the mirror copy is always up-to-date, meaning less of your data is at-risk at any given time. In this mode, when a client runs a query on the production server, the production server immediately sends the transaction to its mirror partner. The production server waits for confirmation from its partner, meaning it waits until the transaction is replayed on the mirror copy, before telling the client that the transaction completed successfully. This places a significant burden on the overall application, because clients now have to wait for *two* SQL Server computers to run every transaction. This mode is available only in Enterprise Edition.

Asynchronous mode is also referred to as high-performance mode, because it doesn't wait for the dual confirmation. The production server processes client queries immediately, and confirms to the client as soon as it's done so. The transactions are sent to the mirror as fast as possible, but it will typically lag a bit behind the primary copy, so you may have some data at-risk if a failure occurs. The lag can become substantial if the production server is under heavy workload, or if the mirror server's hardware isn't able to keep up.

19.3.2 Mirroring failover

If you're using asynchronous mode, then SQL Server doesn't support any kind of automatic failover. You have to manually tell the system to use the mirror copy instead of the production copy. That's a big downside of mirroring and high-performance mode, because your application may stay offline until someone manually "flips the switch" to use the mirror copy.

High-safety synchronous mode, conversely, requires a third server called a *witness*. This doesn't contain a copy of the database, but instead sits around and watches the two mirror partners (the witness can also be serving up its own, unrelated databases to clients, so it's not completely useless). The witness enables automatic failover, meaning it will "see" the production server fail, and make sure traffic starts going to the mirror copy instead. At that point, the mirror copy becomes the principal copy of the database, and what used to be the production server is now considered the spare.

NOTE The witness can be running any edition of SQL Server, even Workgroup or Express, which means you don't have to pay for a SQL Server license if all the thing will do is sit there and stare at your mirror partners.

19.3.3 Connecting clients to a mirror set

Obviously, for things like automatic failover to work, your clients have to know when to switch servers. Normally, clients connect by using a *connection string*, which is a set of instructions that includes the server name. For a mirror set, that server name would be the principal copy, or what I've been calling the production server. The connection string can also provide the name of the other server, the backup copy where the mirror exists. The OS's data access layer stores this information in memory. Upon making the initial connection to the current principal server, the OS-level data access layer retrieves the mirror partner server's name, caching it in memory. As you might imagine, all of this magic requires a Windows client OS. It won't work with non-Windows systems unless they've been specifically written to duplicate this behavior.

NOTE In a web application, the end-user's web browser doesn't talk directly to SQL Server. Instead, it talks to a web server, which talks to the SQL Server, which means the web server is the "client" in that scenario, because it's the machine connecting to SQL Server.

Here's what a connection string might look like when you specify both mirror partners:

```
"Server=Partner_A; Failover_Partner=Partner_B; Database=AdventureWorks2012;
    Network=dbmssocn"
```

Reconnecting in the event of a failure is not necessarily automatic; applications must be aware of the failed connection, and must initiate a reconnect. This forces the client to start all over, and presumably the connection to the old principal server will fail, forcing the client to try the failover partner. The witness, if you're using one, helps the two mirror partners understand who's in charge, but it doesn't necessarily help clients reconnect. This is the biggest downside of mirroring, because you can't guarantee that clients will quickly and transparently start using the mirror. Read more about this at http://technet.microsoft.com/en-us/library/ms175484(v=sql.105).aspx.

NOTE This is a major point of misunderstanding for mirroring. The witness determines which of your two mirror partners believes it is in charge; this has no impact on which one your clients connect to. In order for mirroring to have truly automatic failover from a client perspective, you may have to make at least small application-level changes to the client application code.

19.4   *AlwaysOn Clustering*

AlwaysOn is a brand name that was introduced with SQL Server 2012 to describe the product's high-end HA options. AlwaysOn Clustering (also called AlwaysOn Availability Clusters) is one of two HA technologies included under the AlwaysOn brand. AlwaysOn Clustering is a new name for SQL Server clusters built atop the Windows Cluster Service, something that we've had for over a decade. But look: a shiny new brand name!!

19.4.1   *Cluster architecture*

With clustering, you start with two or more servers, which we'll call *nodes*. It's possible for a node to be *active*, meaning it will be running a SQL Server instance that is being used by client computers, or to be *passive*, meaning the node sits and waits for another node to experience a failure. Within the cluster, you can run multiple instances of SQL Server, and you can designate which nodes are capable of running each instance. For every instance, you need to have a chunk of disk space where the instance can keep its database files. That disk space is usually provided on a SAN, because the disk space must be "visible" to every node that might run an instance. That way, whatever node is running an instance will have access to the instance's files on disk. Figure 19.1 shows what this might look like in a complex setup.

Let's look at what figure 19.1 is showing. We'll start at the top of the diagram, where you can see four virtual server names and IP addresses. These are defined in the organization's DNS server, so that client computers can resolve the names (Instance1, Instance2, and so on) to the associated IP addresses. The clustering software on each of the four server nodes, shown in the middle part of the figure, can potentially "listen" to any incoming traffic for these IP addresses. NodeA, for example, "listens" to incoming traffic for Instance1, Instance2, and Instance3.

Each node has three instances of SQL Server *installed*, but in our example each node only has one instance *started*. In figure 19.1, I've shown the started instances in a white box, and the stopped instances in a grey box. So on NodeB, the SQL Server services related to Instance 2 are started and running; the services for Instance 1 and Instance 3 are installed but stopped. In clustering terminology, we'd say that NodeB was active for Instance 2, and passive for Instance 1 and Instance 3. NodeB can never become active for Instance 4, because that node isn't physically installed on NodeB.

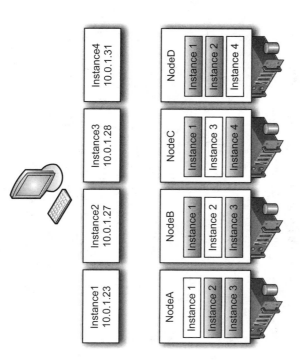

Figure 19.1 AlwaysOn Clustering example. Notice that in each node there are three instances installed, but only one is active (highlighted in white). If one node fails temporarily, the others can step in to cover while it recovers.

At the bottom of the diagram is the SAN, which has chunks set aside for each instance. As we start the explanation, NodeA "owns" the chunk of SAN space reserved for Instance 1's files. NodeB owns the SAN space set aside for Instance 2's files, and so on. Any of the nodes can potentially touch the files for any instance, but by mutual agreement they agree to stay hands off everything except what they're currently using.

19.4.2 Data file redundancy in clusters

Pay special attention to the fact that this HA technology *does not provide redundancy for the database files.* They're all located on the SAN, which becomes a single point of failure. In reality, most SANs are built with their own redundancies, the same as spare power supplies, disk arrays, and so on, so SANs are generally thought of as a safe place to keep your data. But there's only one copy of data for each instance, and that's a potential point of failure. What if the database becomes corrupted? The SAN is still running, so it can't necessarily help with that, but you'll lose the entire database until you can restore from a backup.

19.4.3   *Cluster failover scenario*

Now consider a failover situation. Let's say NodeB dies for whatever reason. A *heartbeat* signal runs continuously between the cluster nodes, so its buddies will realize when NodeB flatlines. Depending on how you've configured the cluster, either NodeA or NodeD could take over for NodeB, since NodeB was running Instance 2 and both NodeA and NodeD have copies of that instance. Suppose NodeA takes over. All of a sudden, NodeA starts its copy of Instance 2's services. NodeA takes over the SAN chunk reserved for Instance 2, and NodeA begins responding to incoming traffic on IP address 10.0.1.27, which is assigned to Instance2. In about a minute or so, Instance2 will be back online, running on NodeA instead of NodeB. NodeA might have some disk and cleanly hand off control of Instance 4 to, say, NodeC, the only other node capable of running Instance 4. This kind of failover takes longer, but it is cleaner, with less data at-risk, because the nodes can cooperate in the handoff.

You can also manually initiate a kind of failover, which you might want to do for maintenance purposes. Suppose you're ready to install a service pack on NodeD. You manually command the failover, which gives NodeD time to write pending changes to disk and cleanly hand off control of Instance 4 to, say, NodeC, the only other node capable of running Instance 4. This kind of failover takes longer, but it is cleaner, with less data at-risk, because the nodes can cooperate in the handoff.

19.4.4   *Clustering pros and cons*

These kinds of clusters are, sadly, expensive. They require a lot of hardware (SANs, networking equipment, and so on) in addition to the servers themselves. They're complex to set up and maintain, and there are a lot of moving pieces in the clustering software. They don't provide data file redundancy, either. On the upside, they provide good HA for hardware failures, and they give you the flexibility of having each node to active work while serving as a backup for its neighbors.

You have to size each node for the amount of work you expect it to do. For example, if you want NodeA to provide decent performance when running Instance 1, 2, and 3, then it has to have sufficient processing power. When it *isn't* serving all three instances, that extra power is wasted.

These days, I tend to steer customers away from these clusters, mainly because SQL Server 2012 introduced something better: Availability Groups.

19.5   *AlwaysOn Availability Groups*

AlwaysOn Availability Groups were introduced in SQL Server 2012, and they closely resemble the HA technology in Microsoft Exchange Server. You start with a bunch of servers, which we'll continue to call nodes. Unlike clustering, these nodes don't need any shareable disk space, although you might still elect to connect them to a SAN for their database files. The point is that each node needs its own private, personal storage space. They'll never take control of each others' disk space.

You define an availability group that spans the nodes, and then assign one or more databases to the group. Each node is said to host an availability replica, either the

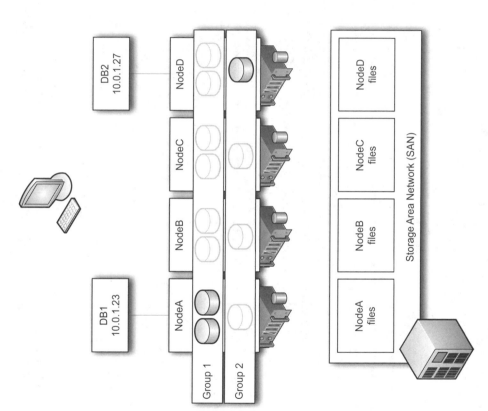

Figure 19.2   AlwaysOn Availability Group architecture, showing two availability groups running on four nodes. Each group is accessible through a separate virtual IP address.

primary replica or a secondary replica. SQL Server 2012 supports up to four secondary replicas per availability group. Every database you add to the availability group is called an *availability database,* and they all live together. Only one node hosts the primary replica at any given point, and it is the primary server for all databases in the group. The databases fail over as a unit. It's possible for a single server to host multiple availability groups, meaning things can get quite complex. Figure 19.2 shows what it might look like.

Here, NodeA, NodeB, NodeC, and NodeD all participate in two availability groups, which I've named Group 1 and Group 2. Notice that there are virtual server names, DB1 and DB2, and corresponding IP addresses. Any of the nodes can respond to these IP addresses, but right now NodeA is responding to 10.0.1.23 and NodeD is handling 10.0.1.27; those IP addresses are virtually connected to the availability groups. As you can see, NodeA hosts the primary replica for Group 1, while NodeD hosts the primary replica for Group 2. Group 1 contains two databases, while Group 2 contains only one. All four servers have their own storage areas on the SAN.

NOTE   SQL Server 2014 introduces the ability to keep an AlwaysOn replica in Microsoft's Windows Azure cloud service. That means you have a cloud-based backup of your data running in Microsoft's data centers. You'd pay for storage and compute time in that replica, but you wouldn't pay for the data being copied in (you don't pay for inbound data in Azure). You'd only start paying for bandwidth if you needed to fail over to that replica.

19.5.1   *Availability group replication*

As changes are made to the databases by NodeA and NodeD, those changes are replicated to the other nodes in the availability groups, using a process similar to database mirroring. The process can work in synchronous or asynchronous modes, the same as mirroring. This gives each node an up-to-date copy of all three databases. They use their own private SAN storage to keep those files. You can see how this offers better data file redundancy than clustering, because each database physically exists in four different places (you could even put some of them on a different SAN for even better redundancy, and that's what I usually recommend).

This replication can even happen over long distances if you have sufficient WAN bandwidth, meaning you can easily keep a copy of your data across town. The nodes in an availability group share nothing other than a common network connection, making it easier to separate them.

19.5.2   *Availability group failover*

The nodes in an availability group are always in touch with one another through a heartbeat signal, much like the heartbeat used by clustering. (Availability Groups are built on top of a portion of the Windows Cluster Service, so they share some capabilities with clustering.) When the node hosting the active replica flatlines, another node promotes itself to active and takes over. It starts responding to traffic on the virtual IP address, and within *seconds*, you've failed over. It's much faster failover than with clustering, because every node is already running SQL Server. They don't have to wait for services to start up.

19.5.3   *Availability group bonuses*

Because the secondary replicas are all up-to-date copies of the database, running on a separate SQL Server, you can put them to use. Remember, in clustering, the backup nodes don't keep SQL Server running, because only one node at a time can "see" the database files on the SAN. With availability groups, every node has its own private, up-to-date copy of the database.

You can configure backup operations to always back up from a secondary replica, freeing resources on the primary. That effectively means you can run backups *during production hours* (!!!) without impacting production (!!!). That means you can run backups all day long, protecting your data even more. You might also configure reporting functions, which only need a read-only copy of the database, after all, to connect to a secondary replica, offloading further work from the primary.

When applications connect to SQL Server, they can include an *intent* statement in the connection data. That intent states what the application intends to do: read data, or change data. You can configure the availability group so that incoming read-intent connections are automatically routed to a secondary replica, saving the primary for write-intent connections. That's an amazing way to increase the capacity of SQL Server, by moving traffic to another whole server.

19.6 HA beyond SQL

There are many approaches to HA aside from those contained in SQL Server itself. Technologies like VMware vSphere FT and Marathon Technologies' everRun MX are designed to take a SQL Server instance running in a VM, and replicate its disk, memory, and CPU state to an identical VM running on another host. If the main VM (or its host) fails, execution transfers to the other VM, with little or no lag time.

Both Microsoft Hyper-V and VMware vSphere support live migrations of VMs, too. So if you have SQL Server running in a VM, you can move that VM to another host, if desired.

These HA techniques present different levels of redundancy to protect against different kinds of failures, and they all have their associated pros, cons, and costs. They're worth looking at, just so you know what options you have for meeting various business needs that might come your way.

19.7 HA comparison

By way of summary, I thought it would be useful to sum up how the different SQL Server-based HA options stack up against each other. This is a simple comparison, but it'll help highlight the main business-level differences. Table 19.1 lays it out for you.

Table 19.1 Comparing HA techniques in SQL Server

Technique	Ease of setup	Relative cost	Hardware redundancy	Database redundancy	Recommendation
Log shipping	Easy	Low	Yes	Yes	Deprecated; do not use for new projects
Database mirroring	Easy	Low to moderate	Yes	Yes	Single-threaded in standard version; not real-time
Clustering	Complex	Expensive	Yes	No	Traditional approach; doesn't harden data; can get expensive
Availability Groups	Moderate	Moderate to Expensive	Yes	Yes	Recommended: provides most options and best redundancy

As I mentioned earlier, I've been pushing my clients toward AlwaysOn Availability Groups. They're far easier to set up than AlwaysOn Clusters, and they provide the maximum amount of redundancy, including the data itself. They're more geoflexible than clustering, giving you the option of splitting across datacenters (provided you have solid infrastructure in place to support it). They also give you the most options to have standby resources performing production work, meaning you're wasting less money on hardware, VMs, and SQL Server licenses.

Good alternatives exist outside SQL Server itself. Providing redundancy at the VM level gives you a ton of flexibility; I've lightly touched on those topics here, but your options vary a lot depending on the products you have in your environment.

20 Virtualizing SQL Server

Organizations, for the past several years, have been on a mission to virtualize every-thing, it seems, especially servers. It isn't hard to understand why: virtualization offers a lot of flexibility, more compact data centers, interesting options for HA, and more. Over those last few years, myths and inaccurate information have been per-petuated about virtualizing SQL Server. Let's clear it up and see how well SQL Server responds to being virtualized!

20.1 Why virtualize?

There are dozens of reasons to virtualize a server. VMs can be easily moved from host machine to host machine, helping to rebalance workloads, make maintenance easier, and even provide for fault tolerance. Once a server is running on a VM instead of on a physical machine, you might not even care where its physical host is located. Microsoft, for example, makes it possible to migrate VMs from your own datacenter into their Azure cloud-based datacenter, giving you interesting options for accessibility and high availability.

Virtualization can also help meet organizations' political or business needs. Sup-pose you have a database that stores customer credit card information. You'd probably be subject to the Payment Card Industry's Data Security Standard (PCI DSS), which might entail specific server- and database-level configurations. You might not want those configurations to be shared by *other* databases that your orga-nization uses. In fact that PCI DSS-compliant server might need to be managed by entirely different administrators and auditors. Virtualizing lets you split that sensi-tive database off onto its own server, without requiring you to go out and buy, install, and maintain a physical box.

Understand that SQL Server has supported a kind of virtualization for a very, very long time. As shown in figure 20.1, SQL Server's ability to run multiple instances of itself on a single server OS means that you can effectively have multiple copies of SQL Server running on one machine (physical or virtual), and those instances can be completely separated from each other. My PCI DSS example requirement could likely be met by running a separate instance, rather than running an entirely separate server.

This virtualization model still has *some* weaknesses. Without special clustering configurations, for example, you can't quickly move a SQL Server instance from one host to another (although with Windows Cluster Service, you sort of can). There's also a single point of administration for the Windows OS itself, and Windows administrators have a certain amount of all-powerful control over SQL Server, since SQL Server is obviously running on Windows. In instances where you need to separate that administrative capability a bit, hypervisor-virtualization lets you do so.

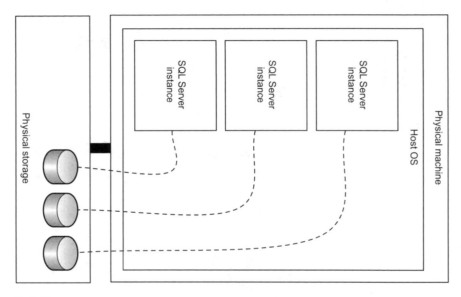

Figure 20.1   SQL Server virtualizes by running multiple side-by-side instances.

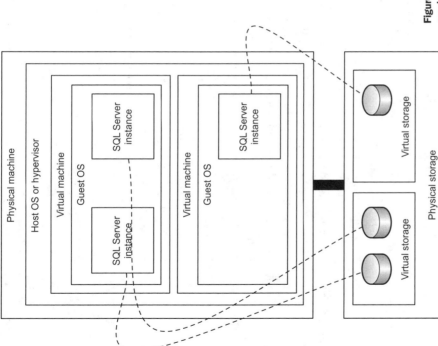

Figure 20.2 Hypervisors emulate physical hardware.

20.2 *Understanding virtual and physical hardware*

As shown in figure 20.2, hypervisor-based virtualization ("real" virtualization, as opposed to running side-by-side SQL Server instances) uses the hypervisor to emulate physical resources like memory and a processor. Each VM believes it's running on its own physical computer, and the hypervisor manages access to the underlying physical hardware.

As you can see, virtualization has a lot more layers. There are more OSes running, plus the overhead of emulating hardware. Virtualization is always less efficient than using physical machines, but because server computer hardware has become so powerful, we can afford to be a bit less efficient in exchange for having more flexibility. The trick in virtualizing SQL Server is to understand where those lowered efficiencies come into play, and understanding what you can and can't do in various scenarios.

CAUTION The advice I'm going to offer in the remainder of this chapter is, obviously, generic. It doesn't apply universally to all situations, and you should, above all else, follow the SQL Server-specific guidance from your hypervisor vendor. Virtualizing is complex, and becoming increasingly complex, and is increasingly being designed to allow workload-specific tuning and tweaking.

20.3   *CPU and memory in a virtual environment*

When I started building SQL Server machines, physical machines, mind you, we tended to overbuild them. Because it's fairly difficult to upgrade a server's physical hardware, we'd stock machines full of CPUs, full of memory (RAM), and everything else. That way the machine could scale up as much as we'd ever (hopefully) need. But it meant we were deploying a ton of wasted computing resources, and that is a key fact to keep in mind when you virtualize SQL Server. You probably do *not* need as much server oomph as you might provision for a physical server.

20.3.1   *Sizing CPUs*

SQL Server, for example, can run smaller and even medium-sized workloads just fine with a single processor core. With physical servers, I almost always had more cores than that, because it's tough to add processors after the server is deployed. With virtualization, it's pretty easy to roll out new cores to an existing VM: it's literally just a configuration setting and a VM restart. So when it comes to CPU, *start small.* Give your SQL Server VMs as little CPU as possible, then ramp up until you're covering your workload. Keep in mind that the jump from one core to two cores can be a big one, as two cores opens up the possibility for SQL Server to start parallelizing queries. It's often worth experimenting to see if your workload benefits from that.

You do need to pay a bit of attention to what other workloads the host computer is handling other than SQL Server. If I've figured out that a given SQL Server VM needs two processor cores, then I want the host machine to have two cores that can be more or less dedicated to SQL Server, unless I know my SQL Server workload isn't continuous and that it won't always need continual use of those cores. That's all part of the performance management of a virtualized environment, though. It's true of any workload, not just SQL Server.

> **CAUTION**   Newer versions of SQL Server are licensed by the processor core, which means reconfiguring a VM to add a core also means you'll be responsible for paying additional SQL Server licensing fees. Be sure you understand the licensing implications in your environment.

20.3.2   *Sizing memory*

Modern hypervisors support something called *memory overcommit*, although different vendors refer to it using differing terminology. The idea is that you can assign more virtual RAM to a host's VMs than the host has physical RAM. A host might have 10 GB of RAM installed, and assign 2 GB each to 10 VMs. In that example, you've overcommitted memory by a factor of 50%, which falls within common real-world practices. The idea is that the hypervisor shifts memory around to give it to whatever

VMs need it, with the understanding that VMs rarely use *all* of the memory they're assigned.

I dislike memory overcommit for SQL Server. That's due in part to the fact that SQL Server tends to try to use all the memory you let it, which by default means all the memory available in the computer (virtual or physical). If you're only *pretending* to give SQL Server that actual memory, you'll incur overhead as the hypervisor has to shift things around to meet SQL Server's needs. Rather than dumping a bunch of RAM on SQL Server and hoping for the best, I try to figure out how much RAM it needs for my workload, give it that much, and make sure the same amount of physical RAM is available to back it up.

Some of the tricks hypervisors use to share memory between VMs don't work well with certain SQL Server configurations, which further drives me to *not* overcommit RAM to my SQL Server VMs.

That said, I have numerous customers who do use memory overcommit with their SQL Server VMs, and they're very happy with the configuration. In most cases, they've specified a minimum memory level that they know meets their average continual workload, allowing the hypervisor to provide more RAM when workloads spike.

A lot of what you do with memory, in this regard, depends on your hypervisor's capabilities, your own virtualization management skills, and your exact workloads. Experiment, remembering that one of the cool parts about virtualization is that you can change VM configurations more or less on-demand, so you're not stuck with a configuration that isn't working well.

20.4   *Disk I/O in a virtual environment*

This is one of the trickiest areas for virtualizing SQL Server, and it's one of the most difficult for me to write about without getting *really* specific about particular hypervisors. Let me start by trying to explain what can go wrong with disk I/O in a virtual environment. I'll be relying on an example that's pretty simplistic, just to lay out the framework for the discussion.

Let's explore some of the layers shown in figure 20.3:

- *The physical machine, or host, is the physical computer.* It runs a host OS, which contains the hypervisor that makes all the virtualization magic happen.

- *The host has its own physical storage.* These days, that's usually a remote SAN accessed by means of a specialized network, like iSCSI or Fibre Channel (FC).

- *The host runs one or more VMs.* The configuration for these is usually defined in some kind of configuration file, which is stored on the host's physical storage.

- *The VMs run guest OSes, like Windows Server, and typically run applications like SQL Server.* That guest OS, any applications, and any application data are stored on virtual storage. Typically, a virtual disk is a special file stored on the host's physical storage. The hypervisor manages the file, and the VM "sees" the file as if it were a physical hard disk.

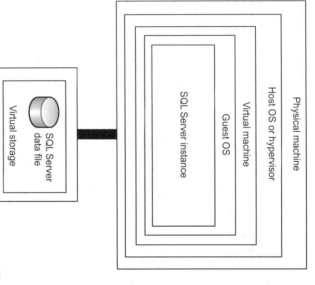

Figure 20.3   Typical virtualized SQL Server

When SQL Server writes an 8 KB page of data to disk, it goes through these layers:

1   SQL Server asks the Windows OS to write the data to disk.

2   Windows passes the data to its disk controller, a piece of virtual hardware provided by the hypervisor.

3   The hypervisor interprets the write activity, and makes the appropriate updates to the virtual disk file.

You've got three entities involved in every read or write operation: SQL Server is managing its data file, Windows is managing what it *thinks* are physical disk I/O operations, and the hypervisor is taking that activity and managing a faked-out disk structure.

With some workloads, this is no problem. With other workloads, the extra layer of the hypervisor puts a noticeable performance kink in the system. An alternate approach is shown in figure 20.4.

In this design, I've installed a virtual *Host Bus Adapter*, or HBA, inside the SQL Server VM. (HBAs are used for FC SANs; if you use an iSCSI SAN, you'd just have another virtual Ethernet adapter in the SQL Server VM.) Now, SQL Server can see the organization's SAN directly. SQL Server asks the virtualized Windows OS to write directly to the SAN. The hypervisor, here, isn't involved in managing SQL Server's data files. This removes a middleman from the disk I/O, and can improve disk throughput considerably from SQL Server's perspective. This is a fairly common approach in the organizations I work with. Many of them have seen significant disk I/O improvement by switching to this model instead of the more traditional virtual storage model.

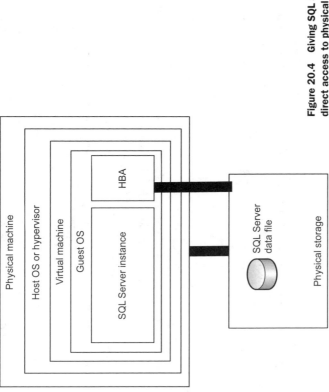

Figure 20.4 Giving SQL Server direct access to physical storage

All that said, things have become a lot more complex. Virtualization vendors are constantly pushing ahead and improving performance of virtual storage, all while adding flexibility that doesn't exist in physical storage models. So you should take my example as a general description of potential bottlenecks, and take the time to understand exactly how your virtualization model deals with storage.

20.5 *Tricks with performance monitoring in a virtual environment*

One of the most frustrating parts about virtualizing SQL Server is that it breaks almost everything you know about SQL Server performance monitoring. In general, you have to be leery of monitoring performance *inside* a VM. Just because the virtualized OS sees the CPU as being at 80%, for example, doesn't tell you much about CPU utilization. It could be that the hypervisor is only *providing what it's been asked for*, and so while the VM sees the CPU as being at near-max, it doesn't mean there isn't more CPU lying in reserve. The same applies to memory, and to a large degree disk I/O, unless you're using a storage model where SQL Server is attaching directly to physical storage (like a SAN), in which case the VM's disk I/O figures should be fairly accurate.

In fact, that's a good rule: don't trust a VM to tell you anything accurate about virtualized resources, but trust it to know what's going on with real, physical resources. So how do you manage SQL Server performance? Yeah. Er. Um. It's complicated.

You'll probably need to find some commercial tools that know how. Seriously. Microsoft doesn't ship anything natively with SQL Server, although Microsoft's System

Center Operations Manager product is coming along nicely in terms of monitoring virtualized workloads; other vendors offer somewhat more mature solutions. The trick seems to be monitoring both the physical host *and* the VMs, so that you can correlate inside-the-VM performance to what-the-host-is-dealing-with performance. You'll know if the VM is maxed out because the host is maxed out, if the VM merely hasn't been given any of the available resources, or if the VM hasn't been allocated enough resources. Performance monitoring at this level is, frankly, incredibly complicated and it's beyond the scope of this book. If you're dealing with a virtualized SQL Server, my suggestion is to find vendors who can help you deal with performance and accept the cost of their tools as part of the cost of doing business. Remember, virtualization brings many benefits, but at least some of those will be partially offset by increased management costs.

20.6   *Hands-on lab*

You won't have a hands-on lab for this chapter, but take a moment to find and read the SQL Server-related virtualization guidance from your organization's hypervisor vendor. VMware's guidance document is at www.vmware.com/files/pdf/sql_server_best_practices_guide.pdf.

21 Moving, migrating, and upgrading databases

The more you work with SQL Server, the more likely you are to need to move, migrate, or upgrade a database from time to time, and in this chapter I'll show you some of the main techniques for doing so. I'll be focusing strictly on moving (or upgrading, or whatever) an entire database, completely intact, without making changes. You might need to do that if you're relocating a database to a new SQL Server instance, for example, or if you're upgrading versions of SQL Server.

I won't be covering situations where you need to modify the database in some fashion, such as when you're upgrading the version of the application that uses the database. That's beyond SQL Server itself.

21.1 Refresh: detaching and attaching databases

If you set up a VM-based lab when you started this book, then you should remember all about attaching databases, but here's a quick review.

SQL Server keeps your data in a file, on disk, that has a .MDF filename extension. Optionally, some databases may have data in one or more secondary .NDF files as well. Also, each database will have a transaction log file in a .LDF file. By default, SQL Server has these files open for its own exclusive use at all times (well, so long as SQL Server is running, at least), making it impossible to copy these files. To get SQL Server to let go of a database's files, closing them and making them available for filesystem operations, you *detach* the database.

In SQL Server Management Studio, right-click a database, select Tasks, then select Detach.... SQL Server will ask you to confirm the operation, which might fail if there are users actively connected to the database. In fact, as shown in

197

Figure 21.1   Check for active connections before detaching a database.

figure 21.1, you can see if there are any active connections, and if you select the Drop Connections checkbox, SQL Server can terminate those connections for you, all in one step.

You also have the option to Update Statistics before closing the database files, which will leave the database updated and ready to go when you reattach it. If you plan to move the database to a different version of SQL Server, don't bother updating statistics, because different versions of SQL Server can't typically use stats generated by other versions. The new version will delete and recreate the statistics automatically.

Once detached, the database files—make sure you grab *all* of them, not just the .MDF file—can be moved to their new location. You can use whatever file-copy mechanisms you want, including Windows PowerShell, the Command Prompt window, and Windows Explorer. There's nothing special about the database files at this point. They are just files.

Once they're in their new location, you can attach them to an instance of SQL Server. Connect to that instance in SQL Server Management Studio, right-click the Databases folder, and choose Attach.... You'll be prompted for the file location (or locations), and the database should attach and become available for use.

Now for the caveats! Keep in mind that databases aren't fully self-contained: typically, they rely on one or more logins, which are mapped into the database's internal database users. Logins exist at the server level, and if the new SQL Server instance doesn't have the correct logins, then users won't be able to access the database.

You can't recreate the logins and hope for the best. SQL Server maps logins to database users by using an internal *security identifier,* or SID, the login's name. Figure 21.2 illustrates how logins are mapped to database users.

In this example, two of the server logins, CONTOSO\DonJ (which, based on the name, is a Windows login) and johnd (probably a SQL Server login) are mapped to database users in the MyApp database. The mapping is made by the logins' SIDs, which aren't normally visible in the SQL Server Management Studio console.

Let's say we detach the MyApp database and move it to a new SQL Server instance. Those same logins (based on SID, not on name) need to exist on the server. You can't simply create a new login named johnd, because when you do, SQL Server will assign a new SID, which won't match the one that the database is looking for. So what can you do?

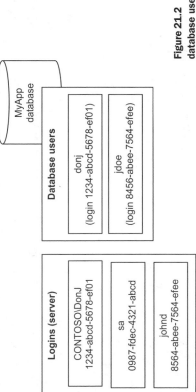

Figure 21.2 Logins map to database users by SID.

You have two options.

- If you've created johnd but it isn't being used by a database on the new instance, you can change the SID of the login to match what the database is looking for.
- If johnd doesn't exist on the new instance, you can create it and assign the SID that the database is looking for.

We'll begin with the second option: start by finding out the SID for the logins used by the database. On the *original* SQL Server instance, run the following query in the server's Master database:

```
SELECT name, [sid]
FROM sys.server_principals
WHERE [type] = 's';
```

This will list logins by name, and include their SID. Write down the SIDs, copy them to a Notepad file, or whatever you like. Then, create the login on the new SQL Server instance, assigning the SID you copied:

```
CREATE LOGIN login_name WITH PASSWORD = N'Login_Password#',
sid = 0x2F5B769F543973419BCEF78DE9FC1A64,
DEFAULT_DATABASE=[master], DEFAULT_LANGUAGE=[us_english],
    CHECK_EXPIRATION=OFF, CHECK_POLICY=OFF;
GO
```

You'll see where the login's name, password, SID, and default database are assigned. This creates a SQL Server-type login; the process is similar for a Windows Authentication login (look up the CREATE LOGIN command in SQL Server Books Online).

To fix existing mislinked database users, you'll use a stored procedure. Make sure your query window is focused on the database in question, and run this within the database you've moved:

```
sp_change_users_login @Action='update_one', @UserNamePattern='<database_user>',
@LoginName='<login_name>';
GO;
```

You specify the database user name you're trying to fix, and the login name it's meant to map to. SQL Server will find everything and change the SID in the database to match the one on the existing login. It's also possible to get a list of database users that aren't properly linked to a login. Again, with a query window focused on the database in question, run:

```
sp_change_users_login @Action='Report';
GO;
```

You can read more about this *orphaned database user* situation, and how to prevent and fix it, at http://technet.microsoft.com/en-us/library/ms175475.aspx.

21.2   *The Copy Database Wizard*

SQL Server's Copy Database Wizard can be a lot easier than detaching and attaching a database, in part because it's capable of handling the whole login-user mapping stuff for you. Both the original instance and new instance of SQL Server must be running and accessible to your computer. The Wizard does run from within SQL Server Management Studio, so for a *large* database, I'll often run this right on the server. That way, I'm not copying data from the source to my computer, and then from my computer to the target. Instead, I'm copying right from the source to the target, which is usually quicker.

Start by right-clicking the database, choosing Tasks, and then selecting Copy Database.... The Wizard will prompt you for authentication information for both the source (origin) and target (destination) instances. As shown in figure 21.3, the Wizard can automate the detach/attach process for you, or perform the copy by using SMO. The latter allows the source database to remain online.

You'll run through the remainder of the wizard's screens to specify the source database, the destination database name, and other options. http://msdn.microsoft.com/query/dev10.query?appId=Dev10IDEF1&l=EN-US&k=k(SQL11.SWB.CDW.COMPLETE.F1)&rd=true has full details about how the Wizard works, including information on security requirements if you're copying between servers.

21.3   *Overview: SQL Server Integration Services*

The Copy Database Wizard actually creates and runs an SSIS package. Older versions of SQL Server called this *Data Transformation Services* (DTS), but the basic idea is the same: it's a kind of script that tells SQL Server how to move or copy data from one place to another, with fairly advanced abilities to modify or transform that data on the way.

A discussion of SSIS is beyond the scope of this book, but I want you to know that it exists. The technology is useful when you need to do anything more complex than a straight instance-to-instance copy (which the Copy Database Wizard does), but SSIS is a complex technology in its own right, with more than a few books written about it.

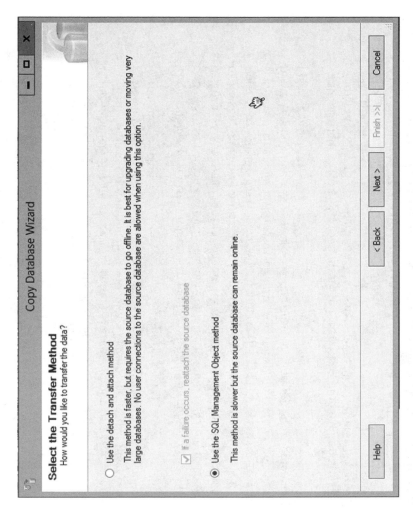

Figure 21.3   The SMO method allows the database to remain online.

21.4   *Database upgrades*

Most organizations I work with tend to leave their databases on whatever version of SQL Server the database is already on. They try not to upgrade, often because the application vendor specifies a certain version of SQL Server for a certain version of their application, and they won't necessarily support the customer if they use a different version of SQL Server. It's common for me to see environments running SQL Server 2000, SQL Server 2008, SQL Server 2008R2, and so on. Yeah, it's a mess.

When organizations I work with *do* upgrade SQL Server, they typically do a *migration*. That means they set up the new instance and copy the database from the old instance, often using one of the two main techniques I covered in this chapter, such as the Copy Database Wizard. These side-by-side migrations, as they're often called, come with numerous advantages. For one, you can migrate over and over and over without affecting the source database, which can remain in use. That lets you test the process as often as you want with little or no production impact. When you're satisfied that everything's working, you can "cut over" to the new instance and retire the old one. Another advantage is that the two instances can be running on entirely different versions of Windows, making this an opportunity to upgrade the server's OS as well as

SQL Server. You can even migrate across SQL Server editions. You get a ton of flexibility, which is why folks like migrations so much.

NOTE It's possible to do a migration on the same server, by installing a new instance of SQL Server on the same physical or virtual machine as an existing instance. But be aware that certain shared components (for example, client connectivity components) will always be updated to that new version, which could potentially cause problems for any older instances running on the same machine.

The term *upgrade* generally refers to an in-place upgrade, meaning you install a new version of SQL Server on top of the old one, with the new instance inheriting the settings, databases, and so on of the old version. It's harder to roll back with this method: short of backing up and restoring the entire server, you're pretty much stuck if it doesn't work. Microsoft also has rules for what it supports for in-place upgrades. It even offers a SQL Server Upgrade Advisor (search http://downloads.microsoft.com for the appropriate version) that can scan an existing instance and advise of potential in-place upgrade problems.

SUGGESTION Nearly everyone in the universe vastly prefers migrations over upgrades. Try to do migrations. It's safer, more flexible, easier. Better in every way.

If you *must* do an in-place upgrade, use the Advisor. Figure 21.4 shows an example of the reports it produces, which includes advice on things that must be done before the upgrade, after the upgrade, or at any time. You'll even be warned about features supported by the old version, which aren't supported by the new version, so that you can evaluate your options if you're using those features.

While the Upgrade Advisor is good, I wouldn't regard it as 100% comprehensive, 100% infallible, or 100% guaranteed. It's an *advisor*, not a consultant. Before upgrading, *back up everything*. Back it up *twice*. Make sure the backups work by restoring them to a lab computer, and performing your upgrade on that lab computer first. Test the upgraded instance to make sure your applications continue to work. Then, and only then, consider upgrading your production instance—after asking yourself *again* why you're not doing a side-by-side migration instead!

21.5 Compatibility levels

Compatibility level is an option within each database in SQL Server: in SQL Server Management Studio, right-click the database, select Properties, then look on the Options page to see the Compatibility Level. This setting tells SQL Server to treat that database as if it were running on an older version of SQL Server. The setting doesn't guarantee compatibility with an older version, but it does cause SQL Server to revert certain behaviors to match how an older version would have behaved. You can read more about this

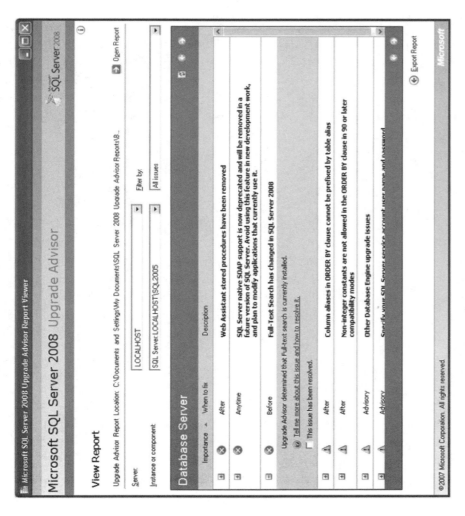

Figure 21.4 Upgrade Advisor report from SQL Server 2005 to SQL Server 2008.

feature, and see a list of changed behaviors, at http://technet.microsoft.com/en-us/library/bb510680.aspx. In SQL Server 2008R2 (SQL Server version 9.0, or compatibility level 90), datetime and smalldatetime values are evaluated according to U.S. English rules when creating or altering partition functions. That's sorta-kinda a bug, and in SQL Server 2012 (version 10.0, compatibility level 100), the behavior was updated to use the current language setting instead of U.S. English. If your application code is expecting U.S. English to be used, then the new behavior could potentially cause problems, so you might use the compatibility level setting to have SQL Server 2012 behave as if it were SQL Server 2008R2.

Compatibility level is all-or-nothing; you get *all* of the behaviors associated with the version you select. You can't pick and choose.

21.6 *Hands-on lab*

This lab is a bit more complex (and will take longer) than the ones I've given you to this point, so you can regard it as optional. But it's good practice for many of the things you've done up until this point, so if you can find the time, it's worth it.

Install a new instance of SQL Server (Express is fine) named MYSQL2. Then, move or copy your AdventureWorks database from your original instance to the new one. Use whatever method you like. In fact, try them all!

SQL Server performance checklist

I want to wrap up with a checklist of performance items. This is a list I tend to follow whenever someone calls me and begins with a vague statement such as, "the SQL Server computer is running slowly." That doesn't give you much to go on, does it? A checklist helps me stay consistent, and to not overlook simple stuff. Keep in mind, too, that SQL Server isn't always at fault—many complex applications include other servers that may contribute to performance problems. But, if you can narrow the problem down to SQL Server, then this checklist will help you solve the problem.

I should emphasize that this list focuses mostly on things that I, as an administrator, can do something about, especially when the database or server in question is supporting an application for which I don't "own" the code. I'm focusing on the things I can do strictly on the server, without touching any programming. If you do have access to the code, or have a coworker who does, there's obviously a lot more that you can dive into.

- *Is the server in basically good health?* Sometimes a failed disk, bad network card, or other hardware problem can impact performance more than you might realize.

- *How are the server's basic CPU, network, memory, and disk performance counters?* If they're maxed out, or even running unusually high, you need to find out why. Is there an unusually high workload for some reason, or has the every-day workload outgrown what the server can deliver?

- *Are the database's file sizes adequate?* Autogrowth on a file that's run out of room is a massive performance killer. Take the time to manage file size manually to avoid autogrowth.

- *Are the database files on a contiguous area of disk space?* If possible, take SQL Server offline and defragment the disk to make sure.

- *Are the indexes in good health?* Check their fragmentation levels and reorganize or rebuild if necessary. Remember that rebuilding takes longer and consumes more resources, but delivers a healthier index.

- *Is the transaction log being maintained?* I'll sometimes come across massive transaction log files that are constantly autogrowing, because nobody is taking the time to truncate the log after database backups are made.

- *Are a lot of blocks or deadlocks happening?* You can check in Performance Monitor; if there are, then the application code might not be well optimized for the level of concurrent workload.

- *Is the tempdb on a fast disk system?* It should be and ideally on one that isn't shared with anything else.

Because indexes are one area that you're usually okay to mess with, even if you don't own the application code, I'll also spend some time investigating indexes.

- Capture some traffic and use the Database Engine Tuning Advisor to ensure all indexes are being used. Remember, indexes that aren't speeding up SELECT queries (or WHERE clauses) may be slowing down everything else.

- Clustered indexes should be built on small keys, and you'll usually find that to be an automatically incremented integer.

- Any column referred to by a foreign key constraint should be indexed.

- Are there any small, super-common queries that might benefit from a covering index?

- More indexes with fewer columns are usually better than fewer indexes having more columns each. When creating an index having multiple columns, the most restrictive column should be included first.

- Indexes primarily help with WHERE, ORDER BY, DISTINCT, and GROUP BY query clauses, so look at queries using those clauses to see where more or different indexes might be beneficial.

- Look for a high number of large table scans. These often indicate missing indexes or badly maintained indexes.

- Almost every table should have a clustered index, so check to make sure they all do. If one doesn't, it should be an extremely small table that is ideally not referred to by any other tables. That's a rare situation.

- Do all indexes have an appropriate fill factor setting? Remember, a smaller fill factor helps indexes from becoming fragmented too quickly, but reduces index performance by increasing disk I/O.

This checklist should get you started on identifying major performance problems and arriving at a solution.

Never the end

You're at the end of your month of lunches for SQL Server administration, but you're really at the very beginning of your SQL Server journey. There's a lot more to learn, especially if your goal is to become a real DBA. I'd like to use this last, short chapter as a way to point you in the right direction for your next steps.

- Start at http://SQLPASS.org, the Professional Association for SQL Server. Cofounded by Microsoft, this community organization is probably the largest and most active in the world. It holds free or low-cost SQL Saturday events worldwide, a global PASS Summit every year, and numerous other in-person events to help you learn and grow. It provides access to great blogs about SQL Server, help you find Microsoft Most Valuable Professional (MVP) Award winners in SQL Server, and a lot more. There are local and virtual chapters where you can network and connect, giving you a personal community that can help you solve problems.

- For online questions and answers, start with ServerFault.com (more admin-focused) or StackOverflow.com (good for T-SQL or programming questions). You'll also find a good set of forums at SQLTeam.com. Microsoft's official forums are at http://social.msdn.microsoft.com/Forums/sqlserver/en-US/home. (Don't expect to see Microsoft employees answering questions; these are community forums.) I also sometimes use the forums at SQLServer-Central.com.

- Head to www.microsoft.com/en-us/sqlserver/community/forums-and-blogs .aspx for the official word on all things SQL Server, including access to technology-specific forums (like Integration Services) and product team blogs. SQL Server is a huge product with numerous subteams, and it's good to keep up with what everyone is saying.

I'm not a big SQL Server expert myself, and I fully expect that you'll quickly outgrow my knowledge and move on to the real giants in the field. While I've found a little niche in helping folks get started with SQL Server administration, authors such as Itzik Ben-Gan, Grant Fritchey, Kalen Delaney, Orin Thomas, Mike Hotek, and others will take you from there. I'm especially fond of Grant Fritchey's work on SQL Server performance tuning, as he uses a straightforward approach and has a very clean writing style.

If you're worried about becoming some kind of programmer when it comes to SQL Server, you can stop worrying. You *definitely* will be doing programming as a DBA! In fact, DBAs have been doing something for a long time that Microsoft is now calling "DevOps." It involves stepping back and forth over the invisible line between administration/operations and software development, and SQL Server has pretty much always required that broad, flexible set of skills. So pick up a book on T-SQL programming and start reading, because it's a skill you'll use every day.

But for now, I think you've probably got a good starter set of skills. You can definitely maintain a SQL Server instance, and you can take a good shot at collecting information to help a developer correct performance problems. You can do performance fine-tuning of your own, and you know a lot about what's going on under the hood as SQL Server processes queries. Good luck with wherever SQL Server takes you next!

Installing SQL Server

In this appendix, I'll walk you through the process of installing SQL Server and the AdventureWorks 2012 sample database. Note that I will be using SQL Server 2012 Standard Edition, which is commonly used in production environments. Installing other production editions looks almost exactly the same, but installing the Express edition has a few minor differences. If you're installing Express, you should still be able to use this walkthrough to get started. As a reminder, you can download SQL Server Express 2012 from www.microsoft.com/en-us/download/details.aspx?id=29062; I suggest the SQLEXPRADV download for either 64-bit (x64) or 32-bit (x86), depending on the OS your computer runs.

A.1 Setting up your computer

For my lab environment, I prefer to use a VM. Note that if you want paralleliza-tion to work, your VM will need to be assigned at least two virtual processors. That only impacts one lab in this book, so it's not a big deal if you can only give it one virtual processor. You can use Hyper-V if your computer supports it, or a product like VMware Workstation. On a Mac, you can use something like Parallels or VMware Fusion.

I recommend using a newer OS, like Windows 7 or Windows 8. You can also use a server OS, such as Windows Server 2012. If you don't own a copy of one of these, you can get a free trial from Microsoft's website. You can, of course, install SQL Server directly on a Windows 7 or Windows 8 (or later) computer that you already own.

I do suggest a 64-bit (x64) OS, although if you only have access to a 32-bit OS, SQL Server will still work just fine.

A.2 Installing SQL Server

Start by double-clicking the Setup executable, whether that's one you downloaded (if you're installing Express) or that you found on the SQL Server installation DVD. You'll begin at a kind of "task list" screen for production editions; click the Installa-tion task to find Setup and get things running.

Figure A.1 shows what you should see first: the SQL Server presetup prerequisite check. Hopefully, you'll have everything installed that you need; if you're missing something, follow the instructions and install whatever you're asked to. Usually, that will include a version of the .NET Framework and other basic Microsoft software. Note that SQL Server 2012 requires .NET Framework 3.5; on Windows Server 2012 R2 and Windows 8.1, that isn't installed by default. It should be present, however, and ready for installation as an optional feature. You can read http://blogs.msdn.com/b/sql_shep/archive/2012/08/01/windows-2012-and-net-3-5-feature-install.aspx for instructions.

After you click OK, SQL Server will check the online Microsoft Update website for updates to the setup routines. You'll usually want to let it do this, so that you can have the latest software. As shown in figure A.2, SQL Server may find an update or two for you to install.

Once that's done, as shown in figure A.3, SQL Server will install SQL Server Setup. Yeah, that seems strange, but it's what has to be done: Setup has to install the real Setup, so that it can set up SQL Server. How many setups would Setup set up if it could only set up setups?

Once Setup is installed, it will launch automatically and start by checking several preinstallation rules. You'll notice in figure A.4 that I got a warning, probably because the Windows Firewall is installed on my computer. The warning in this case is reminding me that Setup won't add any exceptions to the firewall, so unless I do so manually,

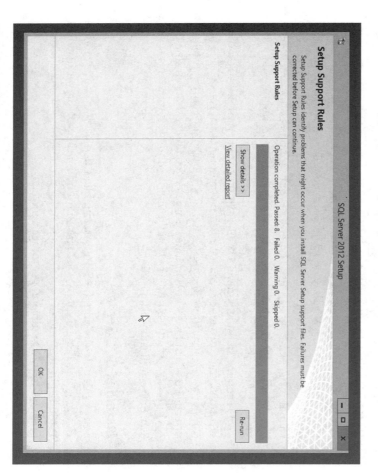

Figure A.1   SQL Server starts by checking prerequisites.

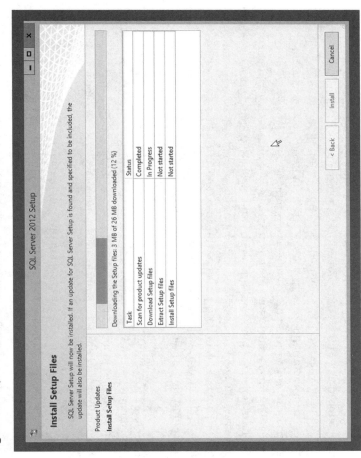

Product Updates

Always install the latest updates to enhance your SQL Server security and performance.

| Product Updates |
| Install Setup Files |

☑ Include SQL Server product updates

Name	Size (MB)	More Information
SQL Server 2012 SP1 GDR Setup ...	26	KB 2793634

1 updates (26 MB) found online.

The Setup updates (26 MB) will be installed when you click Next.

Read our privacy statement online

Learn more about SQL Server product updates

< Back   Next >   Cancel

Figure A.2 SQL Server will download setup updates for you.

Install Setup Files

SQL Server Setup will now be installed. If an update for SQL Server Setup is found and specified to be included, the update will also be installed.

| Product Updates |
| Install Setup Files |

Downloading the Setup files: 3 MB of 26 MB downloaded (12 %)

Task	Status
Scan for product updates	Completed
Download Setup files	In Progress
Extract Setup files	Not started
Install Setup files	Not started

< Back   Install   Cancel

Figure A.3 Setup will install the Setup files.

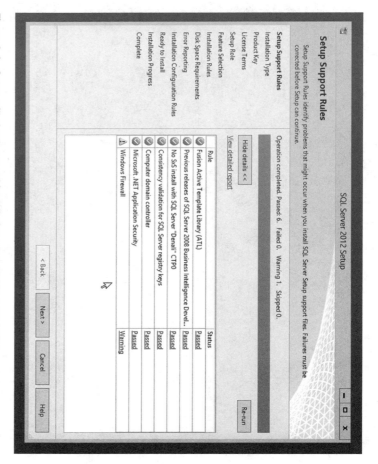

Figure A.4   Setup will check several installation rules before proceeding.

nobody will be able to connect to my server. That's a detail my server administrator handles, so I'll pass on the reminder to her.

Next, Setup will ask what you'd like to do. As shown in figure A.5, you can install a default instance of SQL Server, or a named instance. I've chosen to install a named instance called SQL2. You can see in the table at the bottom of the screen that an existing instance, MSSQLSERVER, is already installed. If you're installing SQL Server Express, it should default to installing a named instance called SQLEXPRESS. I recommend letting it do that.

My next prompt is for a license key. As shown in figure A.6, you also have the option of installing a free edition, such as an evaluation, which might expire. SQL Server Express might not show you this screen. I'll enter my product key and click Next to proceed. If you enter a product key, it will usually determine what edition of SQL Server is installed, so make sure you double-check the key before using it.

Figure A.7 shows the next step, which is the inevitable license agreement. Make sure you read it and understand it (or get a lawyer to help) before proceeding.

The next screen, shown in figure A.8, is a shortcut offering of sorts. You can elect to do a feature install, where you pick the bits of SQL Server you want, or you can install everything. The full install is pretty large, and it's rare in a production environment that you'll need everything, so I usually do a feature install.

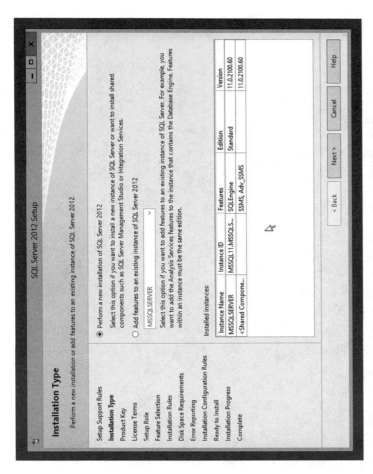

Figure A.5 Decide if you want to install a named instance, or the default.

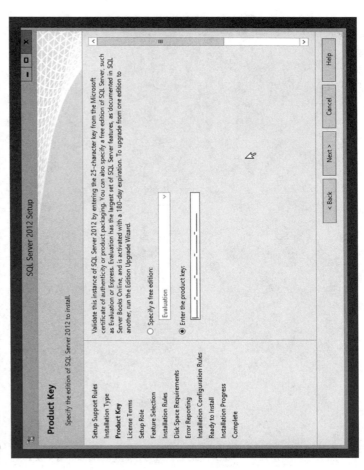

Figure A.6 Enter your product key to proceed.

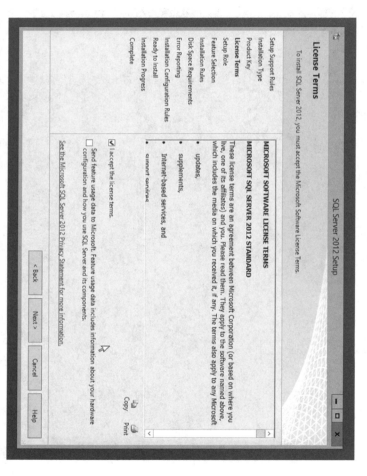

Figure A.7 Accept the license terms to proceed.

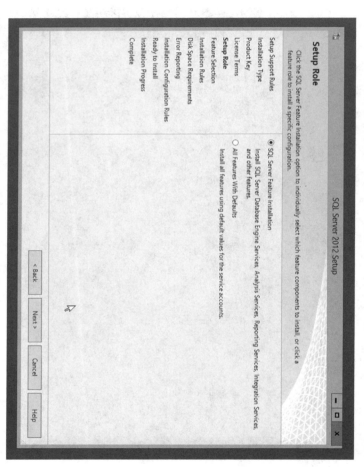

Figure A.8 I usually select the Feature Installation option.

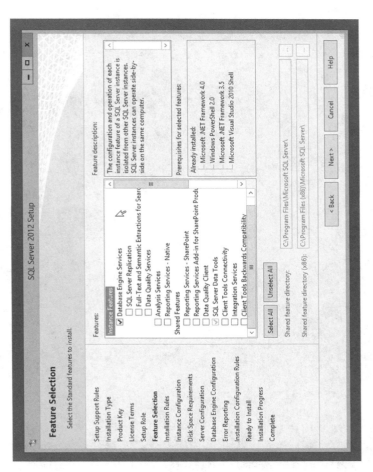

Figure A.9 Select the features you want to install.

Figure A.9 shows where I get to select the features I want. I'm going to install only the core database engine, which is pretty common on a production server. I already have the management tools from a previous installation (the existing instance on this computer), and if you scrolled down the feature list you'd see those tools with a gray check mark, indicating they were already installed. Note that SQL Server Express has a smaller feature list.

Step 10, shown in figure A.10, is where Setup checks to see if any of the files it needs to play with are in use. If they are, you'll be required to restart your computer at the end of the installation, and this is where you'll receive that warning.

The next step, shown in figure A.11, is very important. This is where you give your named instance a name, and where you choose the root installation folder. Setup will create a folder hierarchy for your instance in this location, so it's okay to install multiple instances to this same root folder.

Setup will then show you how much disk space this will all take, as shown in figure A.12. Make sure you're comfortable with the amount of free space you'll have left.

The next screen, shown in figure A.13, is also important. Here, you'll specify the user accounts and startup types for the SQL Server services that are required by the features you chose. If you're setting up a lab environment, it's pretty safe to leave these at the default, although I do like to change SQL Server Agent to start automatically, and

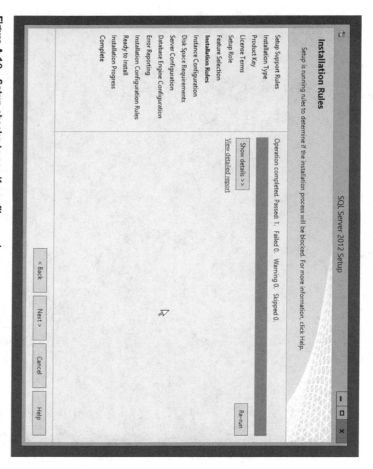

Figure A.10   Setup checks to see if any files are in use.

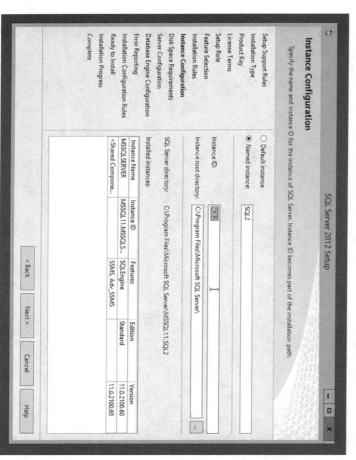

Figure A.11   Don't forget the instance name that you provide here!

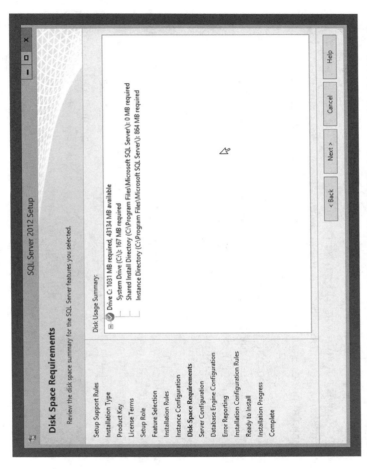

Figure A.12 Setup provides you with a disk space requirement.

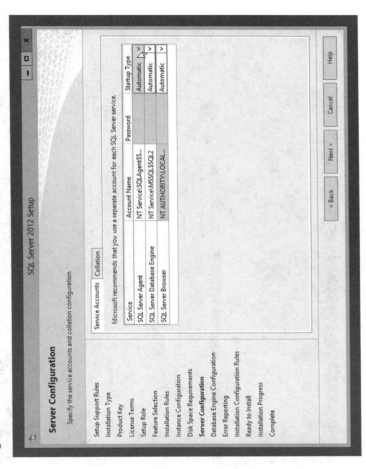

Figure A.13 Choose the service parameters for SQL Server's services.

I often set the Browser to Manual since I don't use it. In a production environment, it's becoming more common to configure a user account or a Managed Service Account to run the services under; you'll need to consult with your directory services folks to see which they prefer to use. You'll learn more about how these user accounts are used in chapter 2.

We're almost done, and figure A.14 has the last main configuration screen. Here, you'll select the authentication mode SQL Server will use. In production, you'll need to know what the applications using SQL Server expect, and many will require Mixed Mode, which is what I've selected. If you choose that, you must provide a password for the built-in, all-powerful sa account.

In a lab environment, you can leave it at Windows Authentication. Either way, you'll need to add a Windows user or group as an administrator of SQL Server. The Add current user button will add whomever you're currently logged on as.

The next screen, shown in figure A.15, asks if you want error reports to be sent to Microsoft. Your organization should have a policy about that, because many Microsoft products offer the option.

As shown in figure A.16, SQL Server will perform one last round of checks to make sure everything looks okay to install based on the information you've provided. Be sure to deal with any errors, as you can't safely proceed without resolving them. Figure A.17 shows your final screen, where you'll confirm what Setup is about to do.

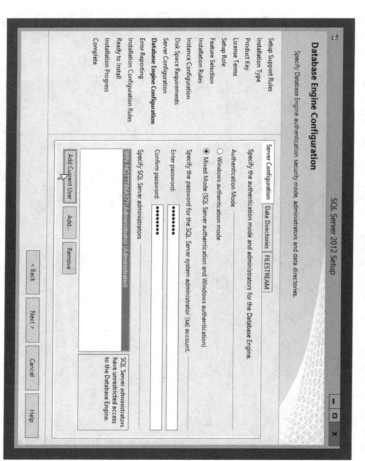

Figure A.14   Choose your authentication mode.

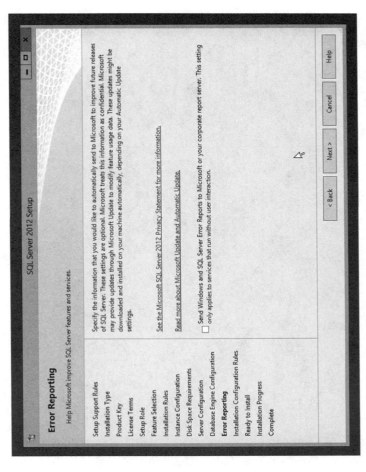

Figure A.15   Choose an error reporting option.

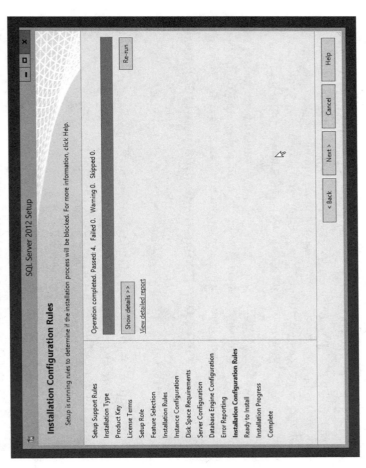

Figure A.16   The final installation check.

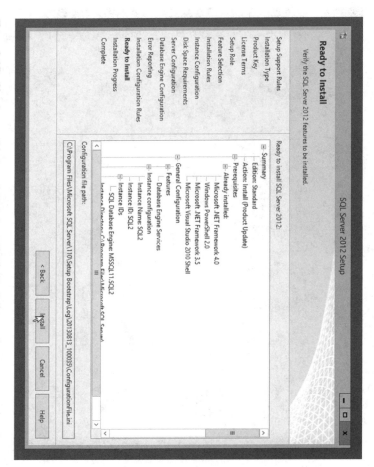

Figure A.17 Check everything carefully before clicking Install.

You're off and running! Figure A.18 shows the progress bar you'll be watching for anything from a few minutes to what seems like an eternity, depending on what you've asked to be installed.

With any luck, you'll complete without error. Figure A.19 shows that I'll need to restart, something that happens a lot to me when I install another instance on a computer that already has one instance running on it. Take care of that restart, and SQL Server is up and running.

Once you restart (if necessary), SQL Server should be ready to use.

A.3   *Installing the AdventureWorks 2012 database*

This isn't a necessary step in a production environment, but in a lab environment the AdventureWorks 2012 database gives you a fully populated database to play with, making labs more interesting.

NOTE   If didn't install SQL Server 2012, make sure you try to get a matching version of AdventureWorks. (There's an AdventureWorks 2008 sample database also.) Most should be available from the same CodePlex.com website where AdventureWorks 2012 is located. It's usually safe to use an older database on a newer version of SQL Server. The worst that can happen is that it simply won't work—you shouldn't damage anything by trying.

Installing the AdventureWorks 2012 database

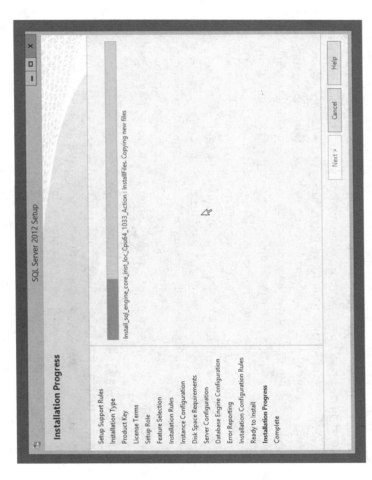

Figure A.18 Watching Setup install SQL Server.

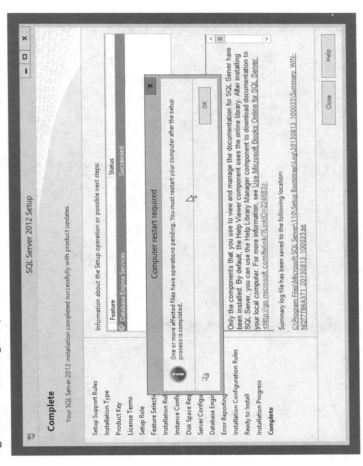

Figure A.19 Setup complete, and time to restart.

The trick is in getting the right download. AdventureWorks is Microsoft's all-in-one sample, so it offers a lot of variations, such as one for data warehousing (the DW variant). I went to http://msftdbprodsamples.codeplex.com/releases/ and found a link for all of the AdventureWorks releases, including 2008, 2008R2, and 2012. Note that the DW variant isn't what you want. I went to http://msftdbprodsamples.codeplex.com/releases/view/93587 to get the right download. The Recommended Download on that page was AdventureWorks2012_Database.zip, which is what I wanted. Pay close attention to filenames; you don't want the LT (light-weight) version, and you don't want the DW (data warehousing) version.

There are brief instructions on the page for attaching the downloaded database to SQL Server, but I'll walk you through it. Obviously, start by downloading it. What you'll end up with is a ZIP file; right-click that to extract all the files. I suggest extracting them to a permanent location, such as C:\Data.

Then open SQL Server Management Studio. In newer versions of Windows, I like to pin this to the Task bar so I can find it easily. It should be located in SQL Server's installation folder if you can't find it; in Windows 8, go to the Start screen and type **SQL** to try and find it. The first thing you'll see when you run it is the connection screen. As you can see in figure A.20, I'm connecting to my local computer (localhost) and the SQL2 instance I just installed (localhost\SQL2). I have it using Windows Authentication, meaning it's connecting using my logon credentials.

In the Object Explorer, which is usually on the left, right-click Databases and select Attach..., as shown in figure A.21.

Click the Add button to add the AdventureWorks 2012 data file, which has a .MDF filename extension. If you've placed that file somewhere under your profile folder, such as in your Documents or Desktop folder, the folder picker may have trouble finding it. That's why I tend to create a folder specifically for the database, under the C:\ drive, just so it's easy to find. Figure A.22 shows what you should see after choosing the

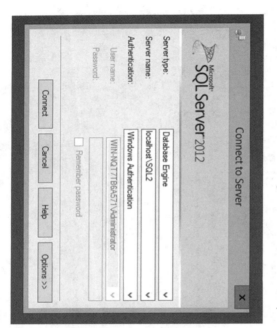

Figure A.20   Connect to your SQL Server instance.

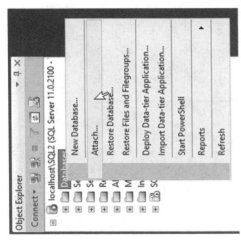

Figure A.21   Select the option to attach a database.

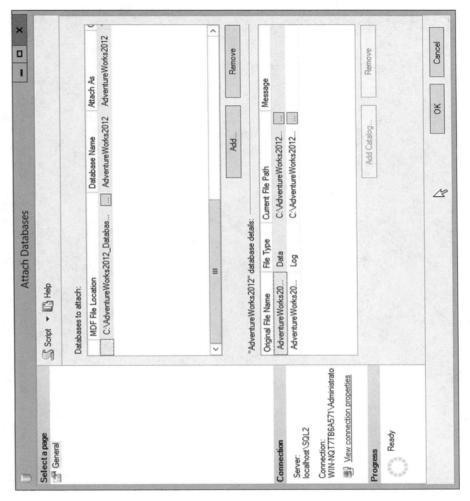

Figure A.22   Select the AdventureWorks 2012 database files.

file. Notice that the corresponding log file, with a .LDF filename extension, has been selected automatically.

Now click OK. As shown in figure A.23, you should be able to expand the Databases node in Object Explorer and see AdventureWorks2012 connected and ready to go. You only have to do this once; it'll be there from now on when you open SQL Server Management Studio.

I should point out that everything I've shown you about attaching this database is suitable only in a lab environment. In a production environment, you wouldn't store your database on the C:\ drive—and you probably wouldn't be attaching a sample database in production, either! Chapter 4 discusses appropriate locations for database files, along with other concerns.

At this point, your lab should be set up and ready to go.

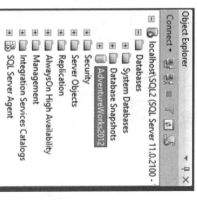

Figure A.23 The database is attached and ready to go.

index